THE LOIRE

Landscapes of the Imagination

THE LOIRE

A CULTURAL HISTORY

Martin Garrett

OXFORD
UNIVERSITY PRESS

2010

OXFORD
UNIVERSITY PRESS

Oxford University Press, Inc., publishes works that further
Oxford University's objective of excellence
in research, scholarship, and education.

Oxford New York
Auckland Cape Town Dar es Salaam Hong Kong Karachi
Kuala Lumpur Madrid Melbourne Mexico City Nairobi
New Delhi Shanghai Taipei Toronto

With offices in
Argentina Austria Brazil Chile Czech Republic France Greece
Guatemala Hungary Italy Japan Poland Portugal Singapore
South Korea Switzerland Thailand Turkey Ukraine Vietnam

Published by Oxford University Press, Inc.
198 Madison Avenue, New York, New York 10016

www.oup.com

Oxford is a registered trademark of Oxford University Press

Co-published in Great Britain by Signal Books

Library of Congress Cataloging-in-Publication Data
Garrett, Martin.
The Loire : a cultural history / Martin Garrett.
   p. cm. — (Landscapes of the imagination)
Includes bibliographical references and indexes.
ISBN 978-0-19-976838-7 (hardcover : alk. paper)—ISBN 978-0-19-976839-4 (pbk. : alk. paper)
1. Loire River (France)—History.   2. Loire River (France)—Description and travel.
3. Loire River Valley (France)—History.   4. Loire River Valley (France)—Civilization.
5. Loire River Valley (France)—History, Local.   6. Loire River Valley (France)—Description
and travel.   I. Title.
DC611.L81G37 2011
944'.5—dc22   2010029656

1 3 5 7 9 8 6 4 2
Design & production: Devdan Sen Images: dreamstime.com: i, xi, 73, 83, 93, 97, 104, 107, 113, 139, 141, 155,
163, 204; istockphoto.com: xxvii, 47, 63; wikipedia commons: xvi, xviii, xxi, xxv, 1, 4, 8, 13, 19, 22, 28, 33, 37,
40, 49, 53, 70, 81, 89, 100, 120, 134, 137, 146, 151, 167, 170, 173, 177, 181, 182, 184, 189, 199

Printed in the United States of America
on acid-free paper

Table of Contents

Preface

The idea of a river is made from a mixture of associations. Some are from books, films or paintings: the white water and leeches of the Ulanga in *The African Queen*, Byron's "arrowy Rhône", the Thames of Whistler or Monet or *Three Men in a Boat*. The Amazon dashes Fitzcarraldo's boat downriver with its gramophone still somehow booming out Caruso's tenor voice. Rat sculls through calmer waters in *The Wind in the Willows*. More directly, we may remember or imagine woods and cornfields and cliffs by the water; fishing or, with Mole, falling in; canoeing or just hearing a gurgling in the night.

In the case of the Loire the associations are likely to be particularly various. It passes, or is connected with, an extraordinary range of landscape from gorges to marshes to vineyards. Its literature includes Rabelais, Balzac, Wordsworth and Henry James. The buildings range from crag-top castles to nuclear power-stations. My own first memories of it, when I was eighteen, are of a river shrouded in mist, and especially of the towers of the château at Chaumont-sur-Loire emerging from the mist. I also remember drinking wine from a plastic cup (apologies to connoisseurs of fine Loire wines) and eating melting cheese while sitting in long grass near the abbey of Fontevraud. I think the wine was Saumur. A bell was ringing from the abbey, I like to think. Later memories include, near Chaumont again, trying to cycle along bumpy sandy tracks by the Loire; floating, in a ferociously hot summer, in the Lac de Maine with a view of Angers in the distance; sunset on the estuary. Nevers, on the middle Loire, has particularly mixed memories: not only the attractions of its cathedral, ducal palace and almond croissants, but the especially large and persistent species of gnat which haunts the bridge across the Loire in summer, turning pedestrians into flailing windmills. On the campsite near the bridge, an electrical night-storm in August 2008 made me wonder, briefly, whether I would be swept away by the river before I could finish writing about it. Books also have their associations: re-reading Balzac's *Eugénie Grandet* on the TGV from Angers to Lille; shepherding my split, soft-covered 1914 edition of Henry James' *A Little Tour in France* through its and my travels.

This book follows the direction of the Loire from source to sea, but the variousness of the places it waters makes bend-by-bend coverage impossible. The tributaries of the Loire would also make that difficult: they not only swell and change the main river as they join it, but themselves flow past many interesting towns, villages, castles and churches. This is particularly true of the Rivers Allier, Cher, Indre and Vienne. And so I write about many of their sights too. When the Loire at last enters the Atlantic, I also linger for a while over the beaches, marshes and resorts which fan out along the nearby coasts.

As usual I would like to thank my family—Helen, Ed, Lottie and Philip—for their help and support. As with my earlier books published by Signal, James Ferguson contributed many insightful suggestions. Patient and helpful listeners to Loire-talk over coffee have included Christine Corton, Jennifer Fellows and Robert Inglesfield. John Edmondson was, as ever, full of useful knowledge and good advice. Thanks also to the French hotel, restaurant, museum and railway staff who took an interest in the idea of a cultural companion to their river and its surroundings, or who at least put up with being told about it. And thanks to my lifelong friend, Peter Mills, with whom I first travelled to the Loire.

Introduction

THE MOST FRENCH OF FRENCH
RIVERS

Thomas Coryat, the Somerset walker and wit, was delighted by his first
sight of "that noble river Ligeris, in French the *Loire*" (*Coryat's Crudities*,
1611). Near Briare there were "certain pretty little islands full of trees" and
"on both sides of the river I saw in divers places very fat and fruitful veins
of ground, as goodly meadows, very spacious champaign fields and great
store of woods and groves, exceedingly replenished with wood." Later travellers emphasized the same smiling fertility, the same calm; for some
French observers the river and its countryside became a defining national
feature. At Amboise, says Gustave Flaubert, you are properly in "fertile,
gentle Touraine, the land of *bon petit vin blanc* and beautiful old châteaux,
watered by the Loire, the most French of French rivers." Poised between
northern calm and southern exuberance, neither prose nor poetry but
"sung prose", it has "the sort of beauty which caresses without captivating,
charms without seducing and, in a word, has more good sense than
grandeur, and more wit than poetry: it is France." The Loire, not the Seine
or the Rhône, is the *fleuve national* (*Le Phare*, January 1904); for Rodin it
is "the aorta of our France".

The colours of the river, too, are often reasonable, not passionate. Flaubert refers to its "silvered sinuosity", the poets Baudelaire and Heredia give us the "green" and "blonde" Loire, and Rodin in *Les Cathédrales de la France* (1914) likes its "soft, delicate grey under the clouds", the old bridges of grey stone and the grey roofs of the towns. But all this silvery moderation reflects only one aspect of the Loire and indeed only its middle sections. The river Coryat encountered had travelled about 280 miles from its source in the Massif Central, through a very different land of gorges, torrents and crags, and would continue for another 350 miles, often past scenes like the one at Briare, to, different again, the vast maritime estuary.

As befits the longest river in France—633 miles or 1120km.—the Loire is remarkably various. It comes close to the industrial city of St.-Étienne, goes through western Burgundy and the Sancerre wine-country and the cathedrals and châteaux of Orléans, Touraine and Anjou, and issues, near the great port-city of St.-Nazaire, into the Atlantic from southern Brittany. It runs through hills, marshes and forests, and fields of maize, sunflowers, roses and soft fruit. There is much evidence of human activity—levées, canals linked to the river and taken across it on spectacular aqueducts at Digoin and Briare, the Grangent and Villerest dams, the mighty anchor and crane preserved at Cosne-sur-Loire to commemorate its foundries, several nuclear power-stations and the Total refinery on the estuary at Donges. Yet the Loire is famous also for its wildlife and is often claimed to be the last "wild" river in France. On the river are beavers, otters (successfully reintroduced in the 1970s) and water-voles, in the forests often wild boar, deer, martens and badgers; the 250 species of birds include herons, egrets, terns, kingfishers, grebes and many sorts of duck. Eels, pike and bream are among the fish of the Loire and its tributaries, although numbers have suffered in recent years, especially in the Loire estuary, because of agricultural and industrial pollution.

Victor Hugo, somewhat heretically, was bored by the Loire poplars. "The poplar is the only tree which can be described as stupid. It obscures the horizons of the Loire," producing a landscape as tedious as "a tragedy written in alexandrines"—the traditional verse-form of French neoclassical literature. More often the poplars and willows have been admired, together with the often nearby forests of oak, pine and beech, and a vast range of smaller plants. Some of the best descriptions of flora on the river occur in the novels of Maurice Genevoix, who lived for much of his life at

Châteauneuf-sur-Loire: from the undulating aquatic myriophylla or milfoils "stretching their long deep-red stems", rough against the skin, to the simple joy of "a veritable forest of rushes" on an island near St.-Benoît-sur-Loire.

"Brusques et terribles colères": the Dangerous Loire

To regard the Loire as always quiet and moderate is also to ignore its more dangerous side: what Genevoix calls its "deceptive languor", its "brusques et terribles colères" ("sudden, terrible anger"). Low levels of water, mainly in summer, make whole stretches of the Loire difficult or impossible to navigate. But at other times of year there is a strong risk of flooding. Strong currents flow around the islands and—another major problem for navigability—the many sandbanks. From the seventeenth century onwards canals were built to help combat these difficulties. From as early as the ninth century, in the central and western Loire especially, people built levées; by the late eighteenth century 25 foot-high banks ran along much of the river between Nevers and Anjou. But the worst floods could not be contained so easily. Among the most devastating were those which arrived, strangely punctually, in 1846, 1856 and 1866.

In London the *Annual Register* gathered flood reports and statistics from the French newspapers. At Roanne in 1846 the Loire "carried away, on the night of the 18th October, forty yards of the embankment, with a noise similar to that of a cannon fired amongst mountains, and the water rushed down" on the town, flooding streets and squares and rising in places "to the fifth storey of the houses". In Roanne alone 200 houses were destroyed "and of 400 boats laden with merchandise, lying in the Loire or in the canal... 270 were sunk; 33,000 pieces of wine and 3,000 hogsheads of spirits of wine, valued at a sum of 2,000,000 francs, have been lost." Boats, including some of the recently introduced steamers, rescued people from roof-tops; many must have died, but no reliable figures were available. At Nevers, in the "immense lake" formed by the Loire and its tributary the Nièvre, "here and there were seen floating timber, trees, and cattle; and cries of distress were heard at every point." In 1856 250,000 acres of land were inundated and the bridge at Cosne-sur-Loire was broken; the *Annual Register* reports that "at the Orleans railway station the water reached the fourth storey. At Tours railway station it was ten feet deep... The waters filled the immense slate quarries at Angers, and threw ten thousand people out of work. In some places whole villages were swept away." Napoleon III's government provided financial aid and set up committees to advise on Loire defences. The levées were built up again, but could do little against later major floods like those of 1879 and 1910. In the twentieth century stronger defences were introduced and water levels controlled by such devices as the dam at Villerest, above Roanne. But the problem has certainly not been solved. Floods on much of the Loire in November 2008 did not lead to loss of life and property on the scale of the nineteenth-century disasters, but vast areas of land were still covered.

Some dangers, of course, are of human making. The Loire has been convenient for the disposal of murder-victims or political opponents, most notoriously in the *noyades* of Nantes, where in 1793-4 the ferocious revolutionary Jean-Baptiste Carrier drowned several thousand people. The young Honoré de Balzac seems to have contemplated throwing himself into the river at Blois, or at least his partly autobiographical hero Félix de Vandenesse thinks about it in *Le Lys dans la vallée.* During a journey from Paris to Tours he feels such anguish at his mother's coldness towards him that he runs onto the bridge. "My suicide," notes the older Félix drily, "was prevented by the height of the parapet." Balzac, who loved the Loire as the river of his native Touraine, would later have felt that it was splendidly apt that he should die in it; but his death at Blois would have deprived us of his accounts of Félix's attempt and of the shining, if treacherous river.

TRIBUTARIES

The Loire, during its long course, crosses twelve of the *départements* of France: Ardèche, Haute-Loire, Loire, Saône-et-Loire, Allier, Nièvre, Cher, Loiret, Loir-et-Cher, Indre-et-Loire, Maine-et-Loire and Loire-Atlantique. As many of these names suggest, the Loire is connected with some other important rivers. They include, to name only a few of the bigger ones, the Allier, Cher, Indre and Vienne. The Allier is 256 miles long. It rises in the mountains thirty-five miles south-west of the source of the Loire and goes on to the cities of Vichy and Moulins. It is still a very powerful river when it joins the Loire at the Bec d'Allier, near Nevers. The other three major tributaries of the Loire rise in the Massif Central and arrive, not far from each other, between Tours and Saumur—the Cher after 219 miles, the Indre 166, and the Vienne 226. A good number of the towns and châteaux which we tend to think of as on the Loire are in fact a few miles away on these tributaries. On the Cher are the châteaux of Montrichard and Chenonceau, and the church at St.-Aignan with its notable twelfth-century frescoes of Christ in Majesty and the healer St. Gilles. The small, moated and much-photographed château of Azay-le-Rideau is on the Indre, as are Loches and Ussé, and Chinon is on the wide, tree-lined Vienne. Earlier in its course the Cher passed through the cathedral city of Bourges and the Vienne, much further south, passed through Limoges. The Indre spends much of its time in quiet, rural places, including those near Nohant which feature in several of George Sand's novels: deep tracks, thickets, misty ponds. And then there are the many lesser Loire tributaries like the Beuvron threading its way through the heaths and forest of the Sologne, or the Authion among the strawberry-fields in Anjou, or the Borne passing the Orgues d'Espally, the "striking pyramidal mass of basalt pillars like the pipes of an organ" near Le Puy (*Bradshaw's Illustrated Hand Book* for France, 1856). There are also the canals, linked especially to the Roanne-Briare stretch of the river.

The tributaries have their own significant tributaries: the Gartempe joins the Creuse which joins the Vienne, as does the Clain, the river on which Poitiers is built. The Maine, whose confluence with the Loire is just south of the city of Angers, is itself very short but combines the waters of the Mayenne and the Sarthe, a 178-mile river which has passed through Le Mans. The Sarthe in turn receives le Loir—not to be confused with la Loire—a 194-mile river which winds, often closely wooded, to the north of the Loire.

The disadvantage of these tributaries for the Loire is the immense amount of extra silt and flood-water they deliver to it. The advantage for the visitor is yet more interesting places to go: to diverge from the Loire, enjoy some Allier or Authion, and return.

RIVER LIFE

Maxime Du Camp, strolling "joyous and carefree" with Gustave Flaubert in 1847, "chattering and keeping quiet, singing and smoking" by the broad shining Loire between Montsoreau and Saumur, noticed large boats in the distance with their swollen sails. They looked like "those ancient galleys which the zephyrs propelled with their breath, and which tritons escorted, blowing into their conches." Often vessels were less divinely wafted. Water levels were unpredictable—there were floods and, especially after the sev-

Chaland: a reconstruction

enteenth century, shallow or dry river-beds. Travel upstream was always hard work. The *chaland*, developed from early medieval times onwards, was the vessel best equipped to deal with these problems: a flat-bottomed, square-sailed craft, up to a hundred feet long. The mast could be lowered. The cargo of such craft included coal, wine, hemp, faïence from Nevers and Roanne, wood, stone, salt.

Chalands were almost certainly what Du Camp saw, unless they were the similar but larger *gabares*. A much smaller version was called a *fûtreau* and there were also, among many other types of boat, *sapines* of pine-wood which travelled downstream from the upper Loire and then were broken up, *galiotes*, *péniches*, *pataches* (originally the name for customs men's boats), and huge *charroyères* for carrying livestock and hay. Logs came up from Burgundy lashed together as *flottages*. And there were stationary *bateaux-lavoirs*, floating huts for washerwomen.

Some of these boats have survived and there are also many reconstructions. But chalands and the like had disappeared from much of the river by 1910. They were a decreasingly practical way of transporting goods, often overloaded or held up by the vagaries of the river: no competition for the railways and then the roads. There are stretches of the Loire which now seem strangely empty. Such quietness was once exceptional, although Elizabeth Strutt, in 1833, records a "serene" moonlit night on the river near Tours; "not a ripple of the noiseless Loire interrupted the full concert of the frogs, who seemed imparadised by thousands in the marshy spots reclaimed by the river." By day the frogs would have found it more difficult to make themselves heard. The loud slap of washing against boards was a familiar sound until well into the twentieth century. Loirelubbers and landlubbers exchanged pleasantries and unpleasantries. According to a 1908 glossary of Anjou speech, a boatman might term a riverine peasant, among other things, a "castaud", "pic", "pampre" or "vire-bouse". "Castaud" is of uncertain origin. The other three are "woodpecker", "vine-branch" and the more evidently insulting "cowpat-turner". In return the boatmen were called "mariniasses" or "pirriers". (*Pirriers* are people who live on butchers' scraps.) They called themselves "chalandoux" or "mariniers". There were also rivalries between different groups on the river. Canal workers fought with river-workers. Boatmen operating from Montjean described as "péteux" ("cowards, scared rabbits") those from St.-Clémentin-des-Levées. Worse, these cowards subsisted, apparently, on a diet of beans.

Language was, of course, only one aspect of the distinctive culture of the boat people. The men dressed in "loose trousers and a short smock of blue serge or canvas... held at the waist by a pin (often of silver)," a coloured scarf, "a felt hat with a wide brim, laced under the chin" and willow or poplar *sabots* (Richard Wade, *The Companion Guide to the Loire*). Stereotypically they were, as Wade says, "rough, tough and devout" and "fond of drinking and whoring".

In the 1820s river traffic underwent a dramatic change which infuriated, sunk or offered alternative employment to such traditional sailors. In 1822 the steam-boat *Loire* made its first trip down the estuary from Nantes to Paimboeuf. It was some eighty feet long, carried 250 passengers and was travelling from Nantes as far as Angers by 1824, when the return journey took two days. Another steamer reached Orléans in 1825 and soon boats and companies proliferated. In the 1840s steamers took fourteen or fifteen hours to travel from Tours to Orléans and between nine and ten to make the easier return journey.

Fierce rivalry meant that boilers were stoked to bursting-point. There were terrible accidents like the explosion on the *Vulcain* at Ingrandes in

An "inexplosible"

1837, when boiling steam and water poured into the first class compartment, killing a number of passengers including a group of four children of the Bernard family (a fifth survived). Their mother was badly scalded and her maid, who had tried to save them, died afterwards. Other mishaps were less accidental. In 1832 the intoxicated crew of a steam-boat at Champtoceaux rammed the rival *Ville d'Orléans* and allowed their anchor to smash into it, causing much damage and dismay. The malefactors were keen to board, armed with bayonets belonging to the soldiers they were transporting, but luckily their officers managed to restrain them.

As a result of such incidents both conduct regulations and boat design were improved. From 1837 "inexplosibles" travelled the river: a new type of steamer with a boiler less prone to overheat. Some were up to 150 feet long with comfortable saloon and restaurant. Smaller "inexplosibles" managed the more difficult waters upriver from Orléans to Nevers between 1839 and 1852, when the Haute-Loire company gave up the struggle. By this time all the steam-boat companies, like other commercial users of the river, were in difficulties because of the coming of the railways. Between 1843 and 1850 they arrived—blow upon blow—in Orléans, Tours, Saumur, Angers, Nantes. Few of the steamer companies survived the 1850s.

The canals, built between the seventeenth and nineteenth centuries to bypass difficult sections of the river, also fared badly against the railways. Much of the Loire with the exception of the estuary is today the preserve of pleasure-boats: a very different situation from that in Thomas Coryat's day, when the river was still a major artery of France. Then salt travelled upstream, wood mainly downstream, wine both ways, to the châteaux built, with such convenience in mind, near the water.

CHÂTEAUX: FROM KEEPS TO PALACES

Mark Girouard, in a useful (if, he admits, "over-tidy") account of the origin and early proliferation of châteaux (*Life in the French Country House*, 2000), explains that

> The leaders of the warrior bands which flooded into France in the fifth, ninth and tenth centuries carved out domains for themselves, which they ruled by force of arms. They acquired their own castle or castles, and their own bands of armed and mounted companions who rode round with them and fought with and for them. They rewarded these companions by carving smaller domains out of their own big ones, and giving them to their followers. On these smaller domains were built smaller castles... held in return for oaths of service.

There is little trace of these castles—they usually consisted of not much more than a wooden tower—but some of their stone successors remain. *Donjons* or keeps in both materials are associated with Foulques Nerra, Count of Anjou from 987 to 1040, ancestor of the Plantagenets. In his long wars against the Counts of Blois the aptly named "Black Falcon" was a great builder as well as a great burner and destroyer. According to his grandson Foulques Rechin, he built thirteen fortresses; his keeps survive at Loches and probably at Langeais. Later châteaux often developed around or near the original building. At Montrichard, for example, the eleventh-century keep which had replaced Foulques Nerra's wooden construction was joined by curtain walls, a chapel and a governor's lodging. The bulky keep of Beaugency is near the fifteenth-century château of Joan of Arc's "companion in arms" Dunois.

Châteaux continued to be strongly fortified during the long struggles between the Kings of France and of England which followed the succession of the Count of Anjou as King Henry II of England in 1154. (Henry's son King John lost most of his continental empire, but the struggle resumed in the fourteenth century for the "Hundred Years' War".) But at the same time the castles, between which kings and lords habitually travelled, were sites for courtly entertainments including poetry, music, dancing, jousting and less refined jesting and tumbling. Towers were elongated for both defensive and aesthetic reasons—the ideal version, only a little exaggerated, is often to be seen in the background in the Books of Hours illuminated for Jean, Duc de Berry (1340-1416). At Berry's own Mehun-sur-Yèvre near Bourges, Girouard points out on the evidence of both the illumination and the ruins, "The old formula, so frequently grim—round towers, massive walls, crenellations, a moat—has been transformed... [T]he towers dissolve at their summits into slender cages of stone and glass, even the crenellations... were carved with trefoils and foliage." Some of the functions of the multi-purpose Great Hall of the earlier Middle Ages were taken over by smaller rooms: bedchambers, oratories, places suited for business, conversation or the contemplation of *très riches heures*.

For the Loire regions the fifteenth-century phase of the wars with the English was particularly important. Driven out of Paris, Charles VII held court mainly at Bourges—he was known, derisively, as "le roi de Bourges"—or at nearby Mehun-sur-Yèvre, or in Touraine. He preferred to live mainly in these areas even after the French recapture of Paris in 1436. The royal connection with the region persisted for another century. Charles VII's cousin Charles, Duc d'Orléans, presided over a cultured court at Blois after he was at last ransomed from the English, who held him for twenty-five years following his capture at Agincourt in 1415. He was both a patron of poets, including François Villon, and himself a versatile poet in many forms, his main subject "amour, prince de mondaine doulceur"—earthly delights. Little is left of the duke's Château of Blois, simply because subsequent princely owners insisted on setting on it their own architectural mark. Charles VII's successors, from Louis XI (reigned 1461-83) to François I (1515-47) spent much time on the Loire, especially at Amboise and Blois. Experiments with Italian decorative elements began there and at Chambord following the French intervention in Italy of the late fifteenth and early sixteenth century.

During the course of the sixteenth century, however, the centre of

dominica .i. quadrage   nficabo cum longitudie
sunocauit me sime.   dierum adimplebo eum.
et ego craudiam cu   Qui hitat ma d ps.⁊
eripiam cum et glo   iutorio altissimi in pro

affairs began to shift more decisively to Paris and the Île de France. Louis XIV's Versailles cemented this tendency in the following century. Royal visits to the Loire became much rarer and some houses were visited only occasionally by their owners and fell into neglect. (Even Blois was nearly demolished under Louis XVI.) There were, of course, exceptions; such châteaux as Montgeoffroy and the now mostly lost Chanteloup flourished in the late eighteenth century as did "Madame de Pompadour's Ménars on its bright terraces" (Edith Wharton). But after the Revolution, as quite often before, many of the buildings were in a sorry state. At Chambord, says Longfellow, "all is mournful and deserted. The grass has overgrown the pavement of the courtyard, and the rude sculpture upon the walls is broken and defaced" (*Outre-mer: or, a Pilgrimage to the Old World*, 1835).

This situation was transformed, at least for the better known houses, by a variety of factors: the establishment in 1837 of the Commission des Monuments Historiques, the growth of tourism, republican nostalgia for the *ancien régime* and the efforts of wealthy or determined owners. One such was Joachim Carvallo, who after 1906 transformed the gardens at Villandry from overgrown confusion to restored Renaissance splendour. In 2007 about 800,000 people visited Chenonceau, 700,000 Chambord, and 330,000 Villandry.

TROGLODYTES

> We passed Montlouis, a village having never an house above ground; but such only as are hewn out of the main rocks which are of excellent freestone; here and there the funnel of a chimney appearing through the surface amongst the vineyards which are over them; and in this way they inhabit the caves, as it were sea-cliffs, one side of the river for many miles together.

John Evelyn, in 1644, had his first encounter with troglodytic living. Houses, chapels, wine-cellars, ovens, stables, barns, garages and sheds have been cut into the pale tufa of Touraine and Anjou for many centuries. Wine can be kept at an even temperature. You can shelter during storms, battles or invasions, quarry stone from your back wall, produce *pommes tapées* or *poires tapées*—apples and pears cooked, crushed and dried by the traditional troglodytic method.

The underground developments could be extensive. Matilda Betham-Edwards, introducing Arthur Young's *Travels* (1792) in 1889, describes "a vast cave, in shape like an amphitheatre, containing half a dozen cottages or human burrows." At Rochemenier there is a whole troglodytic village, dug in this case not into tufa but into the soft shell-marl known in France as *falun*. Even larger is the Vignemont quarry at Loches. For hundreds of years workers and their families lived as well as quarrying here. They grew mushrooms. They sought refuge from soldiers and brigands: one sixteenth-century intruder, in a reconstruction here, has burrowed his way in but is about to receive a hefty blow over the head from a troglodyte with a stick. Other models and displays follow the quarrying process. Often this must have involved tremendous, echoing noise. Now, however, the cold caverns feel like a vast natural gallery of colours and textures. Sound is supplied by visitors' voices and the percussive "sound sculptures" of Will Menter.

Of the subterranean places still put to practical use one of the most memorable belongs to the Marc Brédif wine-company in Rochecorbon, just north of the Loire near Vouvray. Its store-rooms and galleries are adapted from a former quarry. The round tasting-room with its rough-hewn ceiling looks like an ancient crypt, a site for torchlight ritual. It is used, of course, for no purpose more arcane than sampling Vouvray.

Troglodytism demonstrates for Arthur Young the dryness of the climate. "In England the rheumatism would be the chief inhabitant." But even in France at the time caves were not always regarded as desirable homes. People were often there as much from poverty as from choice. Betham-Edwards reports that "already in 1875 the darkest and most comfortless subterranean chambers had been abandoned, and on revisiting the country fourteen years later, I found neat, new dwellings springing up, the homes of peasant farmers built by themselves." Some chambers stayed abandoned, while others were later made habitable enough for the liking of estate agents, Parisians and foreigners.

FOOD: RIVER OF PLENTY

Elizabeth David, the indefatigable educator of British tastes, listed some of the joys of Nantes in an article of 1962 (reprinted in *An Omelette and a Glass of Wine*, 1984): "Winkles and whelks, cockles and oysters, spider crabs, scallops, shrimps, langoustines, mussels, prawns," clams and sea-truffles make "the open-air market-stalls... a fishy paradise, smelling of iodine, salty, dripping with seaweed and ice." Moving on to the restaurants, she absorbed small Breton mussels, "cooked in their own liquid until they opened; fresh cream was poured over them; they were sprinkled with chopped fresh tarragon; and brought to table piled up in a tureen."

Other areas have their delights. The Le Puy green lentil, grown in the Haute-Loire, is used in soup, in salads, with meat, fish, bread, and has been granted the AOC (*Appelation d'Origine Contrôlée*) reserved mainly for distinguished wines and cheeses. The Loire in general is known for bream, tench, pike, and eel. In *French Provincial Cooking* (1960) David celebrates "the famous *beurre blanc*", a popular sauce "made solely from a reduction of shallots, which are to Angevin cooking what garlic is to Provence, and wine vinegar whisked up with the finest butter." In Touraine she experienced stuffed clams, *dodine de canard* ("a very rich cold duck galantine"), pork "garnished with… enormous, rich juicy prunes," "wonderful wine-dark *matelotes* of eel" and *alose à l'oseille*—grilled shad with sorrel sauce. Tours is famous also for *rillettes*: pork cubed and then cooked in its own fat, pounded down with a mortar, kept in jars and often eaten on toast. The version traditional in Le Mans uses goose as well as pork. Always mentioned with *rillettes* are *rillons* (or sometimes *rillauds*), where the pork is cooked for longer and not pounded.

Another item of *charcuterie* associated with Touraine but familiar elsewhere is *andouillettes*. Arthur Koestler, canoeing on the Loire in 1957, paused on a "lone beach facing the mouth of the Allier" to lunch on "andouillettes de vire (chitterling stuffed with sausage meat which looks in cross-section like mottled quartz), goat cheese and peaches" (*Drinkers of Infinity*, 1968). The goat cheese may have been Crottin; its most valued variety, made in a village near Sancerre since the sixteenth century, is Crottin de Chavignol.

Tarte Tatin, an upside-down caramelized apple tart, originated in the Sologne. According to tradition it was created accidentally by Stéphanie Tatin, of the Hôtel Tatin in Lamotte-Beuvron, in 1898. *Crémets*, white cheese mixed with egg-whites and cream, are a popular dessert from Anjou. (Cheese was not part of the original recipe.) The *pithiviers* is an almond-cake named after its place of origin, 25 miles north of Orléans.

La Maison Troisgros, the restaurant of the Troisgros family in Roanne, is one of the best-known restaurants in France. Three generations of the family have been involved since 1930. In 1979 Richard Wade, in his *Com-

panion Guide to the Loire, noted that "If you like truffles with your scrambled eggs; juniper berries with your thrush pâté; lobster cooked in ways undreamed of… and if you have a long pocket, this is where you want to be." The menu has evolved since then—Michel Troisgros, the present owner, has been influenced by Japanese and other cuisines—but continues to win awards and to require said pocket.

WINE: "DIVINE LIQUOR, AND CELESTIAL JUICE"

The serene female personification of the Loire on the Place Royale fountain in Nantes not only pours water from her urns but, very suitably, is crowned with vine-leaves and grapes. Given the immense variety of wines available along the Loire and its tributaries, wine commentators struggle slightly to come up with a general verdict. Roger Voss (*Wines of the Loire*, 1995), however, feels that "Loire wines are often understated, aiming to please rather than overwhelm." Even the richest of them—"the reds of Chinon and Bourgueil, the sweet whites of Quarts de Chaume and Bonnezeaux—rely as much on elegance as weight, on balance as much as on power."

The vine has been cultivated here since about the fourth century AD; its importance to Ligerians is underlined by the frequency with which St. Martin of Tours is credited, as Voss points out, with planting vineyards. *Martiner* traditionally means, in Touraine, to test the year's wine. The principal grapes for white wine are Muscadet (used also as a name for the resulting wine), Sauvignon blanc and Chenin blanc. Cabernet Franc produces red wine, including Chinon. Cabernet, Gamay and Grolleau are "responsible for very large quantities" of what one critic rather grudgingly calls "more or less amiable rosé, one of the region's great money-spinners" (*Hugh Johnson's Wine Companion*, 4th edition, 1997). The rosé has perhaps improved, but like other French wine has been subject to fierce competition from other parts of the world.

There was an even greater variety of grapes and wines before the devastating arrival of phylloxera from the 1850s onwards. Many vineyards in the southern parts of the region never recovered. (St.-Pourçain-sur-Sioule is one of the few southern wines which still has a following; Johnson quips that "it is almost all consumed today to mitigate the effects of the treatment of the spa of Vichy".) Less than 100,000 hectares of land are now used for vine growing, compared with at least 200,000 before phylloxera. But some very popular names remain, most obviously Muscadet in the Loire-Atlantique, Vouvray in Touraine, and the wines of the Sancerrois and the neighbouring Pouilly-Fumé. The Muscadet vineyards are the most extensive; the main *appellation* is Muscadet-Sèvre-et-Maine. It has not always been so familiar abroad. According to the yachtsman Captain Leslie Richardson in *Brittany and the Loire* (1927), "the local dry white wine called Muscadet," which he drank with a meal of pike (*brochet au beurre blanc*), eel, asparagus and duck, "was little known outside of Nantes." Clearly his belief that "the Nantais themselves consume, with ease, the entire output" was a little exaggerated but paid tribute to the palatability of the wine. "Vouvray" denotes a wide range of different tastes. The sparkling version "tends to be a little richer and rounder than champagne… There is more flavour of grapes about it, if a little less subtlety," concludes Hugh Johnson in *Wine* (1992 edition).

As well as the wine-critics' discerning discriminations, we have Rabelais' "discourse and pleasant tattle of drinking" by the parents of Gargantua and their thirsty company in Touraine. Sir Thomas Urquhart's seventeenth-century translation renders, with appropriate exuberance, the

Loire vineyards

cries of multiple speakers once "began flagons to go, gammons to trot, goblets to fly, great bowls to ting, glasses to ring":

Draw, reach, fill, mix, give it me without water. So my friend, so, whip me off this glass neatly, bring me hither some claret, a full weeping glass till it run over. A cessation and truce with thirst. Ha, thou false fever, wilt thou not be gone?… I drink for the thirst to come. I drink eternally… I sup, I humect, I moisten my gullet, I drink, and all for fear of dying. Drink always and you shall never die. If I drink not, I am a ground dry, gravelled and spent. I am stark dead without drink, and my soul ready to fly into some marsh amongst frogs… I have a remedy against thirst, quite contrary to that which is good against the biting of a mad dog. Keep running after a dog, and he will never bite you; drink always before the thirst, and it will never come upon you. There I catch you, I awake you. Argus had a hundred eyes for his sight, a butler should have (like Briareus) a hundred hands wherewith to fill us wine indefatigably… *Natura abhorret vacuum*… Come, therefore, blades, to this divine liquor, and celestial juice, swill it over heartily, and spare not! It is a decoction of nectar and ambrosia.

To be dry for a moment having consulted a concordance: the word "vin" occurs 178 times in Rabelais' work.

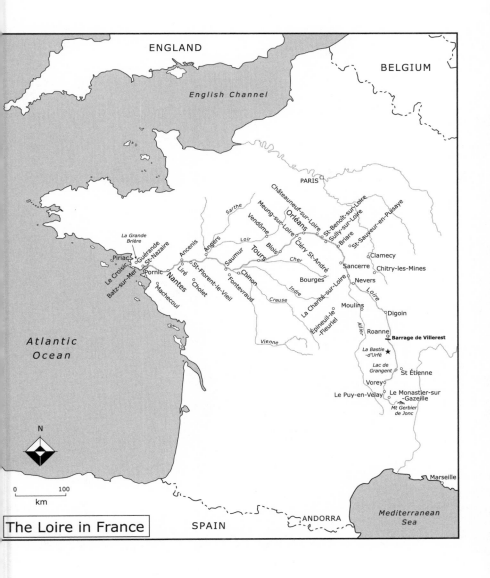

The Loire in France

ENGLAND
BELGIUM
English Channel
PARIS
Sarthe
Châteauneuf-sur-Loire
Meung-sur-Loire
Vendôme
Orléans
St-Benoît-sur-Loire
Sully-sur-Loire
St-Sauveur-en-Puisaye
Loir
Angers
Blois
Cléry St-André
Briare
Ancenis
Saumur
Tours
Cher
Clamecy
La Grande
Brière
Piriac
Guérande
St-Nazaire
Liré
St-Florent-le-Vieil
Chinon
Sancerre
Chitry-les-Mines
Le Croisic
Pornic
Nantes
Cholet
Fontevraud
Indre
Bourges
Nevers
Batz-sur-Mer
Machecoul
Creuse
La Charité-sur-Loire
Loire
Épineuil-le-
-Fleuriel
Moulins
Digoin
Atlantic
Ocean
Vienne
Allier
Roanne
Barrage de Villerest
La Bastie
-d'Urfé
Lac de
Grangent
St Étienne
Vorey
N
Le Puy-en-Velay
Le Monastier-sur-
Gazeille
Mt Gerbier
de Jonc
Marseille
0   100
km
Mediterranean
Sea
The Loire in France
SPAIN
ANDORRA

Chapter One
STRUGGLING WITH THE ROCKS
FROM THE SOURCE TO ROANNE

The Loire rises among the Vivarais mountains of the *département* of Ardèche. The Mediterranean is eighty-five miles away and at first the river runs towards it, parallel with the Rhône. But an extinct volcano, the Suc de Bauzon, soon blocks the way, diverting the Loire north-west. It continues to the Lac d'Issarlès, a volcanic crater which supplies the hydro-electric plant eleven miles away at Montpezat. It passes one of the first of very many ruined hill-top castles: Arlempdes on its basalt rock, beloved of nineteenth-century painters and engravers. "Wimpling over the stones at Goudet," Robert Louis Stevenson reported, it is still "an amiable stripling of a river, which it seems absurd to call the Loire." Streams continue to join and swell the river as it moves on towards Le Puy-en-Velay, the first city on its course, and its precipitous crags. At Le Puy the Loire, its tributary the Borne, and the Dolaison which feeds the Borne, "roll their shallow waves over rocky beds" (Louisa Stuart Costello, 1842). Deep gorges follow, over one of which rise the rock and castle of Lavoûte-Polignac. This too was once a romantic ruin but was rebuilt after the Polignac family, its ancestral owners, bought it in 1888.

The gorges deepen further as the Loire twists on to Vorey. Still there are dramatic views of, and from, high castles, villages and churches: the restored Romanesque church and monastic ruin at Chamalières-sur-Loire, the castle of Rochecorbon above Bas. After Retournac the Loire is joined by its first significant tributary, the southern Lignon or Lignon du Velay, which rises not far from it near Mont Mézenc. Further north the Loire opens out into the Grangent reservoir, where people come to swim, sail and water-ski: a popular escape from the big city of St.-Étienne to the east. Beyond the lake the river moves on towards the plain of Forez, with the peaks of the Forez mountains to the west. The plain struck the traveller Douglas Goldring in 1911 as "an unhealthy, humid, misty expanse". Honoré d'Urfé, three hundred years earlier, delivered a very different idealized version of his native Forez and the nymphs and shepherds wandering by its River Lignon—not the "southern" Lignon but another tributary, the "Lignon forézien", which joins the Loire near Feurs. The spa of Montrond-les-Bains, on the right bank of the Loire before Feurs, has a more direct remedy for the "unhealthy" element Goldring perceives. According to Vivian Rowe (*The Loire*, 1969), it "specializes in the treatment of stomach ailments and liver complaints, arthritis, anaemia and obesity, and perhaps hypochondria, by means of hot springs."

After the low Forez the gorges return until Roanne. "This is the river's last struggle with the rocks," as Goldring puts it. After Roanne it will run mostly through plains and more moderate hills. But before the city one grand sight remains: the great concrete curve of the Barrage de Villerest, completed in 1984. Its reservoir, the Lac de Villerest, is over twenty miles long. A beach, campsites and a golf course have been installed partly to compensate local people whose land was submerged when the lake was created. But perhaps the most exciting activity here is to watch the vast, surging, spraying arcs of white water when the floodgates are opened, as they were during the floods of autumn 2008. Usually life is more serene. The canal from Roanne to Digoin begins its orderly course. Vineyards, among the first of many along the Loire, appear to the west on the reddish granitic slopes of the Côte Roannaise.

Mont Gerbier de Jonc and the Sources of the Loire
In May 1911 Douglas Goldring journeyed from Le-Puy-en-Velay to the source of the Loire by tram, crowded bus, foot and horse-drawn "wag-

onette". On the way up to Le Monastier he walked with "a bull-necked man in brown corduroys... with a bottle of wine sticking out of each pocket" who kept warning him that his "destination was *diablement* cold." Twelve miles up from Le Monastier, having helped push the wagonette "a great part of the way", Goldring came to the cold, desolate village of Les Estables, beneath Mont Mézenc: now a rather happier place, a cross-country ski resort. At a grim local inn—the tourist office "châlet"—he felt cold and lonely and discovered that he had lost the gold coin which was supposed to cover all expenses until he got back to Le Puy. (An innkeeper at Goudet later took pity on him and provided him with sustenance and a bed.) But his mood changed completely when, at about 5 a.m., he looked out of the window and saw sun, green slopes, daffodils, violets and clear blue sky. Soon he was out among the larks and glittering rivulets, on the way to Mont Gerbier de Jonc, at the foot of which the Loire begins.

The mountain is an abrupt peak shaped, Goldring notes, like a pine-cone. The summit is 5,200 feet, but the ascent is easy because it rises from a plateau already 4,700 feet above sea-level. As Graham Robb points out in *The Discovery of France* (2007), the summit has also been five hundred feet lower since its collapse in 1821. But the view remains spectacular. Robb describes it near the beginning of his book: "to the east, the long white curtain of the Alps...; to the north, the wooded ridges of the Forez and the mist descending from the Jura to the plains beyond Lyon; to the west, the wild Cévennes, the Cantal plateau and the whole volcanic range of the upper Auvergne." Nearly a thirteenth of France is "spread out like a map". As so often, the Loire is at the heart of the country. But Robb's main point is how remote, disparate and unknown that country has been for most of its history. In the eighteenth century (and much later) several of the regions visible from Le Gerbier "barely knew of each other's existence" and spoke very different dialects, so that "to walk in any direction for a day was to become incomprehensible." Such places were dangerous for outsiders. At Les Estables there were worse things to worry about than Goldring's temporary "blues": Robb tells the story of the young geometer, a member of a team sent out in 1740 to gather data for a new, accurate map of France, who was "hacked to death by the natives". "To isolated villagers, a man in foreign clothes who pointed inexplicable instruments at barren rocks was up to no good." He was credited with sorcery; under his influence the crops might fail and the animals die.

Mont Gerbier de Jonc

Goldring descended, safely, in search of the "tiny trickle" of the Loire. He discovered it, unexpectedly, in a farm where he ate bread and cheese with "sour red wine". He asked the farmer, who was swilling out his barn with water from a wooden pipe, for information. The water running from a trough through the pipe was, of course, "the veritable source" and Goldring claims that he decided, forthwith, to follow the Loire from there to the estuary. He did so, and wrote in the process one of the most interesting and readable books on the subject, *The Loire: the Record of a Pilgrimage* (1913). (Goldring, 1887-1960, went on to have a varied career as a travel-writer, poet, anti-war novelist, publisher and magazine-editor.) But the trough at the farm is not the only "veritable source". Three springs have their champions: the alleged "true", "geographical" and "authentic" sources. These and many others permeate the granite at the foot of the mountain, producing streams which together form the Loire.

Le Monastier

Robert Louis Stevenson came to the département of Haute-Loire in the early autumn of 1878. He recalled his impressions in "A Mountain Town in France" and *Travels with a Donkey in the Cévennes*. He felt at home in the countryside "wild and tumbled, rather than commanding; an upland rather than a mountain district". On the whole both the landscape and the people around Le Monastier—near the Gazeille, a tributary of the Loire—seemed convincingly Scottish. The natives, he wrote, have "abrupt, uncouth, Fifeshire manners, and accost you, as if you were trespassing, with an '*Où'st-ce que vous allez?*' only translatable into the lowland 'Whau'r ye gaun?'" Like Stevenson's Scots they kept the Sabbath; "not to attend mass would involve social degradation." The young men, too, tended to emigrate, if in this case less out of poverty than in search of new experiences. For Stevenson as for Goldring, who visited Le Monastier in 1911, it was the local lace-makers who brightened the rather dour atmosphere, although by Goldring's time the industry was in decline as a result of changes in fashion.

Within a few days, as Stevenson explored the area, churlish "Whau'r ye gaun" had given way to polite "*Quoi, vous rentrez au Monastier ce soir?*" In the town "every urchin seemed to know my name, although no living creature could pronounce it." The lace-makers were full of questions about his homeland. How remote the Haute-Loire still was in 1878 is suggested by their conviction that if the language spoken in Britain was not French, it could only be *patois*. Stevenson proceeded to give "illustrations of my native jargon", which the lace-makers declared to be the "most preposterous and jocose" sounding patois they had ever heard. "At each new word there was a new explosion of laughter, and some of the younger ones were glad to rise from their chairs and stamp about the street in ecstasy… 'Bread,' which sounds a commonplace, plain-sailing monosyllable in English, was the word that most delighted these good ladies of Monastier; it seemed to them frolicsome and racy, like a page of *Pickwick*; and they all got it carefully by heart, as a stand-by, I presume, for winter evenings."

Douglas Goldring found the situation of Le Monastier "remarkably fine"—dominated by "the line of red, craggy rocks of La Moulette, that burst like jagged bones out of the smooth green turf." But the town itself was "squalid, dirty, and unprepossessing". He was prepared to admire the Romanesque church and the remains of the monastery which gave Le Monastier its name, but thought little of the houses "built of black lava-rocks stuck roughly together and roofed… with red tiles" and less of "the naked squares full of garbage, dirty children, and adventurous pigs." The adventurous Stevenson was not so easily put off; he was about to encounter harsher conditions in the high Cévennes, sometimes sleeping rough.

In Le Monastier Stevenson bought, for sixty-five francs and a glass of brandy, the "diminutive she-ass" Modestine. He soon found that he would have to carry much of the luggage himself, but for twelve memorable days they "jogged along with our six legs by many a rocky and many a boggy by-road," covering "upwards of a hundred and twenty miles" across several "respectable ridges".

LE-PUY-EN-VELAY: "THE CONVULSIONS OF THE QUATERNARY"
The country around Le Puy is, observed Arthur Young in his 1792 *Travels*, "all in its form tempestuous as the billowy ocean". The city is set, as Ian Robertson puts it in his *Blue Guide* to France, "amongst a denticulated landscape of volcanic cones thrown up during the convulsions of the quaternary." Various prominent buildings, including the cathedral of Le Puy, rest on such high cones or rocks. The Romanesque chapel of St. Michel stands on Rocher Aiguilhe—"almost a pillar of basalt," says John Ruskin, "crowned by an aerial church". The high castle of Polignac, a few miles away, has its "abrupt and precipitous rock" as described in Anthony Trollope's story "The Château of Prince Polignac", a comic piece involving local courtship rituals and misunderstandings on an excursion from Le Puy to the château. The Rocher Corneille, above the cathedral, has been crowned, since 1860, by the "colossal and all too conspicuous" (Robertson) statue of Notre-Dame de France, forged from Russian cannon captured at the Battle of Sebastopol.

Young saw by the road "basaltic pentagons and sexagons"; "gypsum and lime-stone abound... the very meadows are built on lava: every thing, in a word, is either the product of fire, or has been disturbed or tossed about by it." Half a century later Ruskin reacted with characteristic enthusiasm and knowledge to the "violent verticalness" of the crags around him. In his 1840 diary he recorded investigating, after dinner, "basaltic beds above town, well formed, containing zircon in considerable quantity, well crystallized." He scrambled up through terraced vineyards and crumbling, slippery basalt to admire "rolling grey clouds far over the east, with crests of rose colour shadowing the heaving hills; the town in full light, a little scattery in effect, but very bright." "The place would," he concluded, "take a month to sketch."

Ruskin, a young man (as eventually an old man) of extreme likes and dislikes, found his accommodation, and the inhabitants, less pleasing than the geology: "Abominable inn, all filth and lime dust, and town disgusting. Crowded mass; quantities of nuns; but nuns and women and children all ugly, decrepit and diseased." The following day he felt more sociable, chatting with a group of grape-pickers who wondered whether he came from Paris, Russia or Normandy. But he still seems unlikely to have agreed with George Sand's Marquis de Villemer (in the novel of that name, 1860) that people in Velay are essentially "honest and proud", however rife seem to be squalor, violence and superstition. Sand had spent much more time in the area than Ruskin and took an interest, at once anthropological and romantic, in folk customs and beliefs. And she needed an appropriately pure setting to contrast with the corruptions of Paris elsewhere in the novel. The inhabitants partake, says the marquis, of both the harshness and the beauty of their land and their sky.

Le Puy: the Cathedral
The Cathedral of Notre-Dame is a pilgrimage church: both for its position on one of the routes to Santiago de Compostela and for its own Black Virgin and fever-curing stone (originally part of a dolmen). Pilgrims should arrive braced by virtuous effort. Louisa Stuart Costello recalled that "After half an hour's climbing, almost on hands and knees, up alleys paved with broad pieces of lava, irregularly piled on each other, through streets narrow, dark, filthy and inodorous beyond all manner of description, we reached the first flight of steps which leads to the cathedral" (*A Pilgrimage to Auvergne*, 1842). There at last it stands: "the true, old fortress church; dark, heavy, and massive; with few windows, and with no large portals", yet with "no crudeness, but on the contrary finish, great elegance, and fine symmetry of form" (Elise Whitlock Rose, *Cathedrals and Cloisters of Midland France*, 1907).

The cathedral has often been felt to look or feel eastern or "mystical". Once it was believed to show the clear influence of Muslim or Mozarabic Spain; now, as Xavier Barral i Altet points out in his authoritative book on the cathedral (2000), the style is seen as Romanesque, in line mainly with southern French and Italian models. Although there have been later addi-

tions like the dome over the crossing, a good range of Romanesque elements remains, including the twelfth-century doors and a Byzantine-influenced wall-painting of a the tall, calm, St. Michael, his long spear thrust apparently casually into the dragon. (In the "war in heaven" of *Revelation* 12, Michael and his angels fight the dragon or Satan.) A much later painting was discovered in 1850 in what is now the Chapelle des Reliques, reached from the north aisle. Prosper Mérimée found it under whitewash, the substance he spent much of his career lamenting, preventing or scraping away. Four of the Seven Liberal Arts emerged: a subtly coloured late fifteenth-century fresco personifying Grammar, Logic, Rhetoric and Music as richly robed female figures. They sit enthroned against a background of soft green hills. Men who have exemplified the arts in question sit slightly lower. The grammarian Priscian writes in a book, taking dictation from Grammar. Aristotle, a grander, more princely figure in red and ermine, reasons under the guidance of Logic. Cicero is with Rhetoric. Tubal-Cain, maker of instruments of bronze and iron (*Genesis* 4.22) is with Music, who holds a portable organ. The artist, Barral and others have concluded that the artist was probably Flemish.

The riches of the cathedral were increased by gifts from royal visitors and donors: both expressions of piety and ways of consolidating support for the French monarchy in this mountainous, often lawless land. In 1239 St. Louis gave the cathedral the immensely valuable gift of a thorn from Christ's Crown of Thorns, which he had purchased from the Byzantine emperor. Part of the True Cross followed in 1283, given by Louis' son Philip III. Kings continued to ascend the high rock and in 1475 Louis XI (extender of the kingdom and devotee of shrines and saints) donated a new crystal reliquary for the thorn. He also provided money for the spectacular restoration, in silver gilt, of the "portable dwelling of the Virgin, called 'chadaraïta'." The word probably derives from a Greek verb meaning "to contain".

But it was the Black Virgin herself who attracted most of the pilgrims, royal and otherwise. Tradition says that St. Louis, the crusader, obtained this statue too in the Middle East and presented it to the cathedral in 1254. Barral, however, concludes that the statue was of local, Auvergnat origin and may have been carved in the tenth century. It was not originally black. Probably it darkened with age, and was periodically repainted to maintain its blackness. One theory about the "black virgins" in a number of European churches is that they are an allusion to the *Nigra sum, sed Formosa*—"I am black but beautiful"—of the Song of Solomon.

The original Black Virgin was burnt by revolutionaries in the Place du Martouret in June 1794. Barral cites a tantalizing eye-witness account of the statue's destruction: as bluish smoke issued from the coverings of the Virgin, it was noticed that there was a "little door" on her back. From the hollow within fell "a sort of parchment rolled into a ball". One of the destroyers, the naturalist Bertrand-Morel, "wanted to retrieve it out of curiosity, but he did not dare to, fearing that he would be taken for a fanatic"—in other words a believer. There is room for limitless speculation on the contents of the manuscript. Doubtless it can be fitted into some Da Vinci Code. Less speculatively, the church authorities installed another Black Virgin, of uncertain date, in 1844. George Sand's Marquis de Villemer is sceptical: "they say that this one is apocryphal, and does fewer miracles than her predecessor." But she continues to attract devotion.

A number of other treasures were lost in the Revolution, and the chadaraïta had already been melted down earlier in the eighteenth century. A priest managed to buy the Holy Thorn in 1792 and took it with him to

St.-Étienne. A fragment of another thorn, allegedly from the same crown, later arrived as a replacement. A more important survival at Le Puy was the Bible of Theodulf, made in about 800 for Charlemagne's adviser, the Bishop of Orléans. As well as the biblical text it includes scriptural writings probably by Theodulf. Some of the parchment has been stained purple; gold and silver illumination is used for textual emphasis, and decorations include a variety of birds and vegetation.

SIMONE WEIL IN LE PUY: "INTERROGATIVE AVIDITY"

The philosophical, religious and political writer Simone Weil (1909-43) grew up in Paris. We might expect her to have stayed there, writing, perhaps, in the same cafés as Sartre and Beauvoir. But she offended Célestin Bouglé, assistant director of the École Normale Supérieure, with her independent thinking and manner, and in 1931 was despatched, for her first teaching job, to the girls' lycée in distant Le Puy. As well as philosophy, she gave lessons in Greek, Latin, history of art and history of mathematics.

According to the four former students who published a memoir together in 1951, everything about her, including "the awkwardness of her gestures" and "her penetrating look, through thick glasses," radiated "total frankness and forgetfulness of self." The poet Jean Tortel remembered, for Weil's friend and biographer Simone Pétrement, his similar first impressions of an unusual, slightly frightening person, "extremely ugly on first sight, face thin and very pronounced under her great black cloth beret, straight hair spilling out, body simply not there—covered by her cape apart from her stout black shoes." She would peer through her spectacles, leaning myopically forward, "with an intensity, and a sort of interrogative avidity, which I have never elsewhere encountered." And yet "the avidity was made up for, and as it were contradicted, by the imploring crease of her mouth, her large, over-moist lips which seemed always to be making a request—both smiling and desperate."

Away from school, Weil also involved herself in workers' education, as she did more extensively on her frequent visits to St.-Étienne. Little scandal attached to such activities. But the same was not true of her support for the unemployed men who had been set to under-paid stone breaking in the square outside the girls' lycée, Place Michelet. At their request she went with them, on 17 December 1931, to present their demands at the Mairie and at a municipal council meeting. Inevitably it was the articulate Weil who did most of the talking. But what really led to trouble was that she had gone to a café with unemployed workers and was in the habit of shaking hands with them on her way into school. Speaking up for such people was rather surprising conduct for a schoolmistress; fraternizing with them was beyond the pale as far as some local newspapers were concerned.

The Academic Inspector or education chief of Le Puy tried to explain to her, in avuncular tones, that it was not possible to behave here as one might in a big city. There would be several attempts to move her on to such a place—which, as she pointed out, she had originally requested. But nobody could force her out because she had technically done nothing wrong and was acknowledged to be a diligent and successful teacher. At one point the girls she taught persuaded their parents to sign a petition demanding that she be allowed to stay. Her own best answer to criticism was the sarcastic article she contributed to the teachers' union journal of Haute-Loire on 21 December. Apparently, she says, the educational administration believes in castes, in Untouchables. "There are people with whom a high school teacher can mix, if she really must, in the secrecy of a securely closed room, but with whom she must not, at any price, be seen shaking hands by the pupils' parents." These people are not crooked bankers or politicians but workers who are suffering because "the crisis [the Depression] has prevented them from exercising their trade."

Arguments dragged on for some weeks, briefly reaching the national press. Anger was fuelled by misinformation: Weil was a rabble-rouser, she was a hypocrite who, it was falsely claimed, wore silk stockings. She was often accused of working for Moscow. Attacks were also sometimes anti-Semitic: Pétrement cites a piece in the conservative *Mémorial* which calls Weil "red virgin of the tribe of Levi, messenger of the gospel of Moscow." She was condemned in a sermon at Le Puy cathedral. And then most people lost interest in the case. In the short term little or nothing had been achieved for the unemployed. But the dispute was one of many contributions to the changed political climate in which a Popular Front government—an alliance including socialists and communists—would eventually be elected in 1936.

After Le Puy Weil taught in schools in Roanne and Bourges. Her involvement with trade union activism and education continued. Searching as ever, she first engaged with communism and then came to doubt it as a solution to social inequality. Later in the 1930s she was closely involved with Roman Catholicism, but sought a synthesis between it and other religions and philosophies. She died in London in 1943, while working for the Free French, from tuberculosis and—saintly or suicidal—malnutrition.

St.-Étienne: "The moon rose red through smoke"

"The moon rose red through smoke as we drove into St. Étienne—a complete French Manchester," John Ruskin noted in October 1840. Three years later Murray's *Handbook* thought it "a French Birmingham" and "by no means an inviting place to tarry in: little regularity is preserved in the building of streets so suddenly thrown up; and the fine white sandstone of its houses, many of them 5 and 6 storeys high, is soon tarnished and blackened by the coal smoke which constantly hangs in clouds over it." It "has the merit, rare in France, of being well lighted with gas"; no doubt it needed to be if people were to see through the murk.

By the 1840s the city had already long been known for products as different as ribbons and small arms. During the Revolution it was even renamed Armeville; it is claimed, Murray reports, "that at a push 300,000 muskets might be produced in 12 months." But it was the coal industry which was to cause most smoke. Coal production had reached nearly 300,000 tonnes in 1812 and rose to over a million by 1836 and 1,700,000 in 1847. After some temporary setbacks the figure rose to four million tonnes in 1873 and, after the efforts of the First World War, close to five million. Initial growth was helped by the development of railways. In 1827 the first railway in France linked St.-Étienne to Andrézieux, a distance of thirteen miles; at first it was used for horse-drawn carts of coal, which were loaded onto boats on the Loire at Andrézieux to proceed down-river. The line also carried passengers after 1832 and steam-engines were introduced in 1844. Lines to Lyon and Roanne opened in 1832 and 1835.

Textiles, chocolates and bicycles were also produced in and near St.-Étienne. Power was supplied usually with the help of the Furan, a tributary of the Loire which runs through the city—now invisibly, having been channelled underground. Escoffier chocolate was made from 1770. The Pupier works opened in 1860 and by 1913 there were twenty-six *chocolateries*. The population of the city was 31,540 in 1821 and 148,650 in 1911; the modern conurbation has over 290,000 people. Such rapid expansion made for a continuously changing environment: building, demolition, gouging the land for mining, roads, railways and tramways. The photographer Félix Thiollier (1842-1914) recorded the change. Some of the people in his pictures wield sledge-hammers, unload goods or work on slag-heaps, but often they are dwarfed by their battered, blackened surroundings or only half-visible though dust, steam or smoke. Simone Weil worried later that the workers were increasingly controlled by their environment, not it by them. She saw the latest technology—pneumatic drills, borers—when she went down a coalmine at Sardou, near Rive-de-Gier, east of the city. She was allowed to try out a pneumatic drill and wrote about the experience in *L'Effort*, a local trade-union newspaper, for 19 March 1932 (quoted in Simone Pétrement's biography). Weil felt that where once the pickaxe was like an extra limb for the miner who used it—it was naturally adapted to the way he moved—now he was "part of the body of the machine, joining it like an extra wheel, and vibrating to its endless shaking." This seemed to her a more pressing problem than labour relations or who owned the mines. If the nature of work continued like this, social revolution would change nothing.

Miners decorate a St.-Etienne façade

Weil nevertheless hoped to ameliorate workers' conditions. She continued to explain social theory to sometimes bemused, but usually attentive audiences at union rallies and meetings. Albert Camus' vision of life in the city was bleaker. In 1942-3, while recuperating from tuberculosis, he lived near Le Chambon-sur-Lignon and sometimes travelled the thirty-five miles north to St.-Étienne for medical treatment. For him the city summed up the hopelessness of life and his own uncertainty about the future. (He was re-working *La Peste* and would soon become more actively involved in the Resistance.) In his *Notebooks* he describes poor, weary people for whom war had made conditions even worse. On the trains, with their battered cases, "all the French look like emigrants." At the station people ate "appalling food without complaint" and rushed off into the dark city. They worked long hours and had little to show for it. In St.-Étienne, in the morning mist, sirens "summon people to work amid a mess of towers, buildings and thick chimneys." Slag mounted towards the dark sky "like a monstrous sacrificial cake". The city and its suburbs were, Camus decided in a later entry, "a condemnation of the civilization which gave birth to them. A world where there is no longer any place for people, for joy, for active leisure, is a world which ought to die." And Europe will die if when peace comes it "does not signify a return to beauty, a restoration of love."

Finally heavy industry declined. The collieries closed in the 1980s or earlier. One which was active until 1973 can be visited—the mining museum at Puits Couriot. Many other aspects of local industry can be studied at the Musée d'Art et d'Industrie and the Musée du Vieux St.-Étienne. The city also has a good museum of modern art, whose collection ranges from Bernard Pagès' arrangements and juxtapositions of bricks and logs, sticks and corrugated iron, to still-lifes by Picasso and a large round *Nymphéas* by Monet. The moon no longer rises red through smoke.

FIRMINY-VERT

Ruskin was soon out of St.-Étienne, going

in delicious frosty sunlight, by an ascent of an hour and odd, up a beautiful quiet piece of green valley in the granite, fringed with pine, fresh grass beneath, knolled and rich and watered by white streamlets, one or two small cottages crouched in its hollows—altogether excessively Tyrolese: opening on an elevated plain of green sward, with patches of dark pine forest.

The *Stéphanois* (the name Étienne derives from Stephanus) still like to leave for such places and especially for the Loire. Le Corbusier, however, wanted people to stay in towns. He sought to create the "radiant city" where people, housing, sports facilities and churches would exist in one harmonious environment. In the 1960s at Firminy, south-west of St.-Étienne and just east of the Lac de Grangent and the Loire, Le Corbusier's Firminy-Vert was built on the site of an iron-mine. He designed a youth-centre, a housing-block, a sports stadium and a church. Eugène Claudius-Petit, mayor between 1953 and 1972 and a Le Corbusier enthusiast, said that the plan would prepare the way for "a renaissance of the human being, of the family, of society". It would revolutionize "the gestures of everyday life". Doubts have been raised about how far this ideal has been fulfilled. The architect, besides, had less of a say in the overall project than at other sites like his famous Marseille housing unit. Deborah Gans, in *The Le Corbusier Guide* (1987), registers a somewhat mixed impression: "Across the entire site of this townscape, Le Corbusier's sports complex and Unité establish a dialogue focused intently on both the landscape and each other, less concerned with their relation to the other solitary towers than to a timeless, ideal city."

HONORÉ D'URFÉ AND LA BASTIE

Not far from the ancient city of Lyon there is, towards the setting sun, a land called Forez which, small though it is, contains within it that which is most rare in Gaul: for both its plains and its mountains are so fertile and situated in such temperate air that the land can grow anything which the farmer can possibly desire. At the heart of this land is the most beautiful part of the plain, surrounded, as if by a high wall, by nearby mountains, and watered by the river Loire which, its source being fairly near, flows almost through the middle. At this stage the river is not yet swollen or proud, but gentle and peaceful. Several other streams add to it their bright waves, but one of the most beautiful is the Lignon which, in its wandering course... winds through this plain from the

high mountains… as far as Feurs where, the Loire receiving it, and
making it lose its own name, carries it off as tribute to the Ocean.

This is the opening of Honoré d'Urfé's immense romance *L'Astrée*
(1607-24). Its central plot results from the shepherdess Astrée's mistaken
belief that the shepherd Céladon loves another; when she rejects him, he
throws himself into the "deep and impetuous" Lignon and is swept away.
Presumed dead, he is in fact taken up by three beautiful nymphs, whose
chief, Galathée, falls in love with him and, Circe-like, will not let him go
(until the end of the first Book). Astrée mourns meanwhile. But this main
story is interwoven and artfully delayed by poems, other tales, letters and
orations. "Like the river Lignon," as d'Urfé's modern translator Steven
Rendall says, "the narrative meanders sinuously forward, gradually broad-
ening as it absorbs its tributaries, and deferring by countless detours its
arrival at its destination."

D'Urfé (1568-1625) fought for the Catholic League in the late sixteenth-century Wars of Religion, before finally making his peace with
Henri IV in 1602. His Forez, an imaginary fifth-century world where personal relationships, poetry and tending sheep are the main preoccupations,
implies a contrast with the savage fighting which had dominated the real
Forez and many other parts of France in the lifetime of the author. His
shepherds are aristocrats, enacting a more elegant and eloquent life than
their descendants. *L'Astreé* has thus sometimes been seen as a paean for the
aristocratic self-determination which was felt to have preceded the wars
and the growth of royal power. But it also looked forward, influencing,
through its many reprints, the development of the novel. Chateaubriand
(*Voyage à Clermont*) enjoyed the "ingenious fantasy" of mingling nymphs
and naiads with shepherds, knights and ladies. One of its most recent re-
vivals was Eric Rohmer's romantic film *Les Amours d'Astrée et de Céladon*
(2007).

D'Urfé grew up by the Lignon at the ancestral château of La Bastie (or
Bâtie) d'Urfé. The château, once a fortified manor-house, had been altered
and enlarged by his grandfather, Claude d'Urfé (1501-58), who spent five
years as an ambassador in Italy. Among the most evident Italianate features are the loggia and the grotto—a celebration of Neptune in coloured
sands, pebbles and shells. The once notable library, no doubt a valuable re-
source for Honoré d'Urfé, was dispersed in the eighteenth century. The

chapel also suffered: in the 1870s its internal decorations were sold off. The lustrous wood panelling—biblical and geometrical scenes, the work of Fra Damiano da Bergamo (1548)—was installed by the collector Harry Payne Whitney in his Fifth Avenue mansion and then given to the Metropolitan Museum of Art by his heirs in 1942. By the time of the sale La Bastie as a whole was in poor condition after repeated changes of ownership. It was saved from demolition in 1909 only when "La Diana", the historical society of Montbrison, raised enough money to buy it.

Chapter Two

THE GREEN PROVINCES

FROM DIGOIN TO SANCERRE

The Loire emerges from the gorges, pools and hill-top ruins of its first long stretch. Floods and low summer waters continue to make navigation difficult and to combat this the Canal du Centre and the Canal Latéral à la Loire were dug in the nineteenth century. At Digoin they meet both each other and the Loire; the canals have been connected, since the 1830s, by an impressive 800-foot *pont-aqueduc* which spans the river, forty feet below. Downstream, at Decize, the Loire joins the Canal du Nivernais. The canals did not, owing to the coming of railways, prompt the expected economic boom, but are popular with pleasure craft.

Nevers, further downstream, provides the sort of view which will become increasingly familiar on the middle stretches of the river: a hill with tall cathedral, fragments of ramparts, slate roofs, some less attractive modern blocks; a strong stone bridge across a wide expanse of reed-fringed, sand-banked Loire. Here the Nièvre enters the Loire; this much smaller river gives its name to the *département*—the area of western Burgundy traditionally called the Nivernais. Just after Nevers, the Loire is swelled tremendously by its confluence with the Allier, amid gravelly sands, at the

Bec—the "Beak"—d'Allier. Moulins is on the Allier, south of Nevers. Another notable cathedral city, Bourges, on the River Cher, is 35 miles west of Nevers; by water, it is linked to Nevers by the Canal Latéral and the Canal du Berry.

The Loire continues north to La Charité-sur-Loire, which provides another magnificent view. Further on, the river enters the wine-country of Pouilly-sur-Loire and Sancerre. Vineyards furrow the landscape. St.-Thibault, between the steep hill of Sancerre and the river, was, until the mid-nineteenth-century, a port dealing almost exclusively with Sancerre wines. Then, before phylloxera attacked the vines, much of the local wine was red. Today some of the best Sancerres are white; "In contrast to sauvignon blancs from elsewhere," for Eric Asimov of the *New York Times*, "good Sancerres are characteristically restrained rather than exuberant, perfumed with citrus and chalk rather than bold fruit." Perhaps only his fellow experts will be able to trace "aromas and flavors… of lime, grapefruit and lemon, of flowers and sometimes of herbs, and of minerality", but they are easily imagined among the green—or autumn red—slopes.

DIGOIN AND PARAY-LE-MONIAL

Douglas Goldring's unfavourable impression of Digoin (*The Loire*, 1913) was influenced by steady rain, a battle with bed-bugs and "disagreeable station officials". Few travellers have found much to say here, but the town has an important ceramics industry—the subject of the Musée de la Céramique de Digoin—and the central position, as noted above, in a network of waterways.

East of Digoin, the mainly twelfth-century basilica at Paray-le-Monial is by the Bourbince, a tributary of the Arroux which is itself a tributary of the Loire. Huysmans' Durtal, in *La Cathédrale* (1898) admires the "august simplicity" of both exterior and interior. John Flower, finding "balance and harmony", singles out the apse, where "the choir, the ambulatory with its elegant arches and slender columns, and the side chapels meet in a series of semi-circles." The reputation of Paray for monastic devotion early won it the name "Monial". Its later, more specific association was with Marguerite Marie Alacoque (1647-90), who entered the Visitandine order in Paray in her mid-twenties and experienced a series of visions. According to her own account, Christ showed her his Sacred Heart, which could no longer contain within itself its burning love for mankind. Further visions showed her the heart flaming like the sun or burning within Christ's breast. He entrusted her with the mission of establishing the celebration of the Heart to atone for the ingratitude with which his love has been received.

Marguerite Marie's immediate superiors gradually came to accept the importance of her visions. Eventually, in 1765, Pope Clement XIII approved the celebration of the Sacred Heart. The requisite miracles occurred, and the nun was beatified in 1864 and canonized in 1920. Thirty thousand people attended the ceremony when her remains were transferred from the convent to the basilica in 1865 and eight years later the first pilgrimage attracted 100,000 people, including many from outside France. The number of English and Irish people who made the journey was enough to alarm the Protestant press, some of whose censure of the "absurd" and "pagan" veneration of the saint and the Heart were gathered by "Non-Pilgrim" of Manchester. Annoyed at the blessing of pilgrims from Salford and their banner before they set off, Non-Pilgrim's sources gave the visions short shrift: "A mind prone to brooding in solitude, set in a body enervated by sickness, and abased by self-persecution, admirably adapted her for seeing visions and dreaming dreams, and the tendency had begun to develop itself before she took the veil." Pious visitors continued to prefer the religious explanation.

MOULINS: "SPLENDID AND METICULOUS DETAILS"

Edith Wharton recorded a brief favourable glimpse of Moulins in *A Motor-Flight Through France* (1908): "With its streets of light-coloured stone, its handsome eighteenth century hôtels and broad well-paved *cours*, it seemed, after the grim black towns of the south, a singularly open and cheerful place; and one was conscious, behind the handsome stone gateways and balconied façades, of the existence of old panelled drawing-rooms with pastel portraits and faded tapestry furniture." Had she not been "flying", she might also have admired the River Allier and its fine bridge. Over the centuries an unknown number of wooden bridges and four of stone had collapsed, undermined by shifting sands and battered by floods, before the engineer Louis de Régemortes found a solution. Between 1753 and 1763 his workforce of nine hundred men and women, aided by dozens of horses and oxen and four hundred donkeys, embanked the river, modified its course and established the piles of the bridge on a platform. The Pont

Régemortes stayed firm, except when part of it was blown up in order to slow the German advance in 1940.

Some of Wharton's "open and cheerful" life was happening at the Grand Café, which opened in Place Allier in 1899. Its Art Deco fittings survive: huge mirrors, a ceiling fresco which tells the tale of Gambrinus, the mythical inventor of beer. The Café Américain in Cours Anatole-France retains its décor of 1905. But a much earlier city is also evident. Moulins was important for its position on the Allier, linking the south, whether "grim black" or otherwise, and the Loire. It was long the capital of the Dukes of Bourbon, until the duchy was reabsorbed into France in the sixteenth century. There are a few traces of the medieval stronghold of the dukes, including the fourteenth-century keep known, from its incongruous later flat roof, as "La Mal-Coiffée". The Musée Anne-de-Beaujeu is in the Renaissance "pavilion" built between 1488 and 1503 by Duke Pierre II of Bourbon and his wife, Duchess Anne de Beaujeu, who was for a time regent for her brother, King Charles VIII.

The choir of the Cathedral of Notre-Dame, in red and pink sandstone, dates from the late fifteenth century. Some of the stained glass was damaged when the Yzeure munitions factory blew up in 1918 but much remains. A window probably of the 1540s, in the Chapelle St.-Nicolas, shows the adventures of Godefroy de Bouillon: battles in Palestine, the capture of the Crown of Thorns. Godefroi was the legendary ancestor of Geoffroy Aubéry who commissioned the window and is included there with his wife, sons and daughters. The nave and towers are nineteenth-century, built in contrasting dark volcanic stone from Volvic and light limestone from Chauvigny.

The special attraction of the cathedral, however, is the triptych (c.1497-1500) by the anonymous Master of Moulins. When closed it shows the Annunciation in grisaille. Mary, kneeling and reading in a long cloak, is surprised by a flowing-robed Gabriel. The wings open—parted solemnly or theatrically by the guide—on a colourful Virgin in glory. She sits, in blue and deep red robes, with the sun and the colours of the rainbow behind her and a crescent moon at her feet. Angels stretch beneath her an inscription which gives the source of some of these attributes in the "great and wondrous sign" of the woman "clothed with the sun, with the moon under her feet and a crown of twelve stars on her head" in *Revelation* 12:1. Two more angels accordingly hold a crown over her head, and form part of a framing group—she is "gloriously enthroned... among her soft-faced Lombard angels," says Wharton. Mary herself looks down in meditation. The donors of the triptych look towards her from the sides: the duke and duchess, Pierre de Bourbon and Anne de Beaujeu again, their robes and jewels echoing hers. They kneel in devotion and are presented by their patron saints, Peter and Anne. Behind the duchess kneels a smaller figure, her daughter Suzanne. The earthly characters are depicted more realistically than the divine—fairly "warts and all".

Edith Wharton calls the angels "Lombard". It was sometimes believed that the painter was an Italian, perhaps Ghirlandaio. It now seems much more likely that he was Netherlandish or northern French, but there has been little agreement as to his identity. Possibly he was Jean Hey, who was described as "teutonicus" (i.e. Dutch) and "pictor egregius" by the duke's court poet in 1504. A reference to "Maistre Jehan le peintre" in a document of 1502-3 suggests that his name was at least Jean—leaving the field rather open. A convincing case has been made for Jean Prévost (Albert Châtelet, *Jean Prévost: le Maître de Moulins*, 2001). But there is no conclusive proof. Whoever the Master was, his "sculptural precision of form…, the poise of his figures, his brilliant palette, the harmony of his compositions, and his taste for splendid and meticulous details make him one of the outstanding painters of his period in northern Europe" (*The Oxford Dictionary of Art*, ed. Ian Chilvers).

THE FORÊT DE TRONÇAIS

"The night was absolutely calm; grey, ashen water filled the stagnant trench between the overhanging cliffs of trees—like the water in an undersea canyon." Julien Gracq, in the "notebooks" of his travels, describes an abortive summer night-hike into the deep Forêt de Tronçais, thirty miles west of Moulins. The River Cher is beyond the forest, a little further west. It was a dark, moonless night. Quickly the walkers fell silent. They turned back after about half an hour. Gracq reflects on the causes of their sense of anguish: "There are no hours in the deep forest night, no graduated progression from dusk to dawn… but only a state which seems final and detached from time, a cataleptic, rigid state of vegetable matter." This makes night-walks in such conditions funereal; you do not so much cross a forest by night as enter "a dark kingdom, a deep place which knows the passing neither of the hours nor of the wind."

In better light Gracq's group could have seen a forest composed mainly of sessile oaks with beech and hornbeam. The abundant wildlife of Tronçais includes stone-martens, roe deer, badgers and increasing numbers of wild boar. Among the birds are snipe, nuthatch, buzzards, summer-visiting hoopoes, several kinds of owl and woodpeckers black, green and pied. But the good management of the forest was first undertaken for the sake not of such creatures and their watchers but of the French navy. It was part of the ship-building programme begun by Colbert, Louis XIV's provident minister, in 1675. A few trees survive from Colbert's time and over a century earlier. Some of the oaks provide the special high-quality wood used for Bordeaux and Cognac barrels.

NEVERS CATHEDRAL: "A REAL IRREGULAR GRANDEUR"

Pilgrims come to Nevers to see the tomb of the woman termed by Baedeker's *Northern France*, a little patronizingly, "the seeress of Lourdes". Bernadette Soubirous (1844-79), who had been fourteen at the time of her visions of the Virgin Mary, left Lourdes (in south-western France) to enter the convent of St. Gildard in 1866 and died there of bone tuberculosis in 1879. She was canonized by the Roman Catholic Church in 1933. Her body, with light moulded coverings for the face and hands, is displayed in a crystal and gold case in the convent chapel. A small museum narrates her life and shows her umbrella, her striped travelling-bag and the clothes she wore before taking the veil.

Long before Bernadette's time, pilgrims came to the city because it was on one of the pilgrimage routes to Santiago de Compostela. The most significant mediaeval church apart from the cathedral is St.-Étienne, which was built in the late eleventh century. It has often been admired as an example of Romanesque architecture at its purest and simplest. Yet for the local historian L.-M. Poussereau in 1897, the massive vaults and columns gave the church "un aspect sombre et froid"; as Robert Speaight says in *The Companion Guide to Burgundy*, St.-Etienne is "difficult to love". The Cathedral of St.-Cyr and Ste.-Julitte, much more mixed in style, seems more loveable. Elise Whitlock Rose (*Cathedrals and Cloisters of Northern France*, 1914) concedes that as a whole it "lacks harmonious outlines,— with its big Gothic apse to the east and its little Romanesque apse to the west," its too-striking contrast between "round and pointed forms". But it has "a real irregular grandeur and an admirable position". The cathedral is on the hill of ancient Noviodunum, above the Loire and the Nièvre.

The mainly thirteenth- to fifteenth-century church was heavily damaged by stray Allied bombs in 1944. From the earlier Romanesque cathedral survives, at the west end, a large twelfth-century fresco of Christ in Majesty: a tall figure with orange-brown hair and robe, enclosed in a double mandorla, rather Celtic at first sight. During the long process of post-war rebuilding other Romanesque elements and the remains of a mainly sixth-century baptistery were excavated. After the rebuilding of much of the fabric of the church, in the late 1970s attention turned to replacing the lost stained glass. Most of the work was done by a group of nine artists between 1986 and 1992. The result is "a pot-pourri", as Xavier Barral i Altet says in his book on modern stained glass (2006), but an effective one: the artists' separate efforts "come together to form a kind of collage, unified not by submission to architecture but by the denaturalization of the space." Gottfried Honegger's geometrical designs "flood the interior with purple" while François Rouan assembles coloured fragments in the tradition of Matisse. Both Rouan and Jean-Michel Alberola, Barral points out, play with the idea of "windows within windows".

In the crypt at the west end of St.-Cyr is a sixteenth-century polychrome statue group of Christ's Entombment. In St. Luke's gospel Joseph of Arimathaea wrapped the body "in linen, and laid it in a sepulchre that was hewn in stone, wherein never man before was laid... And the women also, which came with him from Galilee, followed after, and beheld the sepulchre, and how his body was laid. And they returned, and prepared spices and ointments." In the sculpted version St. John supports the pale, almost collapsing Virgin. St. Mary Magdalene, the only woman whose head is uncovered—she is identified, as usual, by her long golden hair—looks down at her golden ointment-pot. Next to her Mary Salome stands pensive or in shock, pot in one hand, the other hand on her cheek. On the right, Mary Cleophas looks more horrified. Joseph of Arimathaea and Nicodemus, who brings "myrrh and aloes" in St. John's gospel, stand, with more ritual solemnity but still sadly, at either end. All are deep in pre-Resurrection grief. All look inconsolable. This is one of the most moving of the many similar Entombments which survive from fifteenth- and sixteenth-century Burgundy. There is another, a little cruder and heavier, in the cathedral at Moulins.

PROVINCIAL NEVERS

For a time in the eighteenth century, however, the most famous religious institution in Nevers was the Convent of the Visitation. All that remains now is the Chapelle Ste.-Marie, with its exuberant Baroque façade, in Rue St.-Martin. But the fame was not for architecture but for a fictional parrot, the eponymous hero of Jean-Baptiste-Louis Gresset's *Vert-Vert* (1734). In this popular mock-heroic poem, expanded in 1736 and thereafter much reprinted and translated, the parrot is "no less notable than Aeneas" in devotion and misfortune. Vert-Vert delights the nuns, especially the younger ones, with his singing, his dancing and his teasing—within suitably modest limits. "More pampered than any court parrot," he lives without a care in the world. He never hears an immodest word, knowing rather his canticles and mystic colloquies. So "Father Vert-Vert" lives, dear to the nuns, "as fat as a monk and no less venerable".

Such fortune cannot last. The parrot's fame travels as far as the Visitandines' sister-house at Nantes. In spite of much mock-heroic horror from the young nuns of Nevers, it is agreed that Vert-Vert will be sent along the Loire on a visit. The passengers on the boat—dragoons and Gascons—are quite new to him. So is the way they and the boatmen speak. At first Vert-Vert is astonished by their irreligious lingo, their loud drinking-songs and blasphemies. When he greets a travelling monk "Ave, ma Soeur" the general derision wounds his pride; soon, of course, he learns to use the coarse language of those around him. After all, he is a parrot. Great is the shock of the Mère Prieure and sisters of Nantes when the much-vaunted bird swears by "devils' pipes" and greets them with cries of "Plague rot you!" "Bs and Fs" flow from his beak; "the junior sisters thought he was speaking Greek." Can "nos Soeurs de Nevers" really use such "langage pervers?" He is sent back in disgrace. At Nevers he soon returns to the path of virtue (after, Gresset added in later editions, due punishment of abstinence, isolation and silence). Vert-Vert is mourned long after his death, two years later, from a surfeit of the jam the sisters feed him. They commemorate him in their painting and embroidery.

Gresset chose Nevers for the sound of the name—the assonance and rhyme of "Vert-Vert, le Perroquet de Nevers"—and its location on the Loire down which his hero must travel. He chose it also as a typical small, church-dominated provincial city in itself likely to make his Parisian audience laugh. Nevers—"built like a capital" but "a child can soon walk round it"—has a similarly generic function in the much more serious context of *Hiroshima, mon amour* (1959), the film by Alain Resnais with screenplay and dialogue by Marguerite Duras. *Hiroshima* approaches the suffering caused by the atom-bomb through the love relationship between a woman originally from Nevers and a man she meets in Hiroshima. Nevers, though it is an average provincial town, was significant as the scene of her suffering and earlier love. Her German lover was shot dead while waiting for her on the Quai de Loire, she was shorn and humiliated as a collaborator, and she hid in a cellar until her hair grew back. Her suffering becomes a way of approaching the larger suffering of Hiroshima, or at least trying to. The names "Hiroshima" and "Nevers" are increasingly intertwined.

THE DUCAL PALACE

Luigi Gonzaga, of the princely house of Mantua, became, as Louis de Gonzague, Duke of Nevers between 1565 and 1595. He obtained the duchy through marriage to Henriette de Clèves, duchess in succession to her brothers and father. In the ducal palace we meet Louis de Gonzague himself, seated in his hat and cloak. The "Automate du Duc", a figure based on the best-known contemporary representation, speaks sonorously, and with knowledge of the future, for the benefit of anyone within earshot. He—"Moi, Louis de Gonzague, prince de Mantoue et pair [peer] de France," he intones—welcomes us to his palace; he was its "personne la plus illustre". Naturally he does not have time to talk about the political skill it took to maintain his position though thirty years of religious and civil war.

Instead he mentions his Italian love of magnificence, festivals, architecture and the arts. Nevers benefited most from his interest in pottery and glass. From the 1560s Italian glassworkers in Nevers specialized in glass figurines, and in 1585 Agostino or Augustin Conrade established a workshop for the production of faïence. In 1603 he and his two brothers (with Giulio or Jules Gambini) were granted a thirty-year monopoly on the production of faïence in Nevers. Well into the seventeenth century craftsmen of Italian extraction remained dominant; the word "faïence" derives from the city of Faenza. Often their work featured traditional religious subjects, but there were also copies of Chinese ware, hunting scenes and, during the Revolution, "faïence patriotique" with appropriate signs

and sentiments—Phrygian caps, declarations pro liberty and the republic. Faïence is still made in Nevers and examples from earlier periods are displayed in the Musée Frédéric Blandin.

The palace was built in the mid and late fifteenth century. Sixteenth- and seventeenth-century rulers made it gradually more elegant and Italianate. Some visitors, however, were unimpressed. Thomas Coryat, the Somerset traveller, acknowledged "pretty turrets, and a convenient court, inclosed with a faire wall" but judged the palace as a whole "but meane, being farre inferiour not onely to most of our English noble mens and knights houses, but also to many of our private Gentlemen's buildings in the country." Nathaniel Wraxall, in a period more responsive to the charms of age and romantic decay, perceived "an air of grotesque and rude magnificence" (*A Tour through France*, 1777). Today the interior, restored in the 1990s, seems uncertain of purpose, rather empty. The tourist information centre leads into a museum which has an aquarium, some faïence and a few examples from later enterprises like Formula One racing at the Magny-Cours circuit. The open rooms of the palace proper, dominated by the voice of the ducal "automate", are mainly empty. There are also function rooms and a council chamber; until the 1980s the building housed the Palais de Justice.

The exterior is more harmonious. The façade, much restored in 1850, has bas-reliefs showing scenes from the lives of the legendary ancestors of the Clèves family, St. Hubert and Helias, "the Knight of the Swan". Helias mysteriously arrived and, several years later, departed, in a magical swan-drawn skiff on the River Rhine. A version of his story became that of Lohengrin as told by Wolfram von Eschenbach and Wagner. The white swan became the family badge; François de Clèves, first Duke of Nevers, was welcomed to the town in 1549 with the gift of a silver swan pulling, by a golden chain, a silver ship and knight.

JONGKIND AND NEVERS

Nevers, especially as seen across the Loire, is attractive to painters: the cathedral high over the bridge, the palace-towers further right, old houses and parts of the ramparts including the Tour Goguin to the left. Johan Barthold Jongkind (1819-91), the Dutch painter and Impressionist precursor who spent most of his career in France, first stayed near Magny-Cours in 1860-1 and in Nevers itself several times between 1870 and 1881.

In September 1870, with his companion Mme. Fesser, he had fled Paris just before the Prussian siege began. They had gone first to Nantes, where his sketching, his Nordic blue eyes and his Dutch accent meant that he was taken for a spy. Claude Monet, in an interview of 1900 in which he also credited Jongkind with "the definitive education of my eye", remembered him as "a good, simple man, mangling his French abominably, very timid".

Having been rescued by the police, the couple made a precipitate return to the station and travelled to Nevers, where they had friends. Here too it was a difficult time for painters—Jongkind was once arrested when sketching at Pont Saint-Ours on the Nièvre. He did, however, succeed in producing at least three pencil and watercolour versions of Nevers and the Loire: the cathedral, sand and sandy sky, the deep blue river. By the spring of 1871 it was also, apparently, safe to work outside the city. In March, for instance, Jongkind painted ploughing, against a yellow background, at Pougues-les-Eaux. On subsequent visits he worked at Magny-Cours, Ville-menant near Guérigny and La Charité-sur-Loire.

Pictures of Nevers include a surprisingly unchanged Place Mossé (near the bridge at the foot of the cathedral hill) and Hôtel St.-Louis, where the painter stayed in 1872. And from about this time survives a blurred photograph of Jongkind in Nevers, bearded, wearing a hat with curving brim and clasping a sketchbook. His clear blue eyes, evident even in black-and-white, have a slightly baleful effect. The photograph is reproduced in François Auffret's illustrated biography of Jongkind (2004), a book which is particularly useful since almost all the works just referred to are held in private collections.

BOURGES: THE SIEGE OF AVARICUM

In 52 BC Caesar's legions were making progress in suppressing the Gallic uprising led by Vercingetorix. At an emergency council of war the Bituriges, the tribe whose land lay next in Caesar's path, agreed with the leader that scorched earth tactics were all that could save them. Twenty towns were fired, says Caesar in his *Gallic Wars*. But then, at a second council, the Bituriges persuaded Vercingetorix, against his own better judgement, that Avaricum, their chief city, should not be destroyed. They could not bring themselves to burn "a town which was almost the finest in Gaul, the chief defence and pride of their state" (S. A. Handford's translation).

The Bituriges liked to think that Avaricum, now Bourges, was impregnable since "it was almost completely surrounded by river and marsh, in which there was only one narrow opening." The rivers Yèvre, Auron and Moulon still run through the city. (The Yèvre joins the Cher at Vierzon, eighteen miles to the north-west; the Loire is about thirty miles to the east.) The Romans laid siege to the city, although the ravaged countryside and enemy raids brought them, at times, close to starvation. At the "one narrow opening" a "siege terrace" with two towers was set up. There were various stand-offs with Vercingetorix's army, which was based on a nearby hill surrounded by marshes.

Eventually, one night, the defenders succeeded in undermining the terrace and setting fire to it. "At the same moment the Gauls raised a cheer all along the wall and came pouring out of two gates on either side of our towers." The fight was hard and went on through the night, but eventually the Romans put out the fires and drove their enemies back behind the city-wall. The men of the Bituriges decided now that their only option was to abandon Avaricum and make, across the river-marshes, for Vercingetorix's camp. What foiled this plan, Caesar says, was the women of the Bituriges, who did not wish to be left behind, with the children, to face "a cruel enemy"; they were not strong enough, they pleaded, to run away with the men. When the men tried to leave, the women "started screaming and gesticulating to the Romans" and this had the desired effect of preventing the warriors from leaving.

Finally, Caesar took the town by a simple stratagem. He ordered his legionaries to work with apparent half-heartedness. Preparations to attack were made, as far as possible, out of sight of the enemy. Caesar was thus able to take the Bituriges completely by surprise: swiftly the Romans attacked and lined the wall, trapping them within the city. Massacre ensued. Still seeking vengeance for the Roman traders killed at the beginning of the rebellion, "none of our soldiers thought about making money by taking prisoners." Caesar, chillingly factual, reports that about eight hundred out of the forty thousand inhabitants escaped to join Vercingetorix. The punishment of Avaricum was a reminder—in spite of the temporary Roman reversal at Gergovia in the Auvergne—that Gaul had best submit to the invaders.

Avaricum became an important city of Roman Gaul, capital of the province of Aquitania Prima. The Rue Moyenne is the most obvious descendant of its street-plan. Straight roads radiate in several directions across the plain which the city continues to dominate. In the Middle Ages it became the capital of Berry.

BOURGES CATHEDRAL: "A SPECIAL, SUPERNATURAL LIGHT"

Meaulnes, in Alain-Fournier's *Le Grand Meaulnes*, cycles, depressed, up and down the streets around the cathedral. There it is, rising at the end of each street and above the empty square, "enormous and indifferent". It suits his mood; he thinks that Valentine, the girl from Bourges who should have married Frantz de Galais, has become a prostitute and that it is his fault. In the narrow, soiled streets "here and there was a red lantern, the sign of a house of ill repute." As in the past, filth and viciousness shelter beside the cathedral. "A countryman's fear came upon him, a revulsion against this town church, where all the vices were carved in secret nooks, which was built among the evil places and which offered no remedy for the pure sorrows of love." In 1903 Fournier spent two terms in Bourges at the lycée later named after him. The original building is now the École Nationale des Beaux-Arts de Bourges. The experience was not entirely happy; filthy sheets were one of his main memories.

People in better moods than Meaulnes have responded accordingly to the cathedral. George Sand, on her first visit in 1831, wrote excitedly to her friend Émile Regnault about the contrast between "the great austere walls" and the decoration "thrown" full-heartedly onto them: "strange, wild, magnificent waking dreams of the imagination". The decoration which so amazed her includes that of the north and south portals (c.1160) incorporated from the earlier Romanesque cathedral. The south sculptures, which are better preserved than the north, include statue-columns like those at Chartres, flights of angels and, on the lintel, the twelve apostles in conversation. The five richly sculpted porches of the early thirteenth-century west front have attracted much attention—not least from the Huguenots who smashed the most easily reachable figures in 1562. Restoration, with concrete and mastic, eventually took place in the 1830s and 1840s; the results were mixed, but the work enabled visitors to see whole scenes largely as planned by the original sculptors. The gable above the central portal was completely replaced as were the heads, most of the limbs, and several whole figures of the rising dead on the lintel. Christ in

Judgement regained his arms. (The repairs can be studied in detail in Tania Bayard's *Bourges Cathedral: the West Portals*.)

Henry James was particularly taken with this central Last Judgement, where "The good prepare, with infinite titillation and complacency, to ascend to the skies; while the bad are dragged, pushed, hurled, stuffed, crammed, into pits and cauldrons of fire." The saved proceed left, led probably by St. Francis, towards "Abraham's bosom"—the patriarch firmly holding a cloth in which several souls are already safely contained. The damned move right towards the "pits and cauldrons" of Hell. Beside "the angel of justice"—St. Michael with his scales—"stands a little female figure, that of a child, who, with hands meekly folded and head gently raised, waits for the stern angel to decide upon her fate. In this fate, however, a dreadful big devil also takes a keen interest; he seems on the point of appropriating the tender creature; he has a face like a goat and an enormous hooked nose. But the angel gently lays a hand upon the shoulder of the little girl—the movement is full of dignity—as if to say, 'No, She belongs to the other side'." (In fact the child, representing a soul, is male.) When James left the cathedral he came near to witnessing a horribly real version of the treatment of the damned. Soldiers and citizens were assembling because "a private of the Chasseurs was to be 'broken' for stealing, and everyone was eager to behold the ceremony." For a moment he was tempted to go too. As he turned away, "I reflected that human beings are cruel brutes, though I could not flatter myself that the ferocity of the thing was exclusively French."

Inside, James had admired "a great simplicity and majesty, and, above all, a tremendous height"; Jules Michelet thought Notre-Dame de Paris and the duomo in Milan would fit comfortably inside the cathedral. The sense of height and space was achieved mainly through the technology, fairly new at the end of the twelfth century, of flying buttresses. The effect is increased by the unusual absence of transepts and crossing. The Master of Bourges managed stability, grace and a remarkable sense of unity in the first building campaign, which most scholars date to 1195-1214. The church is also, as James puts it, "inordinately rich in magnificent old glass".

Particularly magnificent is the early thirteenth-century glass. The pro-gramme includes the Old Testament prophets, the canonized bishops of Bourges and Christ's ministry, passion and resurrection. Among later ad-ditions perhaps the most notable is the rose-window commissioned in about 1370 by Jean, Duc de Berry. This is the duke, often called "fastueux"—a lover of show, of splendour—in French sources, for whom the *Très riches heures du Duc de Berry* was produced. The ruins of one of his many châteaux are at Mehun-sur-Yèvre, near Bourges; in glorious pristine state it forms a background to the Temptation of Christ in the *Très riches heures*. There is also good sixteenth-century glass in chapels such as that of St. Denis, full of narrative and incidental detail including a windmill and a diabolical executioner with flowing and curling grey hair, lined brow, black eyes and cruel smile. Michelet as, in 1835, he entered the church for the first time, saw in its depths darkness and scintillating light, "une nuit de saphirs et de rubis". He found himself in "une merveilleuse caverne de Dieu…, in the heart of the ruins of Golconda, illuminated by a special, su-pernatural light, where the living and the dead could wait together for the Last Judgement."

Sand enthused, with a shiver, about the crypt or lower church: while in the upper church the eye is astonished by soaring emptiness, here "it is frightened by stone masses pressing down on every side, as the sepulchre presses down on the corpse. This weighty vaulting, these ribs interlacing without end, these squat pillars, project great strength and provoke, at night, an indefinable sense of terror, like the entrance to a tomb."

BOURGES: JACQUES COEUR

In the mid-fifteenth-century there was a good chance that any vessel to be seen on the Loire or the Cher belonged to, was financed by, or was carrying goods for, one person.

> There was at that time, in the royal administration, a hard-working and sagacious man, Jacques Coeur of Bourges, of plebeian origin but of great and quick intelligence, and with a prodigious skill in handling secular affairs. He was the king's *argentier* [money-man] and the commercial operations in which he ceaselessly engaged enriched him considerably... It was he who—first of all the Frenchmen of his time—armed and equipped galleys which, loaded with woollen goods and other French manufactures, sailed out to the shores of Africa and the Orient, as far as Alexandria in Egypt, and brought back from there silk fabrics and every kind of spice... To this [his wealth and his illustriousness] the most obvious testimony is the magnificent residence which he had built for him in his city of Bourges. It is so beautiful, decorated with so many ornaments, that in all France, I say not solely among the middling aristocracy but even, because of its huge size, where the king is concerned, it would be difficult to find a more magnificent dwelling.

So the fifteenth-century chronicler and former royal counsellor Thomas Basin summed up the achievements of Jacques Coeur (c.1400-56). Basin was not exaggerating. Coeur, the son of a furrier, built up an extraordinary business empire from small beginnings. He became Charles VII's supplier, banker, financier and fixer—the sort of operator seen previously only in Italy. He reorganized taxation and provided jewels, furs, weapons and robes for the court. He financed and directed Charles' capture of Normandy from the English—an event of symbolic as well as practical significance in establishing the king's claim to the whole of France. Coeur was also involved in silver mines, ship-building, paper and cloth manufacture and the lucrative trade in salt. In the process he amassed personal wealth, offices and influence. He has often been seen as an early capitalist.

Bourges continued to be one of the capitals of Coeur's empire. His daughter married the Viscount of Bourges and his son became, in 1446, its archbishop. (Home loyalties apart, Bourges was an immense and

wealthy diocese.) The archbishop was only twenty-two; the pope oblig-
ingly issued an age-dispensation. An even younger brother was Dean of
Limoges and a canon of the Sainte-Chapelle in Bourges, a palace chapel
dedicated in 1405. It was demolished after storm-damage in the eighteenth
century; some of its contents survive, including the tomb of Jean, Duc de
Berry, in the cathedral.

Jacques Coeur's own ennoblement in 1441 enabled him to build on
a fortified site he had acquired on the Gallo-Roman ramparts of the city.
The great house he built here between 1443 and 1450, the Hôtel Jacques
Coeur, preserves an appearance of medieval military strength in the west
front, while on the city side and the interior comfort, decoration and self-
advertisement prevail. The king was duly saluted by an equestrian statue
on the façade, but the figures on either side looking out of false windows
may represent the money-man and his wife. The king's statue was destroyed in the Revolution but these figures survived and were restored.
They look perfectly at ease with their surroundings, relaxed, perhaps a
little complacent. Coeur seems, however, to have lived in the house little,
if at all.

Coeur was not shy about the commercial origins of his greatness. His
house was intended to function as a warehouse as well as a residence, and
bas-reliefs and panels show spinners, fullers and merchant-ships. Some
aristocrats must have looked askance at the jumped-up merchant but many
were in debt to him. He seemed, and clearly thought himself, unassail-
able. He had the inestimable advantage of support from Charles VII's lover,
Agnès Sorel, and her powerful faction at court. Coeur—the "Heart" at the
heart of the kingdom—proudly inscribed his punning and hubristic motto
on his house: *A vaillans cuers riens impossible* ("For the valiant heart
nothing is impossible").

If Coeur did spend any time in his palace, he did not have long to look
up at his motto or enjoy his fine banqueting hall with the ship's keel roof.
His fall, apparently sudden, was the work of a coalition of the many
enemies and enviers such a man was bound to attract. Their task was made
much easier by the death of Agnès Sorel in 1450. Indeed, the first, improbable charge against him was that he had poisoned her. This was soon
dropped, but other accusations multiplied: counterfeiting money, doing
deals with the "Saracens" for his personal advantage, demanding bribes
and embezzlement. Since such practices were standard among officials of

the time—if not perhaps on such an international scale—the charges were difficult to deny. The death-penalty was commuted to imprisonment and an enormous fine of 400,000 écus; his property, of course, was confiscated. Why Charles VII abandoned his once indispensable servant so easily is, like his desertion of Joan of Arc twenty years earlier, a matter of unresolved debate.

The fallen favourite somehow escaped from his prison in Poitiers in 1454. He fled to Provence and then to Rome, where the new pope, Calixtus III, put him in charge of a fleet which was being sent against the Turks. Clearly his organizational and fiscal skills were still in demand. But he was wounded, tried to recuperate on Chios and died in 1456. Charles did relent sufficiently to return some of his estate, including the Hôtel, to his family the following year.

LA CHARITÉ-SUR-LOIRE

In 1825 Victor Hugo wrote an article, "Guerre aux démolisseurs", declaring war on the destruction, abandonment, sale and crass restoration of the historic monuments of France. At La Charité-sur-Loire, downstream of Nevers, for example, a Romanesque church, whose size and architectural richness could stand comparison with those of the most famous cathedrals in Europe, "is half in ruins. It is falling, stone by stone, and as unknown as an oriental pagoda in its desert of sands." (Hugo's notion of pagodas was perhaps a little vague.) "Ten stage-coaches pass through every day but no-one notices the state of the church."

The priory church of Notre-Dame, built in the late eleventh and early twelfth century, was very grand. Its nave and aisles are nearly 400 feet long and 120 feet wide; in France it was second in size only to the Benedictine mother-house at Cluny. It had been dedicated, amid crowds of clergy and laity, by Pope Paschal II in 1107. As he anointed the high altar with chrism (oil and balm), says an early account, "his face shone forth like the face of an angel." Paschal was not there seeking only spiritual joy, however. He had come looking for French support against the Holy Roman Emperor Henry V, particularly in their dispute over the investiture of bishops. A great assembly followed the dedication service; it allowed Suger (c.1081-1151), the future Abbot of St.-Denis and Regent of France, to give an early demonstration of his oratorical skills. But La Charité was usually involved in simpler matters. The monks' reputation was good enough, tradition says, to change the town's name from Seyr to La Charité. The arms of the priory include three open golden money-bags.

The priory never fully recovered from the great fire of 1559 and the siege of the town when it was held by Huguenots in 1573. The fire left the Tour Sainte-Croix and the central doorway separated from the four remaining bays of the nave and the choir. In August 1834 Prosper Mérimée, assessing the damage now that authority had finally heeded Hugo's and others' calls, found modern booths or shacks rammed up against the surviving tower and its sculpture. One of the tympana was divided in two by a floor, firewood was heaped up in front of a bas-relief, while chickens and children were busy spreading dirt. A month earlier, says Mérimée, a soldier had slept in the upper part of one of the booths, sharing his alcove with "a bas-relief representing the Eternal Father seated on the clouds, surrounded by his angels and his saints." The soldier thought little about the decoration, more about the bed-bugs which tormented him during the night. "In the morning, as he packed his bags, he caught sight of the relief and addressed himself to the Eternal Father: 'You're the one,' he said, 'who invented bed-bugs; here's something to say thank you.'" And he broke off the statue's head with his stick.

On Mérimée's initiative a recently rescued tympanum from the tower was moved into the church. It shows the Transfiguration: the vigorous, alert Christ in a mandorla with kneeling apostles and Moses and Elijah on either side. The feast of the Transfiguration was first celebrated by Cluniac monks under the direction of Abbot Pierre le Vénérable in the 1130s and the tympanum probably dates from then or soon afterwards. Its architrave shows the Adoration of the Magi and the Presentation of Christ in the Temple. The Virgin sits upright while Joseph ("decidedly anxious looking," thinks John Flower in his 1994 *Burgundy*) stands behind her chair with his staff. The Magi sweep forward in classical-influenced drapery; Mérimée noted the fine folds, the perfect details of the cloth, the "profusion of embroidery and jewels", but struggled to understand how such proficient artists could carve "hands completely out of proportion to bodies". His realistic assumptions would have puzzled medieval artists; his own puzzlement reminds us how new it was to take such art seriously. The tympanum which remains in place on the tower is more difficult to study. It includes an Annunciation with splendidly-winged Gabriel.

There is a notable view of La Charité from across the Loire: "a

La Charité: "Canaletto-like"

Canaletto-like view of the skyline," suggests Robert Speaight in his *Companion Guide to Burgundy*, "dominated by the two towers associated with the church of Notre-Dame and the walls of the mediaeval château away to the left of the picture." Jongkind renders a more dynamic, more blowy place in his pencil and watercolour study of March 1871, where the dark bridge is the line between the light river and the huge light sky of rapidly sketched drifting clouds.

JULES RENARD: "MY CICADA IS THE GRASSHOPPER"
Jules Renard (1864-1910) lived from the age of two at Chitry-les-Mines, about thirty miles north-east of Nevers. Between 1875 and 1881 he boarded at the lycée in Nevers now named after him. Although he spent much of his career in literary circles in Paris, he retained a deep affection for the Nivernais countryside. From 1895 he rented a seventeenth-century stone house at Chaumot, near Chitry, with views of woods, hills, the River Yonne and the Canal du Nivernais. He called it "La Gloriette" because, he says in his *Journal*, it "means a little pleasure-house, and also because it is a diminutive of glory"—the literary glory he sought and gained, mainly for his plays and for his fictionalized childhood autobiography *Poil de carotte* (1894). Renard and his family lived here for several months of most years,

mainly in the summer. In 1900 he became a municipal councillor for Chaumot and from 1904 Mayor of Chitry. "As Mayor," he remarked, "it's my job to maintain country roads; as a poet, I'd rather see them badly maintained." In May 1910 he died of arteriosclerosis in Paris and was buried at Chitry.

Renard's sharpest insights into country life occur in his *Journal* (1887-1910, posthumously published in the 1920s). He writes about harvest and haymaking; the *curé* with a narrow forehead which looks as if it had been "hammered out on the anvil of his faith"; the man whose job is to stop stray logs blocking the river—timber provided one of the main industries in the Nièvre. The schoolmaster of Corbigny is "dry, dark, authoritarian, relentless", while his colleague from Chitry is a talkative angler. An unemployed boatman plays his accordion on the canal one summer night in 1903; other brief sketches include the villages of Asnan, on its "marvellous, heather-pink hill", and of Grenois "there, quite complete, like a snail-shell". In more practical mood Renard notes that the shops in Corbigny, the nearest substantial town, are empty except on fair-days. If you go in you are greeted with open-mouthed astonishment by someone visible through the garden-door at the back. On a later visit he can't find anywhere to buy a toothbrush.

Some of the best descriptions are of animals, mainly birds. Renard's contradictory feelings about hunting, from hatred to obsession, are registered in the *Journal* and other works. He kills a mole as if he were a god delivering thunder. "Why? Why?" The duck is "a domestic penguin". He sees "turkeys the colour of constipated Englishwomen". More poetically, the sad note of the toad blends with the sound of the country streaming with rain, "something of the sound of a bubble which has just broken on the surface of a pond... something infinitely soft." Such observations are part of Renard's philosophy, as expressed in an entry for August 1897, as "a man of the Centre of France", safe from northern fogs and southern passions both. "My cicada is the grasshopper, and my grasshopper isn't symbolic. It isn't made of gold." He catches it in the fields and uses it to bait his line.

CLAMECY: ROMAIN ROLLAND

From the hill outside Clamecy, Colas Breugnon, the eponymous hero of Romain Rolland's novel (1919), can see his town "girded by the lazy Yonne and the ambling Beuvron", rolling, cultivated slopes and, in the distance, a sea of softly undulating wooded mountains. This River Beuvron enters the Yonne at Clamecy, and is not to be confused with its namesake which joins the Loire at Candé-sur-Beuvron.

The novel is set in 1616; Rolland notes in his afterword that trees and factory-smoke had rather changed the view. The water and the wood were particularly important for Clamecy which was, until the 1920s, a centre for *flottage*: logs from the Morvan were built into huge rafts which were steered up the Yonne—navigable from Clamecy—to the Seine and Paris. Eventually the industry failed because of competition from barges on the Canal du Nivernais, connected to the Loire and its lateral canal, and then from rail and road transport. The Musée Romain-Rolland has models and pictures of the rafts as well as objects and editions associated with the once very well known author. His birthplace and his grandfather's house have become part of the museum, together with the larger seventeenth-century Hôtel de Bellegarde.

Rolland (1866-1944) did not much like Clamecy. His childhood was by no means entirely unhappy but he suffered from breathing difficulties and, he tells us in *Le Voyage intérieur*, a constant fear of death. No doubt this was exacerbated by his mother's anxious concern for his health following the sudden death of his younger sister. Another problem was the fundamental difference between his parents: as R. A. Francis puts it in *Romain Rolland* (1999) his father was "cheerful and extrovert", his mother "intense and severe". Rolland says he felt like a prisoner—or, looking out at a courtyard with walls on three sides and a canal on the other, like a creature in a zoo enclosure. (This small canal was later drained.) He watched boats and clouds, listened to the bells of St. Martin's church and dreamed of escape.

When Rolland was fourteen his family transplanted itself to Paris so that he could study there. He thought little about his native woods and waters. But in spring 1913 a visit to Clamecy, his first for many years, "awoke in me a past which I thought would sleep for ever." According to the address to the reader in *Colas Breugnon*, Rolland was busily planning books on contemporary subjects which would share "the rather tragic atmosphere" of *Jean-Christophe* (1904-12), his long philosophical novel and the work mainly responsible for his Nobel Prize for Literature in 1915. But he was seized by the irresistible desire to write *Colas*, a celebration of his native Nivernais. After years in the straitjacket of *Jean-Christophe*, he felt the need not to transform or explain the world but for "free Gallic gaiety"—the inheritance of his extrovert father.

Colas begins the novel with a persuasive, companionable address to himself in the mirror. He is good-humoured, witty, anecdotal; a trustworthy Falstaff, a Sir Toby who can hold his drink. During his fifty years he has filled his old tanned bag of a body with "pleasure and pain, tricks and quips... straw and hay, figs and grapes, unripe fruit, sweet fruit", with—he and Rolland enjoy the vowels—things "vues, et lues, et sues, et eues, vécues" (seen, and read, and known, and had, lived). Nothing will shake him easily now. His wife is loud and troublesome but he refuses to be provoked, laughs when she shouts; "When it rains, I let it rain." He enjoys whatever can be enjoyed, including food and Burgundy wine: people will always find new ways to wage war, says the Rabelaisian Colas, but will they come up with any better ways to drink? In his work as a woodcarver his rich imagination overflows in panels, fantastic figures and rosy nymphs, laughing townsfolk and roaring lions, garlands and spiral staircases.

Colas also loves his house. It is on the banks of the Beuvron, that "indolent, fat" river—here he relishes the *ers*—"vert, bien nourri d'herbe, de terre et de merde" (green, well fed on grass, earth and shit). The house is just across the bridge from the walled town and the proud tower of St.-Martin with its "embroidered skirt"—the tower is early sixteenth-century Flamboyant. Every time an enemy is spotted from this vantage-point the town closes its gates, leaving the enemy to visit Colas' house. Usually he moves out, leaving the key under the door. Sometimes he comes back to find both key and door gone. So he rebuilds. It might be safer to live within the walls, but with no better view than a wall he would die of boredom. More cautious dwellers' fine timbered houses survive in Clamecy from the fifteenth and sixteenth century. They include the so-called "Maison du Tisserand"—"Weaver's House"—on Rue Romain-Rolland and Rue du Pont-Châtelain. Colas "needs elbow-room", needs to be able, when he's not working, to sit outside and watch the reflections in the water, the drifting weeds and the fish; to wash his "rags", to empty his pot.

By the end of the novel Colas will have lost his house, his wife and his health, but, predictably, not his ability to enjoy life. He shows, as Francis says, "a paradoxical combination of harmony with his environment and

43

willingness to fight against it. As a comic hero, he resolves rather pain-lessly the constant dilemma of Rolland's heroes, whether or not to accept his destiny." Publication was delayed by the First World War; in 1919 Colas could seem either a good example of heroic endurance or an absurd figure whose optimism was belied by recent events. Rolland's *Au-dessus de la mêlée* (1915)—*Above the Fray*—was a controversial call for both sides in the conflict to seek peace; Maxim Gorky saw *Colas Breugnon* as expressing "Gallic defiance" of war and Rolland came to feel that he was not far wrong.

SANCERRE: "THE REFUGE AND RETREAT OF SO MANY POOR BELIEVERS AND CHILDREN OF GOD"

Sancerre, declares Baedeker's *Northern France* (1889), is "an old and ill-built town... finely situated on a steep hill (1000 ft.), in the midst of an undulating country that produces good red and white wines." The wine and the view of the vineyards from the steep hill are the main attractions; the principal vantage-point is the Tour des Fiefs, all that is left of the fortress involved in the great siege of 1573.

In the wake of the St. Bartholomew's Day massacre in Paris Huguenots were attacked in nearby towns including La Charité-sur-Loire. Refugees crowded into Protestant-dominated, well defended Sancerre, which royal and Catholic forces besieged for several months. Jean de Léry, a pastor, survived to describe the siege in *Histoire mémorable de la ville de Sancerre* (1574). The strongest chapter of the book describes the famine. In April people started killing and eating donkeys and mules, with which the town was well supplied "because of its high situation". In May it was the turn of the horses. Every part of the animals was used—and sold, at exorbitant prices, by the owners. Léry reproves "the extreme avarice of some who did not fear the hand of God at a time of such calamity." In June the town authorities attempted to ration corn—half a pound per person per day, then a quarter, then a pound a week—but it had run out by the end of the month. People moved on from horses to cats, rats, mice, moles, and then dogs. Soon they were boiling up anything made of leather. It was found that parchment was palatable if it was soaked, scraped and boiled for long enough; letters, books and documents were eaten this way, even those "a hundred or a hundred and twenty years old". Grass and roots were grubbed up and some people died after eating hemlock. Others warned them of the danger, "but it was talking to the deaf, since their stomachs did not want to understand." Soaked and ground straw was used as substitute wheat; "flour" was made from nutshells heated and reduced to powder. Tallow and grease went into soup or served for cooking oil. And in late June there was at least one case of cannibalism involving the parents of a small child who had died of starvation. Léry was physically sick when he saw the evidence of what they had done: it was much more horrifying, he says, than the flesh-eating he had seen during his ten-month expedition to the "Sauvages Ameriquains" of Brazil. He vigorously defends the couple's punishment—the husband was burnt alive, the wife strangled—as a necessary example to others. He claims that they had committed a series of other crimes, including, in the husband's case, murder.

Léry estimates that eighty-four inhabitants died in fighting, but about five hundred from famine. Eventually in August, after further desperate scenes and news of Protestant defeats elsewhere, the Sancerrois leaders, including Pastor Léry, negotiated their capitulation. Demolitions, financial exactions, looting and a few murders followed the triumphant re-entry of the Catholic authorities. The church was restored, as Léry puts it, to its "idolatry and papist superstitions". He and a number of his colleagues had left for Switzerland immediately after the surrender. From there he pitied "the deplorable state of the poor town of Sancerre, formerly the refuge and retreat of so many poor believers and children of God". It is his duty to observe that their situation came about as much through human sinfulness—avarice, in particular—as through the cruelty of the enemy. Nevertheless God will, he is sure, be merciful towards the survivors.

St.-Sauveur-en-Puisaye: Colette

Sidonie Gabrielle Claudine Colette (1873-1954) was born in St.-Sauveur-en-Puisaye and lived there until 1890. There is a Colette museum, with documents and photographs, in the Château de St.-Sauveur. The Puisaye, at the north-western edge of Burgundy, east of the Loire, is sometimes called "the poor Burgundy" by contrast with its rich, fertile neighbour. In *Les Vrilles de la vigne* (*The Tendrils of the Vine*) Colette describes "a rather sad countryside with gloomy forests, a peaceful, poor village, a damp valley, a bare, bluish mountain which does not provide sustenance for so much as a goat." But her accounts and versions of the house where she grew up (3 Rue de l'Hospice, now Rue Colette) are much more positive. It was built on a steep slope with an upper and lower garden. The lower was "a confined, warm kitchen-garden dedicated to aubergines and pimentos, where the smell of tomato-leaves mingled, in July, with the odour of ripe apricots from the espaliers" (*La Maison de Claudine*, 1922). The upper garden, with its "twin firs, walnut-tree, roses, neglected lawn and dismantled arbour", was a good place for children to play and hide in, and also one of the great enthusiasms of Colette's mother, who is celebrated (and idealized, inevitably) in *Sido* (1930). "Sido" is vital, definite, unconventional, and loving. She is observant of, and attentive to, plants, animals and children. She loves red flowers—geraniums, foxgloves, roses, hortensias, red-hot pokers. Her daughter comes upon her studying the wind or, with a magnifying-glass, the "branched crystals" of the snow she has just scooped up.

Colette sees the rest of her family as less fulfilled than her mother. The more reserved, less known father is too consumed with love for Sido to have a very close relationship with anyone else. He hums and sings, "preceded and protected by his song." The various problems of her brothers and unhappily-married elder sister are also suggested. But on the whole the world of *Sido* is idyllic. From the garden there are glimpses and sounds of other lives: to the south, the neighbour with a white dog whose head he dyes blue and hindparts red each 14th July; to the north the old woman who sings "a little hymn as she ties violets for the altar of our church which was struck by lightning and no longer has a steeple"; to the east, the sad-sounding bell which announces a customer's arrival at the notary's. But the real world is the Colette garden where "children never had fights, where animals and people expressed themselves in tranquillity, a garden where, for thirty years, a husband and wife lived without ever raising their voices against each other."

Chapter Three

CORN AND COMBAT

FROM BRIARE TO THE BEAUCE

At Briare the Loire and the canals are full of pleasure-boats; their progress across the high Pont-Canal, with its views of woods and river, makes an impressive show. The Canal Latéral à la Loire, which runs for 122 miles between Digoin and Briare, was built to bypass some of the more awkward stretches of the river, although the advent of the railways made it largely redundant.

After Briare and Gien the Loire curves on, through a widening valley, towards its apex at Orléans—the point at which it turns decisively south-west towards the still distant Atlantic. The days of Orléans as a significant port are long over, but every two years in September it is crowded with boats for the increasingly popular Festival de Loire. A great range of craft, many of them historical reconstructions, sail, row or are trailered here from all over France and beyond. Those arriving directly by the Loire may have come from as far downstream as the estuary or as far upstream, depending on their draught, as Nevers. There are races and water-jousts, fireworks and artistic light-shows. On the quays are bars, local produce tasting and demonstrations of barrel-making. On and off the water there are concerts:

traditional river-songs with banjos, guitars, accordions, harmonicas and hurdy-gurdys.

South of Olivet, now almost part of Orléans, the River Loiret makes its sudden appearance in the Parc Floral de la Source, which is known especially for its roses and irises. It is now certain, as was long suspected, that this is a resurgence. The waters of the Loiret leave the bed of the Loire near St.-Benoît-sur-Loire and flow, through perhaps 25 miles of underground caves, to the "source". In 1776 the traveller Nathaniel Wraxall described it rising "in a prodigious column" before immediately forming, as it still does, a "considerable" if short river. The spring Wraxall saw, the so-called Abîme or abyss, suffered when the owner of the Château de la Source "enlarged the opening from whence it issues" so that "it now only appears to bubble up scarce above the surface of the ground, in the middle of a shallow, artificial basin." Wraxall had wanted to keep the old romantic setting, the "dark and gloomy hollow shaded by deep woods"; "One cannot view so ridiculous and absurd a metamorphosis without the greatest regret, mixed with indignation." The Loiret responded to the change by forcing through another spring, known as the "Bouillon", which is now the main "source". Having emerged, the river flows eight miles to rejoin the Loire at Pointe de Courpain.

Making west, at this stage south-west, the Loire proceeds towards Beaugency—the "old brown Beaugency in its cup between two heights" admired by Edith Wharton. Here there are an eleventh-century keep, a fifteenth-century castle, and a magnificent 1,444-foot bridge. For centuries this was the only place between Orléans and Blois where the Loire could be crossed. The castle and the bridge—partly blown up to slow enemy advances in 1815, 1870 and 1940—have been much fought over. The siege and capture of the town from the English was part of Joan of Arc's victorious progress along the river, which is perhaps the most well known episode in the history of the Orléanais. An immensely fertile region, including the great agricultural plain of the Beauce to the north of the river, was usefully reincorporated into France. A few miles downstream of Beaugency is an installation, which its supporters believe, is another triumph for the nation: the nuclear power-station of St.-Laurent-des-Eaux, built on an artificial island in the 1960s.

BRIARE

The Briare Canal, part of a system of waterways linking the Loire, Loing and Seine, made the town at one time a significant port. Work began in 1604 under the direction of Hugues Cosnier and on the initiative of Henri IV and his minister Sully. Having halted for many years after the king's assassination in 1610, it was completed in 1642. The Pont-Canal, linking the Canal Latéral à la Loire of 1827-30 with the Canal de Briare, was added in the 1890s: a spectacular piece of engineering from the Eiffel company, designed by Léonce-Abel Mazoyer. It is 2,171 feet long and 36 high; with a full load of water it weighs over 13,000 tonnes. On the pilasters at the town end of the bridge, bronze boats with winged monsters at their prows surge forward, oars powerfully at work.

In June 1940, during the German invasion, emergency talks took place in Briare between the British and French leadership. On the 11th Churchill and a group including Anthony Eden and Generals Edward Spears and Hastings "Pug" Ismay flew in a twenty-seat De Havilland Flamingo, escorted by twelve Hurricanes, from Hendon to Briare. Churchill complained about the (necessarily) indirect route they took—

he wanted to proceed south without further ado; Ismay suspected (*Memoirs*, 1960) that "he had a faint hope of being able to see something of the battle!" They would find their French opposite numbers less avid for conflict.

General Spears had close connections with France. Indeed, he had been a passionate Francophile until 1940. But he was becoming terribly disillusioned as France moved closer to accepting defeat. From the largely empty aerodrome, with Churchill beaming diplomatically and Spears, to judge by his own account, scowling at the "beastly place", they were driven to a nearby château. For Spears, who was ready not to be pleased, it was "a hideous house, the sort of building the *nouveau riche* French *bourgeoisie* delight in, a villa expanded by successful business in groceries or indifferent champagne into a large monstrosity of red lobster-coloured brick, and stone the hue of unripe Camembert." It had, he was "glad to hear, a ridiculous name: *Le Château du Muguet*—Lily of the Valley Castle" (Spears, *Assignment to Catastrophe*, 1954).

Almost at once talks began in the dining-room. The French party included a still-lively prime minister Paul Reynaud, General Weygand who seemed to have abandoned all hope, and Marshal Pétain looking "more woe-begone than ever" (Ismay). The French wanted Britain to commit its forces, including all its fighter-planes, to a last attempt to save France. But Churchill held firm: "This is not the decisive moment. The decisive moment will come when Hitler hurls his Luftwaffe against Britain. If we can keep command of the air over our own island—that is all I ask— we will win it all back for you." Hindsight says he was right, but it did not strike the French leaders as a helpful approach to the situation. Weygand told Reynaud that Britain would have "her neck wrung like a chicken".

Churchill continued Churchillian. Asked by Reynaud what he would do if France capitulated and Germany concentrated its full might on Britain he, "with his jaw thrust well forward, rejoined that he had not thought that out very carefully, but that broadly speaking he would propose to drown as many as possible of them on the way over, and then to *frapper sur la tête* anyone who managed to crawl ashore." Unsatisfactory discussions continued. The only French leader who impressed the British was the newly promoted Brigadier General Charles de Gaulle, who said little during the debates but looked much more resolute than his colleagues. A conference photograph shows a tall, erect, uniformed de Gaulle with a group of smaller, rather shifty-looking men in suits. Spears, who desperately needed someone to restore his old faith in France, studied the future leader carefully:

> For relief I turned to de Gaulle, whose bearing alone among his compatriots matched the calm, healthy phlegm of the British. A strange-looking man, enormously tall; sitting at the table he dominated everyone else by his height... No chin, a long, drooping, elephantine nose over a closely-cut moustache, a shadow over a small mouth whose thick lips tended to protrude as if in a pout before speaking, a high, receding forehead and pointed head surmounted by sparse black hair lying flat and neatly parted. His heavily-hooded eyes were very shrewd.

With little agreed except a plan (a "fantasy," says Ismay), soon abandoned, of fighting in Brittany, the delegates departed. On the way back from Briare no fighter escort could be provided because of heavy cloud-cover over the Loire. Churchill, however, needed to get back to England urgently. His unarmed and unaccompanied plane made it across the Channel only because a German pilot, busy bombing Allied shipping, failed to notice it. Undaunted, Churchill crossed the Channel again a few days later. In Tours he talked once more to Reynaud. Churchill now accepted that it was legitimate for the French army to capitulate, but argued strongly against an armistice. He was back in London for a cabinet meeting at 10 p.m. that night, apparently neither tired nor harassed, says Ismay, after five recent expeditions to France. "He had, as he afterwards admitted, suffered real agony of soul; but he never gave a sign of it." On 17 June Pétain told the French forces to stop fighting, on the 18th de Gaulle broadcast from London calling for continued resistance, and on the 22nd Pétain signed the armistice.

SULLY

Sully-sur-Loire possesses, notes Murray's *Handbook for the Traveller in France* (1843), "an old Castle, resting its front upon the Loire, and separated on the other side from the town by a deep ditch". The round towers look satisfyingly solid but the château has often been inundated by the river; once in the seventeenth century its most famous owner, deeply absorbed in writing his memoirs as the waters rose, is said to have had a narrow escape.

Maximilien de Béthune, Duc de Sully (1559-1641), is less well known than the later royal first ministers Richelieu and Mazarin. His time in office was much briefer than theirs, and was spent in the service of a highly capable king, Henri IV, while the cardinals ruled for the less impressive Louis XIII and the under-age Louis XIV. Yet Sully contributed much to Henri's success and to the centralizing programme of the later ministers. His greatest achievements were financial—less glamorous than the foreign policy with which Richelieu and Mazarin are especially associated. As Surintendant des Finances from 1598, he succeeded in regaining control of the economy after the long chaos of the Wars of Religion. And as well as finance he superintended fortifications, buildings, bridges, roads and artillery. In Paris he completed the Pont-Neuf and built the beautiful Place Royale (now Place des Vosges).

The assassination of Henri IV in 1610 ended Sully's political dominance. He had made many enemies with his reforms, the often heavy-handed way he forced them through, and the Protestantism in which he, unlike Henri, persisted. He remained respected enough for Richelieu to make him a Marshal of France in 1634, but he spent most of his time on his many estates; his financial acumen had given him a very considerable personal fortune. One of his possessions was the château of Sully-sur-Loire. In 1602 he had bought the barony of Sully and in 1606 was created duke. He modernized the château and did some of the writing (and frequent rewriting) of his memoirs here between 1611 and 1641. Sully's aim was to justify his policies and the king's. The short title of the memoirs is the *Oeconomies royales*— "economies" meaning roughly "administration" or "way of running things". The longer title suggests the author's slightly biased perspective: "Mémoires des sages et royales Oeconomies d'Estat domestiques, politiques et militaires de Henry le Grand, l'exemplaire des roys, le prince des vertus, des armes et des loix [laws]..." Eventually it reaches Sully himself, praising the "useful service, fit obedience and loyal administration" of this trustworthy "soldier and servant of the great Mars [Henri] of the French people".

There had been a castle at Sully-sur-Loire since at least the early twelfth century, but most of what can now be seen was built by Guy de la Trémoïlle in the late fourteenth century. The most remarkable survival—

Sully has been much burnt, bombarded and flooded—is the ship's-keel roof-frame of Trémoïlle's great hall, fifty feet high, 115 feet long, and perfectly preserved. Sully is very much dominated, however, by the memory of the great duke. Representations of him abound: a replica of the tomb effigy from Nogent-le-Rotrou; a statue by Pierre Biard, a large, powerful, armoured figure with touches of Neptune and of his old master the king; a great grey-bearded portrait of about 1610. The Grande Salle Haute celebrates Sully and his family. Over the main fireplace is a large painting of the grand buildings and gardens he planned, but did not fully realize, for his birthplace, Rosny-sur-Seine. Beneath Rosny two flaming cannon-balls honour his position as Grand Maître et Capitaine de l'Artillerie de France; they reappear in solid form on the fireplace in the Dining Room.

Among the family portraits in the Grande Salle Haute is that of the fifth duke, who invited François-Marie Arouet (1694-1778) to Sully in the summer of 1716. Arouet, who had yet to adopt the name Voltaire, had been exiled from Paris for writing satirical verses implying incest between the regent, the Duke of Orléans, and his daughter. At Sully, more innocently, he jested to correspondents about the "magnificent wood" where rascally lovers have defaced every tree with their names: a good place

53

too for those who want to "murder partridges". He also wrote some non-satirical poetry, unlikely to get him into trouble, in connection with the "nuits blanches" which were held in the park. He told the Marquise de Mimeure about the "great chamber of elms lit by fairy-lights". Here was served a splendid supper, accompanied by music and followed by "a ball involving over a hundred superbly costumed masked dancers". Voltaire's contribution to the entertainment was to leave *La Nuit blanche de Sully* in the plates of two young noblewomen, Mme. de la Vrillière and Mme. de Listenay: courtly lines saluting the former lady as a naiad, a dryad, a charming bird, and assuring the second that all these cupids and masquers and brilliant costumes show how much everyone wants to please her. This even applies—a slight touch of mockery is allowable—to "these dreadful violins with which they are deafening you".

The Chambre Haute or Grand Salon still has its coffered ceiling from Sully's time. The room displays nineteenth-century paintings which feature the heroic legends of Sully and the rather more charismatic Henri IV. The young future minister, by carrying a prayer-book, escapes the massacre of his fellow Protestants on St. Bartholomew's Day. The new king, portrayed in 1817 by Charles-Achille d'Hardiviller, rallies his outnumbered men at the battle of Ivry; he points to the white plume—the famous *panache blanc*—on his helmet. If the battle-standards are lost in the fray, he is supposed to have told his companions, "rally to my white plume. You will find it on its way to victory and to honour." This became the famous watchword cited by Rostand's Cyrano de Bergerac, another exponent of *panache* in the heart as well as on the head.

St.-Benoît-sur-Loire: the Basilica

Le Port, a small village on the Loire by St.-Benoît, was once, as its name suggests, a significant landing-place. Pilgrim-boats docked here, just before the long, curved island of Les Mahis. Food and drink for pilgrims and monks, wood and stone for building, robes and jewels for visiting kings and courtiers, also arrived here. Off Les Mahis now, much of the activity is provided by beavers and otters.

People wanted to visit the monastery of Fleury or St.-Benoît because—whence the second name—it possessed the relics of St. Benedict, seized from Monte Cassino in the 670s. The abbey school was famous in the days of Charlemagne. The monastery, its library and its buildings became particularly notable, however, under the learned and powerful abbots Abbo (ruled 988-1004) and Gauzlin (1004-30). It was Gauzlin who began the massive tower-porch of Nivernais limestone at the west end of the church, probably after a fire in 1026. He intended it, says an early life, as "an example to all Gaul". Its Romanesque capitals, which may date from about 1030, include flowing vegetal designs, lions and other beasts, and scenes from the Apocalypse and the life of St. Martin.

In the late eleventh century the choir and transept were rebuilt in limestone. This was quarried at Bulcy, taken in carts to nearby La Charité-sur-Loire, and brought down the river from there. The transept contains the fourteenth-century alabaster statue of the Virgin of Fleury. Even more important for pilgrims is the crypt, at the centre of which, surrounded by squat pillars, is the reliquary of St. Benedict. In the Choir is the tomb effigy of the abbey's most important royal patron, King Philippe I (ruled 1060-1108), on a slab supported by four stone lions and with a fifth at his feet. When the king's tomb was opened by the local authorities in 1830 it was found that he had been buried in an oak coffin within a sarcophagus of large stones. The wrappings of the body were of silk, woven with patterns of flowers and leaves. The pale stone of the effigy (originally painted) is in harmonious contrast with the ancient *opus sectile* marble floor, installed here in the time of Abbot Gauzlin (with some additions in 1531): browns, reds, greens, circles, rectangles, lozenges.

Some of the finest capitals are also to be seen in the Choir. They date probably from the 1080s. One group represents St. Benedict and his miracles as described by Pope Gregory the Great in his *Dialogues*. At the entrance to the Choir, on the north side, Benedict faces temptation in the form of a woman from his past. She is brought in by an animal-headed nightmare demon. It was the strongest temptation the saint ever experienced, says Gregory. But in the nick of time the hand of God appears above to bless Benedict; he hurls himself naked into a thorn-bush. Prominent ribs stress his bareness and his asceticism. "His wounds drove from his body what was wounding his soul." At the other end of the Choir, Benedict miraculously mends a sieve through prayer, resurrects a peasant's son, enables his assistant to walk on water in order to save another monk from drowning, and reproaches the tyrannical King of the Goths, Totila. The figures in these groups have been aptly described by Eliane Vergnolle (*Saint-Benoît-sur-Loire et la Sculpture du XIe siècle*, 1985). Their supple, often fluid draperies are rendered in relief rather than by "un graphisme de surface". The faces are "very distinctive, with their jutting chins, square jaws, strong noses descending straight from the foreheads, eye-holes pierced with a trepan, accentuated arches of the eyebrows, foreheads covered by hair."

There is much other interesting sculpture in the basilica. The Early Gothic portal in the fourth bay of the north aisle shows Christ with the Four Evangelists at their desks, writing the Gospels. At the entrance to the Sanctuary a Romanesque capital presents the story of Abraham and Isaac. Abraham's sword is raised in his right hand, while the left grasps Isaac by the hair. Isaac, naked and blindfold, perches on the altar. At the same moment the angel swoops in, his protecting wings thrust forward above the boy's head and towards the sword—lack of space, as well as dramatic considerations, dictates the arrangement. Also in this one moment the angel pulls off Isaac's blindfold; it is all very immediate for the participants but also, since it figures the sacrifice and resurrection of Christ by the Father, an eternal moment of sacred time. A calmer, stiller scene follows in which Abraham holds the ram, which God has substituted for Isaac, ready on the altar. Isaac himself, perhaps more adult-looking now, stands to offer up the sacrifice.

St.-Benoît-sur-Loire: Flying above Language

The poet, novelist and painter Max Jacob (1876-1944), a great talker and player with words, loved the silence of St.-Benoît. Paradox was essential to his work. The poems and prose-poems of *Le Cornet à dés* (*The Dice Cup*, 1917), especially, combine the serious and the comic, the fantastic and the everyday; they are full of puns, parody and free word-association. He was a modernist, a humorist and, for much of the second half of his life, a man of deeply traditional religious faith. A vision of Christ in 1909 began his conversion—to the horror of his Jewish family in Brittany—to Roman Catholicism.

Jacob first came to Saint-Benoît in 1921, seeking a quiet retreat from the febrile literary and artistic world of Paris where he was associated with Cocteau, Picasso, Apollinaire and Modigliani. He stayed, with occasional absences, until 1927, living first in the *curé's* house and then at the former monastery. (The Benedictines were expelled at the Revolution and again, following legal changes, between 1901 and 1944.) Here he worked hard, stopping only for meals, sleep and frequent attendance at religious services in the basilica. This church, which for hundreds of years had been the centre of a mighty and influential Benedictine monastery, was of great importance to Jacob. He worshipped there, showed round pilgrims and tourists, and admired the building: "yellow and pink, enormous, more Assyrian or Egyptian than Roman". He wrote its history, partly as a devotional exercise.

By 1927, however, Jacob was finding life at St.-Benoît too isolated. He needed the contacts and the funds available to him in Paris, to which he returned for another nine years. But in 1936 he fled the world again and came back to live in the Hôtel Robert (now Foyer Sainte-Marguerite) and then, from 1939, in more congenial lodgings in Place du Martroi. He was welcomed back by old friends: "the blacksmith calls me *tu*, buys me drinks and keeps shaking hands with me: 'you'll paint a picture of me shoeing a horse'." Jacob painted landscapes, Paris views, Cubist pieces, and Christs, partly in order to raise some money; he wrote less in his last years, sometimes dreaming by the fireside, he said, "of books I won't write". He expected not to live much longer, particularly once the German occupation began in 1940. He refused to join the mass exodus south. As a Jew he was subject to increasing restriction; Jewish writers were banned from publishing. In theory he was even banned from entering his beloved basilica. His brother-in-law died in a camp at Compiègne and his sister and one of his brothers in Auschwitz. Max Jacob himself was finally taken on 24 th February 1944.

He was sent via Orléans to the camp at Drancy, close to Paris. Friends tried to intervene, using whatever contacts they had. Jean Cocteau wrote an extraordinary and moving appeal to the German embassy. As well as praising Jacob for his friendship and exemplary, retired life, Cocteau proclaims his importance as a poet by nature, involuntarily; as the inventor, with Apollinaire, of "a language which flies above our language, and expresses depth"; as "the troubadour of that extraordinary tournament in which Picasso, Matisse, Braque, Derain, Chirico, joined and opposed their variegated coats of arms." Cocteau speaks as much to posterity as to the Germans. His and other letters may, however, have had the desired effect. The order to release Jacob went out, but too late for the prisoner, who died of pneumonia in Drancy on 5 th March. He was buried first there in a common grave and then in 1949, as he had desired, in the cemetery at

Saint-Benoît-sur-Loire. A permanent exhibition upstairs at the Information Centre displays a good range of Jacob documents and pictures.

Châteauneuf-sur-Loire

The novelist Maurice Genevoix (1890-1980), who was born on the Loire
at Decize, lived in or near Châteauneuf for much of his life. Here he wrote
the First World War memories of *Ceux de 14*, and novels including *Rémi
des Rauches* (1922), where the town is called by its earlier name, Portvieux.
Harmony with nature and specifically the Loire is a main concern of *Rémi*.
The river calls irresistibly to the main character, with its reddish-brown
pebbles, its rustling bulrushes (*rauches*), its "old pines and alders bending
towards their reflections and seeming to float, aerial, between the sky and
the Loire", its pearly whiteness at dawn and opaline purity "in the last
light of dusk". Forty years later *La Loire, Agnès et les garçons* (1962), ends
with a scene perhaps no less poetic, if more everyday, of communal swimming on a warm September evening by the bridge at "Portvieux". The
Loire has provided the two adolescent boys of the title with memories,
meeting-places, context, and come close to drowning one of them—now
he is wisely learning to swim. It has proved at least as important to their
development as their first love, Agnès.

After his father's death in 1928 Genevoix moved the short distance
downstream to St.-Denis-de-l'Hôtel. Les Vernelles was an old house which,
when he found it, seemed on the brink of collapse but appealed to him as
an ideal point from which to watch, swim in and write about the Loire.
In his later years, as member and (1958-73) Permanent Secretary of the
Académie Française, he spent more time in Paris, but continued to use les
Vernelles. It remains a private house; there is a museum, the Maison
Maurice Genevoix, in the middle of St.-Denis.

By Genevoix's time the Loire had become "ce beau fleuve inutile" (this
beautiful, useless river). Its more useful, sometimes less beautiful past is
the subject of the Musée de la Marine de Loire. Founded in 1960, it commemorates the period when Châteauneuf was a major river-port, with
documents, photographs, models, maps, clothing and anchors. The
museum also has a good collection of faïence, some of it decorated with
boating scenes; prints and drawings of local places; a display on Maurice
Genevoix; and washerwomen's equipment including an oaken washing
"beetle" from late nineteenth-century Anjou.

Cenabum and the Gothic Forest

Cenabum was the Loire city of the Carnutes tribe. According to Julius Caesar, it was the Carnutes who sparked off Vercingetorix's major and nearly successful rebellion against Roman rule in 53 BC. They volunteered to begin the fight, ceremonially stacking military standards with those of other Gallic peoples as a sign of solidarity. Led by two thugs—from Caesar's point of view—called Gutuater and Conconnetodumnus, they descended on Cenabum, killing and robbing Roman traders who had settled there.

Cenabum suffered for the actions of the Carnutes. Caesar, whose absence in Italy had encouraged the uprising, moved rapidly through Gaul on his return. His siege preparations persuaded Vellaunodunum (Montargis) to surrender and he continued, unexpectedly soon, to Cenabum. He had a hunch that the inhabitants would try to leave, under cover of darkness, by the bridge which crossed the Loire directly from the city walls. The legions were waiting for them. As the Carnutes tried to evacuate, the Romans fired the gates and stormed into the narrow streets. Caesar says that almost all the people in Cenabum were captured—most would be sold as slaves—and the city pillaged and burned. Its rebuilt descendant was renamed Aurelianum, after the Emperor Aurelian, in the third century AD, whence Orléans.

Occupying Romans are less successful in dominating the area in René Goscinny and Albert Uderzo's *Astérix et les Goths* (1963). Somewhere in the vast Forêt des Carnutes gatherings of Druids took place. One theory is that they met at what is now Saint-Benoît-sur-Loire, still a religious centre. In *Astérix* this becomes a convention which includes a competition to be named "Best Druid of the Year". Panoramix, resident of the hero's village—the only one which, book after book, resists Roman rule—naturally wins the prize after displaying the power of his magic strengthening potion. But he is kidnapped by a gang of Goths—strong men with substantial moustaches, their helmets at once Viking and Junker—who have penetrated the forest and intend to force the winning Druid to help with barbarian invasion-plans. The rest of the book involves the adventures of Astérix and his large friend Obélix in rescuing Panoramix. Life in the thick forest becomes confusing for the Romans. The heroes are mistaken for Goths, while the plodding legionaries mystify the real Goths by ignoring them. The two go round for a time disguised as Romans, as a result of which the legionaries all suspect each other of being enemies. There is much bashing of heads. "They are all idiots, and I am their chief!" sobs the Roman general Nenpeuplus, slumped against his tent-pole.

The Forêt d'Orléans, north and west of the city, remains extensive even if less so than the Druid-filled woods of the Carnutes. As a child George Sand (*Histoire de ma vie*, 1856) journeyed slowly through its depths in her aristocratic grandmother's coach or *berline*, a veritable mobile home with its freight of food, "sweets, perfumes, packs of cards, books, itineraries, money and what not". As they lumbered through the forest, she reminisced calmly to her less calm attendant about the days when brigands frequently attacked travellers on the road. Before the Revolution, she remembered, convicted robbers "were hanged on the trees by the roadside, at the very place where they had committed their crime: so that here, on either side of the road, and not very far apart, one would see corpses attached to branches, swinging in the wind over one's head." If you travelled the same road often enough, you got to know individual corpses; she remembered a woman with black hair, surrounded by crows. "Perhaps Grandmother thought I was asleep during this mournful recitation. I was dumb with horror, bathed in cold sweat." For years afterwards she was visited by horrible imaginings whenever she crossed the forest.

THE SIEGE OF ORLÉANS: "NOT EVEN A MAN"
Many people in the city itself might have been hanged or otherwise killed in 1428 or 1429. In autumn 1428 the Earl of Salisbury, veteran of Agincourt and other victories, closed in on Orléans, the main surviving obstacle to the extension of English power south of the Loire. He secured the bridgeheads and settled down to besiege the city. But at the end of October he was fatally wounded at the fort of Tourelles. According to Edward Hall's chronicle, he was killed while observing the city from "a high chamber having a grate full of bars and iron by which a man might look all the length of the bridge." A French master-gunner decided to target this "totyng hole" with "a piece of ordnance"—a small cannon. While he was at dinner, his young son sighted Salisbury and other commanders. He "took his match, as his father had taught him… and fired the gun, which broke and shivered the iron bars of the grate, whereof one struck the earl so strongly on the head, that it struck away one of his eyes and the side of his cheek." In retrospect Salisbury's death presaged the collapse of English fortunes in France.

In *Henry VI*, Part One, which draws on Hall's narrative, Talbot's lament for Salisbury is interrupted by the news that

> the French have gathered head.
> The Dolphin, with one Joan de Pucelle joined,
> A holy prophetess new risen up,
> Is come with a great power to raise the siege.

Salisbury lives long enough to greet this information with a groan. He wants vengeance, not victorious dolphins (*dauphins*—the as yet un-crowned Charles VII) and *pucelles* (virgins). But in reality the timing was less dramatic. The siege had been in progress for over six months before the coming of the army of Joan and her ally Dunois, known somewhat risibly to modern ears as the Bastard of Orléans; he was the half-brother of the poet Duke of Orléans who had been captured by the English at Agincourt.

In February 1429 a French and Scottish relief force failed disastrously in its attack, near Rouvray to the north of Orléans, on an English wagon-train supplying the besiegers. The engagement became known, mockingly, as the Battle of the Herrings—part of the English cargo. But the situation changed rapidly with Joan's arrival in April. She and her men entered the city on the 29th, giving new heart and necessary supplies to the defenders. They went on to the offensive, attacking the English-held *bastides*. A cross-bow-bolt pierced Joan's shoulder during the assault on Les Tourelles, but her refusal to leave the fight made her seem all the more miraculous. On the 28th she had issued her defiant challenge to the English, whom she intended to "throw out of France". On 8 May the siege was raised. Both sides believed that her power, whether divine or diabolical, was at work. She did not herself join in the fighting but rode, seemingly unstoppable, with her white standard painted with Jesus (holding the world), two angels and fleurs-de-lis. Believing in her, the French moved on along the Loire. In one week in June they captured Jargeau, Meung and Beaugency. In July Charles VII was crowned at Reims in the presence of the Maid, still bearing her standard. This was the climax of her career. Her successes now became fewer and royal support for her waned. She was captured in 1430 and went to the stake, unransomed, in 1431. But English confidence in the war never recovered.

Not surprisingly, audiences of *Henry VI* at the Rose Theatre in 1592 were shown that the French victories were the work not of a saintly maiden but of an unchaste, hypocritical schemer. In Act Five it is revealed that she is in the habit of summoning evil spirits to her aid. This devilish Joan has, of course, little in common with the heroic figure rehabilitated by France and the Pope in 1456 and eventually canonized in 1920. Orléans was one of the Maid's earliest cult centres. Her relief of the city is still commemorated every 8 May. This became an occasion for processions, sermons, civic gatherings and feasts. As early as 1435 a hagiographic play about her was performed. Statues abound, including the equestrian piece by Denis Foyatier (1855) in Place du Martroi. There are displays and reconstructions at the rebuilt Maison Jeanne d'Arc (on the site of the house where she stayed in 1429) and the Centre Jeanne d'Arc. In the nave of the Cathédrale Ste.-Croix her story is told in colourful stained glass (commissioned in 1878-9, completed in 1897) full of gesticulating soldiers and angels; the sequence, including her triumphant entry into Orléans, runs above the Stations of the Cross. Charles Péguy (1873-1914), the city's Catholic and socialist poet and polemicist, returned repeatedly to Joan in his work from his *Jeanne d'Arc* plays (1897) to some of the last pieces he wrote before his death at the Battle of the Marne in September 1914.

Joan's appeal is clear but paradoxical. At Orléans, as Vita Sackville-West says in her biography (1936), "Her position as a leader was a unique one. She was not a professional soldier; she was not really a soldier at all; she was not even a man. She was ignorant of war. She was a girl dressed up. But she believed, and had made others willing to believe, that she was the mouthpiece of God." Some people found this uniqueness troubling. As Edward Burns pithily puts it in his Arden (third series) edition of *Henry VI*, "The woman in man's clothes wielding a sword is a pucelle with a pizzle, and therefore a puzzle."

ORLÉANS: SCHOLARS AND MONARCHS

Medieval Orléans was, as the siege attests, a strategically important city, well placed for Paris and on the Loire. It was also the site of a famous university; among its fictional students is the scholar in Chaucer's *The Franklin's Tale* who is as learned in magic as in the law he is supposed to be studying. He knows those "sciences/By whiche men make diverse apparences." He can create illusory scenes of hunting and hawking, jousting and dancing. And, what matters most for the story, he can make the "grisly feendly rokkes blake" of the coast of Brittany disappear. He charges the squire Aurelius a thousand pounds for this service but later, in this tale of serial "gentillesse" and generosity, magnanimously waives his fee.

Rabelais' Pantagruel also finds the students of Orléans somewhat distracted from their official studies. Sir Thomas Urquhart translates, freely but with his habitual Rabelaisian zest: here "he found store of swaggering Scholars that made him great entertainment at his coming and with whom he learned to play at tennis so well, that he was a Master at that game; for the Students of the said place make a prime exercise of it." Sometimes, too—Urquhart expands the passage and the innuendo—"they carried him unto Cupid's houses of commerce... there to recreate his person at the sport of *Poussavant*, which the wenches of London call the *Ferkers in and in*." "As for breaking his head with over-much study he had an especial care not to do it in any case, for feare of spoiling his eyes."

In Rabelais' time Orléans was still, like much of the Loire valley, a significant political centre. In 1560 the sixteen-year-old King François II came here to preside over a meeting of the States General. He also managed a day's hunting in the forest before he was taken ill and, on 5 De-

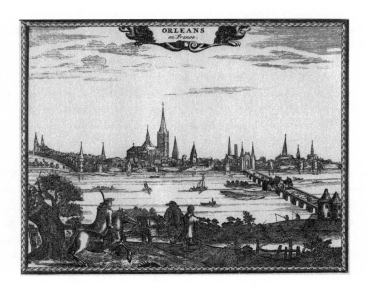

cember died at the Hôtel Groslot, the residence, completed only ten years earlier, of the city magistrate Jacques Groslot. The young king's death was a political setback for the Catholic Guise faction and was hailed as a providential victory by John Calvin: the God who had struck Henri II fatally in the eye in a tournament the previous year now struck his son in the ear. (Severe infection of the ear was the prelude to the brain abscess which killed him.) For François' widow Mary, niece of the Guises, it was a personal as well as a political disaster. She had been Queen of Scots almost since birth and had lived at the French court since the age of five; François died just before her eighteenth birthday. Famous mistakes and misfortunes awaited her on her return to Scotland in 1561. At the Hôtel Groslot a painting (1865) by Pierre Dupuis, in the detailed historical manner of the day, shows François on his death-bed and Mary distraught in blue. The queen-mother, Catherine de' Medici, who will now take power as regent, indicates to the reluctant Guises that they should kneel to her.

The Wars of Religion would begin in earnest a few years later. One of their casualties was Orléans cathedral, sacked by Huguenots in 1586. Rebuilding was begun by Henri IV, eventual restorer of civil peace, in 1599, although it was not completed until the nineteenth century. On the whole, Baedeker's *Northern France* grants, it is "a successful enough reproduction of the late-Gothic manner, while the florid façade... attains a certain amount of dignity in spite of its bastard style." In a side chapel Henri's promise to restore the splendour destroyed by his former co-religionists is celebrated in stained glass. Surrounded by appropriately ruffed dignitaries, he holds a hat with his signature white plumes.

The other building most likely to attract visitors is the Musée des Beaux-Arts. It houses an eclectic, if frequently rather "also-ran", collection. There are some pleasing Dutch and Flemish landscapes, Jean-Baptiste Chardin's honest, forthright self-portrait with round, armless spectacles perched on his nose— the artist's own replica of the version in the Louvre—and sculpture by Rodin and Maillol. Among the most exciting paintings are the *Four Elements* by Claude Deruet (1588-1660), commissioned by Cardinal Richelieu for his château at Richelieu. These are highly inventive accounts of water (frozen and flowing), earth, fire and air (where courtiers fly falcons), in the tradition of idealizing court entertainments. Louis XIII, his wife and two young sons are present in chariots; Richelieu himself is also, inevitably, prominently placed.

CLÉRY-ST.-ANDRÉ

In August 1483 King Louis XI was buried, in accordance with his own instructions, not in the royal basilica of St. Denis near Paris, but in the church of Cléry-St.-André, about two miles south-east of the Loire at Meung. He had a special devotion to the Virgin of Cléry, whose wooden image had been unearthed by a peasant in about 1280. Louis had honoured her by partly rebuilding her church; the earlier one on the site had been all but destroyed by the Earl of Salisbury's troops in 1428. As Dauphin, in 1443, Louis had fulfilled a vow to give the church his own weight in silver in return for his success in besieging Dieppe. And he repaired in triumph to Cléry in 1465, some months after his victory over the Burgundians and his internal opponents at Montlhéry. Two years later he granted the spacious collegiate church the status of chapel royal.

Louis' tomb was designed partly by the painter Jean Fouquet. The king's detailed prescriptions of 1472-3 for his bronze effigy have survived, unlike the effigy itself, which was melted down in 1562 during the Wars of Religion. He is to kneel facing the Virgin of Cléry, holding his hat, wearing the collar of St. Michael, boots, spurs and sword. Reflecting his favourite pastime, he will have a hunting-horn at his back and a greyhound at his side. He even prescribes the nose—a striking feature in his portraits. It must be "aquiline, longish and slightly high". The hair must be long, and on no account must he be bald: a desire churlishly denied in the marble replacement effigy of 1622 by Michel Bourdin (restored 1896), where he has little hair. In general the replacement Louis looks dignified but probably more anonymous than the original.

MEUNG-SUR-LOIRE: POETS AND POLICE

Meung is a small, walled riverside town It is watered by a series of canalised streams, *les mauves*, which, as the Michelin Green Guide enthuses, "gaily lap, gurgle and murmur between the houses." The pleasant setting, together with a large measure of coincidence, perhaps explains the surprising number of literary associations of a place which still has only 6,400 inhabitants.

At the Grand-Café in Meung the drinks change with the seasons: half-bottles of new white wine during harvest, grog or warm wine in winter, *anis* in spring, chilled white in summer. Commissaire Maigret, who has retired to this quiet provincial town in Georges Simenon's *Ceux du Grand-*

Café (1938), used to visit the café only occasionally but has now become a regular. He had found himself bored in the evenings. Mme. Maigret, busy as ever in the kitchen, suggested that he went to play cards at the Grand-Café. He was just going to join in once, but the following day a boy came to tell him they were waiting for him at the café. Soon he is one of the "Grand-Café lot". He is not sure whether he enjoys it or not, he feels rather ashamed, but soon he must have his daily fix. Usually the group includes the butcher (a hopeless player), "Citroën" the motor-mechanic (a seriously good player with no patience for partners' failings) and Maigret, whom the others call "commissaire"—they are rather frightened of him. Either the *patron* or the farrier usually makes up the four. They might have gone on playing and drinking, drinking and playing, but this is a detective story and detectives cannot escape from crime even in the peaceful provinces. One April evening, when sunset glows on the sandbanks in the Loire and the group have been drinking their seasonal aperitif, there is a knock on Maigret's door. "Someone's killed the butcher!"

Maigret, of course, works out how his fellow card-player ended up shot in his van at the edge of Meung. But for good reasons connected with what he finds out, he persistently refuses to help either the local police or the suspects. He is free to go back to his garden. Many years later Simenon, in his own retirement, could still see him there: according to the memoir *Un Homme comme un autre* (1973), the novelist had a dream, almost a vision, of an enviably calm man, seen from behind, wearing work-clothes and a battered straw-hat; taller, plumper and more broad in the shoulder than Simenon. He was hoeing his garden. Meung, which features in several of the stories, had remained an ideal site of provincial tranquillity for Simenon, a Belgian who had travelled widely in France in search of such places. Essentially Simenon's provincial France is an outsider's creation, and one that has probably influenced both the myth and the reality— Simenon was popular, prolific, and very good at local colour. There was, however, one less happy note: in the dream Maigret no longer fished in the Loire because the water was too polluted.

Meung was the birth-place of another famous dreamer, Jean de Mehun or de Meun, continuer of *Le Roman de la Rose*. Guillaume de Lorris wrote the first 4,000 lines of the poem in the 1220s or 1230s. Lorris, his place of origin, is at the eastern end of the Forêt d'Orléans. In the 1270s Jean's 18,000 lines expanded Guillaume's allegorical dream-vision into a more complex debate on love and society. In the fifteenth century the literary connection was with François Villon, who was imprisoned and tortured at Meung castle by the Bishop of Orléans in the summer of 1461. The traditional site of his dungeon is a pit in the castle grounds. His offence on this occasion is unknown but he was already notorious for robbery and affray. In the "Épître à mes amis", probably written at this time, Villon asks his friends to get him out of his dark, airless prison; the friends include girls who like lively young men, dancers, "singers who sing for pleasure, without rules" and "makers of lays, motets and rondeaux". In the event it was a royal amnesty that delivered him when Louis XI came to Meung in October.

In the fictional seventeenth century the young D'Artagnan made his emphatic début here in the first chapter of Alexandre Dumas' *Les Trois Mousquetaires* (1844). The people of Meung in 1625 are accustomed to panic and disruption: great lords are for ever making war on each other, the king on the Cardinal, the Spaniard on the king, and thieves, beggars, Huguenots, wolves and servants on everyone. So some townsmen, when they see women fleeing the main street and hear the cries of children, buckle on their breast-plates and bolster their courage by seizing a musket or a bill-hook. But all that has happened is that an assured and "impertinent" nobleman at the first-floor window of the Franc-Meunier inn has had the audacity to amuse his companions with witticisms at the expense of D'Artagnan's evidently laughable horse. He has excited a strong response. The nag was D'Artagnan's father's parting gift, together with a little money, a letter of introduction to M. de Tréville, Captain of the Royal Musketeers, and the advice that, as a Gascon and his father's son, he must above all show courage—fight, indeed, on the slightest provocation. So far the resulting fierceness of his demeanour has made other travellers either suppress their laughter or attempt to show it, like ancient masks, on one side of the face only. But now D'Artagnan draws his sword on the man who mocks him, strives valiantly against a hail of blows from the companions and the host until his sword and his head are broken, and recovers to attempt a new attack. He runs after his galloping enemy with cries of "Coward! *ah, misérable, ah, faux gentilhomme!*" before collapsing again. The young man's irrepressible spirit remains unbroken. Soon he will be arranging duels for noon, one o'clock and two o'clock with his future friends Athos, Porthos and Aramis.

THE BEAUCE: "A TRUER POEM OF THE EARTH"

In Rabelais' *Gargantua* the young giant's enormous mare is responsible for both the name and the nature of the fertile plain north of the Loire and west and north-west of Orléans. In a forest near Orléans she is bothered by ox-flies and hornets. She swishes her mighty tail at them and in the process flattens the forest. Since then "there have been neither woods nor hornets." Gargantua, pleased with the open country thus created, says to his followers "'Je trouve beau ce.' That is why, since then, this area has been called the Beauce."

Julien Gracq, in *Lettrines 2* (1974), does not find beautiful the Petite-Beauce, the part of the vast plain which is near the Loire. There is no longer a Loire valley, only a plateau of corn: "a bare Beauce with stout walled farms" along the "anaemic river... beside which no poplars shiver and which flows at the same level as the corn." As Gracq moves sadly east, even further away from his beloved Anjou, he finds a formless landscape, "a whole confused back-country". It is an unfinished sketch, "a sewage-farm for the Loire rather than a valley". The bored town of Jargeau is in the grip of a "tristesse calviniste" and seems to have nothing to do with the river. It faces away from it onto the great cultivated fields. Among the deserts of barley and sugar-beet the Loire "drags along resentfully, like a rejected woman".

People, not rivers, suffer in Emile Zola's *La Terre* (1887). The novel is set deep in the Beauce, in a village near Cloyes-sur-le-Loir. Cornfields, alfalfa and clover stretch for mile after mile to the horizon. The straight, chalk-white road from Châteaudun to Orléans crosses the landscape. There are a few windmills. Villages are like "stone islets" in the corn. Here land, soil—*la terre* can mean either—is everything. In his sketch for the novel Zola says that the soil is "the heroine of my book. The nourishing soil, the soil which gives life and which takes it back, impassive." *La Terre* focuses on the peasant's obsessive passion for the land, to own it, to own more of it (as the sketch also says) and on the terrible consequences of this passion. Fouan, a farmer, divides his land like King Lear and with similar results. In the pursuit of land his family are prepared to go to any lengths. This is a savage picture of country life, involving incest, rape and murder, as well as accidents, fires, drunkenness and the straining, sweating daily battle with the land: sowing, ploughing, threshing, muck-spreading. In the most horrific incident a pregnant woman is raped by her brother-in-law, with her sister's collusion, in the hope of aborting the child to prevent it inheriting. Zola admired more idealized country tales like George Sand's *La Mare au diable* but wanted to write "a truer poem of the earth". He was attacked, as usual, for exaggeration and obscenity.

TALCY: "NOT ABSENCE, NOR FORGETTING, NOR THE PASSING DAYS..."

The Château de Talcy, in the Petite-Beauce near Mer, was built mainly in the early sixteenth century. From 1517 it was the property of Bernardo Salviati, whose descendant Isabelle Salviati extended the east wing in the mid-seventeenth century. Salviati belonged to a dynasty of Florentine bankers with links to the Medici. One of his main jobs was to finance the incursions of the French kings into Italy. His château looked more fifteenth-century than sixteenth. Ian Dunlop, in *Châteaux of the Loire* (1969), observes that Salviati was

> more concerned to identify himself with the French nobility than to be up to date with the architectural fashion of his own country [which was influencing royal châteaux of the day], and he built accordingly. Towers were status symbols; pilasters were not. So Talcy is a charming anachronism; looking at the turrets and *chemin de ronde* of the gatehouse, or at the gables and cloisters of the court, one has to remind oneself that this building is later than Chenonceau or Azay-le-Rideau. A sharp eye will detect that most of the machicolations are dummies.

Salviati, whose financial expertise was needed at court, moved in high social circles. Pierre de Ronsard first saw Bernardo's daughter, Cassandra or Cassandre, at a ball in the royal château of Blois in 1545. She was aged fourteen and he twenty-one. Whether or not he actually fell in love with her, "Cassandre" is the ostensible subject of some of his many poems about love, and particularly the *Premier Livre des Amours*. (Other sequences are addressed to Marie and Hélène.) "Élégie à Cassandre" (published 1554) explores the rival claims of the lute and the trumpet—love poetry or royal encomium—and positions Ronsard's work as part of the movement to renew French verse by good use of classical and Petrarchan models. The manifesto of the movement was Joachim Du Bellay's *Défence et illustration de la langue française*. Many love-poets fall short of this stan-

dard: they are too crass or too feeble, they "pay more attention to poetry than meaning," they give us a wench instead of a lady. The "Élégie", both a measured argument about literature and a passionate tribute to "My eye, my heart, my Cassandre, my life", suggests the qualities Ronsard and Du Bellay seek.

"À Cassandre" (1569) recounts, or purports to recount, a much later meeting with the beloved. Time cannot destroy the poet's love. "Not absence, nor forgetting, nor the passing days/Have effaced the name, the graces or the love" printed on his heart since "tender youth". The poem returns several times to the first, piercing, wounding glance. Its effects continue: it does not matter that age, which "breaks down walls and fortresses", has also marked her and him, because "I am not concerned/With what is now, but with the first look," with the first heart-penetrating "arrow" of her grace from which he still bleeds.

The real Cassandre Salviati had married in 1546 and Ronsard himself, unlike his later devotees, probably never visited Talcy. But in the 1570s another poet, Agrippa d'Aubigné (1552-1630), did come. He paid court to Diane Salviati, niece of Ronsard's Cassandre; he will not attempt, he says in *Spring*, to imitate the great verse of the master, but will maintain the equal beauty of the niece, the equal force of his passion. But in the long term he had little time for dalliance. He was a Huguenot, most of his poems were written in the Protestant cause, and he had narrowly escaped the St. Bartholomew's Day Massacre when he came to Talcy in 1572. He had fled Paris the day before the killings, having resisted arrest after a duel in which he acted as second. While staying at Talcy he went to a village in the Beauce where an unknown mounted assailant wounded him in the head. Desiring "to die in the arms of my mistress", he rode forty miles back to Talcy and collapsed when he got there. Diane Salviati tended to him, but while he was unconscious, he later recorded, worldly love was not his concern: he experienced a seven-hour vision of scenes from the history of Protestantism, confirming him in his faith. He remained human enough to write bitter verses when Diane fell out of love with him some time after his recovery. But much more of his creative energy went into the Protestant epic *Les Tragiques* (begun 1577, published 1616) and into fifty years as Protestant soldier and polemicist, the outspoken adviser and then critic of Henri IV. Only at the end of his life, in the 1620s, did he withdraw from France to the comparative safety of Geneva.

In the nineteenth century the château became the property of the Stapfer family. Philippe Albert Stapfer (1766-1840) was a Swiss politician and philosopher who settled in France. His son Albert Stapfer (1802-92) wrote liberal journalism for *Le Globe*, produced one of the first French translations of Goethe's *Faust* (1828), and helped man the barricades in the 1830 Revolution. He knew Mérimée, Stendhal, Mme. Récamier, the opera-singer Giuditta Pasta and many other luminaries of the French Romantic period. Delacroix's dark, spiky, Gothic illustrations for *Faust* originally accompanied Stapfer's version. The Stapfer exhibition which filled the usually placid rooms of the château in 2008 gave a sense of the excitement of the 1820s and 1830s: blow-ups of the Delacroix surrounded by the aptly demonic sounds of Berlioz's *Symphonie fantastique*. After his marriage in 1835 Stapfer led a rather quieter life. At his father-in-law's insistence he renounced his involvement in politics. Having inherited Talcy in 1844 he spent more time there. One of his main activities was as a daguerreotypist; a self-portrait and early pictures of the château are displayed in the Cabinet Stapfer on the first floor.

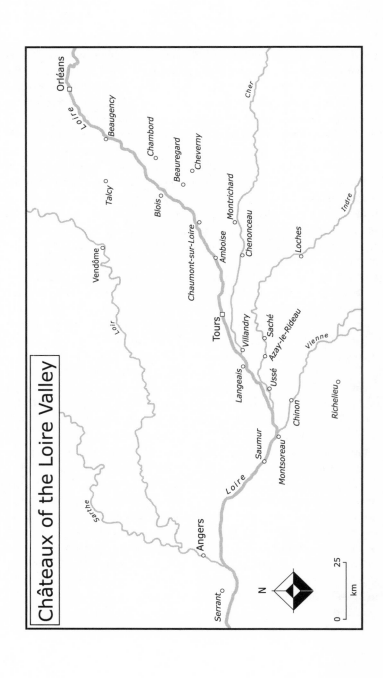

Châteaux of the Loire Valley

Chapter Four

"Many Fair Noblemen's Houses"

From the Sologne to Chaumont-sur-Loire

Between the Loire and the Cher extends the large area of ponds, marsh, heath and woodland (pine, oak, birch) known as the Sologne. Here wildlife is much hunted and much observed. Black terns, kingfishers, cranes and grey herons are often seen, and there are wild boar, hares, beavers, water-voles, four species of newt and three of frog. Everywhere there is water (much of it loud with frogs in spring and early summer). Some of the rough tracks become more like streams in winter, although drainage has been greatly improved in modern times. Problems had begun, in the sixteenth and seventeenth centuries, when medieval oak-forests were cut down and not replaced.

Small rivers thread the landscape. In the eastern and southern Sologne the Petite and Grande Sauldre and the Rère feed the Sauldre which runs on, through Romorantin-Lanthenay, to join the Cher. Further north the Beuvron is joined by the Tharonne, the Bièvre and the Cosson before entering the Loire at Candé-sur-Beuvron. Often these are quiet, wooded streams, sometimes diverted underground, sometimes rather more substantial rivers. Nathaniel Wraxall in 1776 was particularly unimpressed with the Cosson where it "flows or rather stagnates" at Chambord, "black, and full of sedges".

Chambord and several other fine châteaux are built in the thicker forests—convenient for royal and later hunting—at the Loire edge of the Sologne. Blois, magnificently sited on the Loire itself, provided a palace and river-port less than fifteen miles from Chambord. Downstream of Blois the river proceeds, soon after collecting the waters of the Beuvron, to Chaumont-sur-Loire, where the château looks down towards the river across a vast sandy shore. With its round white towers this looks the perfect château; Henry James thought it too perfectly, cleanly restored and "rather like an enormously magnified villa". Even the superb view is insufficient for some: Mme. de Staël, who briefly lived at Chaumont among other places when exiled from the capital by Napoleon, missed her filthy local stream in Paris so much that she claimed to prefer it to any Loire, however bright and clear it might be.

THE SOLOGNE

George Sand, in *Histoire de ma vie* (1854-5), is unenthusiastic about the Sologne. It is an arid land without poetry, ugly, flat, "deadly dull"; "the soil is pale, the heather, the bark of the stunted trees, the bushes, the animals, and especially the inhabitants, are pale, are livid even." Her dislike was born of long, slow childhood journeys through the area in her grandmother's carriage. By the time she wrote, the Sologne was changing at last. The new emperor, Napoleon III, had acquired the château and *domaine* of Lamotte-Beuvron in 1852. Soon afterwards his government launched a transformative programme of road, railway and canal building, plantation of pines and birches, and management of the *étangs* (the hundreds of man-made lakes and ponds). Outsiders brought in money and bought property. Fishing, hunting and farming flourished. Parts of the Sologne even became, in the end, quite tame: in Julien Gracq's Sologne (*Carnets du grand chemin*, 1992) "often the villages seem like the outbuildings of a vanished château, the very memory of which is lost." There are small, neat brick houses. "The street and the pavement always seem to have been swept recently." Nothing produces dust or dirt. The small enclosed gardens have a border of petunias or geraniums.

But in Gracq's youth—he was born in 1910—this was not just a place for careful villagers or carefree hunters. Much of society was divided between landowners and their agents and the poor who worked for them or, as poachers, against them. Lakes were owned and closely guarded. Even taking leeches was poaching; still in the late nineteenth century desperately poor people would wade into the water at night, collect the leeches which attached themselves to them, and sell them for a few pennies in the morning. The best-known fictional treatment of this divided Sologne is Maurice Genevoix's *Raboliot*, which won the Prix Goncourt in 1925. The novel is set in the country between Lamotte-Beuvron and Brinon-sur-Sauldre. Life is organized along quasi-feudal lines. The eponymous hero and his fellow poachers must contend with the landowner and his representatives, the gendarmes and "les gars du St.-Hubert"—members of a national force sent out, disguised as farmers, labourers or woodmen, to catch them.

Raboliot knows the wildlife and the landscape intimately. His father-in-law, the taxidermist Touraille, can tell him even more about the creatures and their names, can show him the "soft, snowy down, swelling at the throat and padding the stomach and thighs" of the sparrow-owl which Raboliot calls a *chavoche* instead of a *chevêche*. (Touraille's original, "le père Beaufils", was a source of information for Genevoix both on poaching and on taxidermy.) But Raboliot, whose very name means "wild rabbit", is more in tune with nature: from the beginning he was "wily, restless, his body slender, his eyes quick and dark… a young wild rabbit, a creature of the woods", whose natural habitat was the thorny scrub, the heathland and the coverts where he could hide behind tall broom. He is alert to the smallest movement of grasses, water and wildlife and—less like a rabbit perhaps—good at concealing his interest when necessary. He poaches, "like everyone in the Sologne, *parbleu*", but less for money or food than out of compulsion.

Raboliot becomes a heroic figure in his struggle with the guards and gendarmes, his closeness to nature and the longing to see his family which brings him, fatally, back to his house after months hiding in the woods. *Raboliot* was published in the period after the First World War when novels with rural settings were especially popular. Genevoix has often been labelled a "regional" writer. But it is evident from his more mystical novel *La Forêt perdue* (1967) that his concerns are broader than the loving realization of locality. The story, which comes "from the depths of time", is set in remote, vaguely medieval and melancholy forest—a world rather like that of Maeterlinck and Debussy's *Pelléas et Mélisande*. The sieur Abdon learns to respect the forest; his son, who obsessively hunts the Great Stag, does not. Abdon's education comes from Waudru, "a little man, almost a gnome", sunburnt, ruddy and old, who materializes in the depths of the forest to protect it and its creatures. He wants to preserve "a world without men, without men's weapons, where the laws of life and death are not transgressed, where the animals can die—be it by claw or by tooth—their true animal death," their "beautiful death".

THE LOST DOMAIN

Alain-Fournier was born, as Henri-Alban Fournier, at La Chapelle d'Angillon, on the Petite-Sauldre in the eastern fringes of the Sologne. La Chapelle becomes La Ferté d'Angillon, the home of Meaulnes, in *Le Grand Meaulnes* (1913). Fournier often returned there to visit his grandparents during the school holidays, but when he was five, in 1891, his father moved further south to become the village teacher at Épineuil-le-Fleuriel, near the River Cher and the Forêt de Tronçais. Fournier's mother was taken on soon afterwards to teach the infants. The school at Ste.-Agathe in the novel, where classrooms and living quarters are in close proximity, is based on the real one.

From an early age Fournier was passionately attached to Épineuil. He would always remember the roughcast red house with roses and nasturtiums at the edge of the village, the hawthorn hedges and the smell of herbs in the garden, the early evening sunlight filtering into the classroom through apple-trees, the white lanes and the local stream called the Queugne. Also nearby were the straight Canal du Berry and the more variable Cher, where some scenes in *Le Grand Meaulnes* are set: transparent and sandy-shored for a summer bathing expedition; flowing peacefully between willows and green meadows with a view, on distant grey hills, of "small turreted castles" among firs. The intensity of Fournier's love for Épineuil, which he and his family left after seven years, was in some ways a burden. His friend and brother-in-law, Jacques Rivière, explained to him that "You had such a beautiful childhood, so filled with imagination, with paradise, that when you left it the meagreness of life dispirited you. It was as if you had already lived your life." Loss and yearning are central to Fournier's novel.

At first the world of Ste.-Agathe is concrete, realistically described. Children gather round the stove in frosty weather. The narrator's mother worries about her new hat. Who is to collect the grandparents from the station? A new adolescent pupil, the tall, highly individual Augustin Meaulnes, becomes François' friend. It is Meaulnes' three-day adventure, when he becomes lost deep in the Sologne, which moves the novel into very different territory. He stumbles then on the "lost domain", inspired partly by the abandoned château and abbey of Loroy, with its tall lime-trees and reedy lake, in the Forêt de St.-Palais near La Chapelle d'Angillon. Here children run free and guests dress in masquerade. Wandering in this place where time seems to have slowed down, Meaulnes comes upon a beautiful young woman playing the piano to a group of children and at once imagines himself married to this "charming, unknown being".

Meaulnes falls in love with Yvonne de Galais; Fournier encountered Yvonne de Quiévrecourt in 1905 and spent much of the rest of his life longing for her. Eventually the dream-like sequence ends. The party breaks up and Meaulnes leaves, feeling already that he will never see Yvonne or the mysterious domain again. He searches, nevertheless, after his return to Ste.-Agathe; the rough country, impassable tracks, woods and ponds make it more plausible that he should have lost the place. François, sympathetic to his friend's idealistic longing, joins the quest. He too becomes a searcher for the "passage" one finds in books, "the old, blocked-up way" whose entrance the weary prince so long cannot find. In the end, thanks in part to François' efforts, they will find the domain, but changed and reduced. Happiness proves elusive. When he first discovered the domain—Les Sablonnières, as it turns out—he reached his height, "a moment of perfection, of purity, which I shall never again attain." A *sablonnière* is a sand-quarry, perhaps suggesting impermanence, the sands of time.

The word *jadis*, "formerly", is constantly repeated in *Le Grand Meaulnes*. We are left with the narrator and his unfulfillable love for Yvonne and for Meaulnes: he has lived through Meaulnes' dreams and secrets, confided in person and then through letters and diaries. The story was serialized late in 1913 and Alain-Fournier was killed near Les Éparges in Lorraine in September 1914. Inevitably it came to seem the novel of a lost generation.

CHÂTEAU DE CHAMBORD: "THE TOUCH OF MADNESS IN ITS CONCEPTION"

The Château de Chambord is "conspicuous", notes Murray's *Handbook for Travellers in France* (1843), for its "vast group of turrets, minarets and cones or inverted funnels". Many people will think it "ugly and fantastic", says Murray, and Douglas Goldring (*The Loire: the Record of a Pilgrimage*, 1913) is disturbed by "the touch of madness in its conception". But certainly it makes a strong impression. "The chimneys of the house appear like so many towers" (John Evelyn); for Henry James, a man of more words, "the towers, the cupolas, the gables, the lanterns, the chimneys, look more like the spires of a city than the salient points of a single building"; "the roof is like the hull of a ship, and must contain a forest of timbers," comments Murray. French visitors were more extravagantly responsive: Chambord is "an arabesque... a woman with her hair blowing in the wind" (Chateaubriand); a wonderful, strange "palace of fairies and knights" (Hugo); a "royaume de Bagdad" (Vigny, writing when Baghdad was synonymous with the romance of the *Arabian Nights*).

It all started, in a sense, as a fantasy: a palace built deep in the woods where François I liked hunting. It also presented an opportunity to experiment with Italian architectural elements. Conceivably Leonardo da Vinci was involved in the project, but he died at Amboise in 1519 before the work could get very far; a more likely candidate, certainly involved later, is Domenico da Cortona. His masterpiece here is the staircase described by Evelyn: "it is devised with four entries or ascents, which cross one another, so that though four persons meet, they never come in sight, but by small loopholes, till they land. It consists of 274 steps (as I remember), and is an extraordinary work, but of far greater expense than use or beauty." Henry James bills the staircase as "a truly majestic piece of humour".

Famous visitors' descriptions, and a long succession of engravings and photographs, have made Chambord one of the most instantly recognizable, or at least familiar, of French monuments. In 2008 the château put on an exhibition about its own image, "Made in Chambord". Pictures of François I at Chambord have been used to sell chocolate, liqueur and *quinquina* or tonic wine. The king is supposed to have scratched on a window here the verse "Souvent femme varie, bien fol qui s'y fie"—"woman is changeable, the man who puts his faith in her is mad." (The king sings it in Victor Hugo's *Le Roi s'amuse* and it becomes "La donna è mobile…" in Verdi's *Rigoletto*.) This is quoted on a poster for Georges Lemaire, Grande Distillerie de Blois, where François merrily raises his glass with a view of Chambord behind him; "La Qualité vraiment supérieure de QUIN-QUINA CHAMBORD," the text continues, "ne varie jamais." In another poster for the same company a Renaissance lady with plumed hat holds high a bottle of quinquina, "the stomach's best friend", while François kneels gallantly before her and lifts his glass for a re-fill. With Chambord in the distance, a less gallant jester swigs quinquina from the bottle.

The exhibition gathered many other examples of the Chambord brand. There was an American advertisement for a Chambord bedspread, part of Bates' Country Collection; because of the royal association, the bedspread was wrapped round a model wearing a tiara. Also making use of the name were glasses, porcelain, cigarillos, wool, alarm-clocks, easy chairs, braces and belts, and a 2007 "Eco-pine" kitchen. Foodstuffs similarly labelled included Loir-et-Cher camembert, *petits fours* and terrine of hare and wild boar. Wondering why an electric system should have been named after Chambord, the curators could only conclude that it evokes the Renaissance and French taste, "vague but attractive concepts" which anyone can use. The house looms in the background of early publicity for the Chambord car made by Ford France in 1951 and then taken over, in 1954, by Simca. It was a commercial failure, unlike Chambord.

The château caters to a different sort of dream in its museum of the Comte de Chambord, the Bourbon pretender ("Henri V") who could not compromise his absolutist ideals sufficiently to gain the throne in 1871. Paintings and statues represent both the promising boy and the stoic, principled fifty-something worthy. On the ground floor of the château a much larger painting of 1824, by Claude-Marie Dubuffe, celebrates his birth. There is much joy among the royals, bearskinned soldiers kneel or marvel, a churchman glows. The miniature artillery given to the prince by his grandfather, King Charles X, is also displayed here: a twenty-seven-piece set with cannons, mortars and gun-carriages; the boy's comically small breastplate can be seen nearby at Cheverny. Supporters bought Chambord for him before the expulsion of Charles X, but he was able to regain possession only after a long legal battle. When he did finally move into the château he could not afford to furnish more than a few of its 400-odd rooms.

Molière at Chambord: Le Bourgeois gentilhomme

In October 1670 the first-floor hall at Chambord was adapted into the theatre where Louis XIV saw Molière's *Le Bourgeois gentilhomme*, with Jean-Baptiste Lully's music. In March 1669 the king had watched the earlier Molière/Lully collaboration, *Monseigneur de Porceaugnac*, in the same setting.

Monsieur Jourdain, the rich bourgeois of the title, dreams of somehow becoming a *gentilhomme*, which meant at the time not just a gentleman but a hereditary nobleman. His masters of dancing, music, fencing and philosophy are happy to make money by encouraging his belief that social advancement relies mainly on external conduct: dance-steps, etiquette and rhetoric. Usually he absorbs his lesson, if at all, to comically disastrous effect. His servant, Nicole, easily defeats him when he insists on fencing with her. When he is introduced to a fashionable lady, Dorimène, he puzzles her by asking her to take a step back: he has learnt that he must make three sweeping bows to her but has miscalculated the distance. He then launches into seemingly unstoppable circumlocutory compliments: "Madame, it is greatly glorious to me to find myself lucky enough to be so fortunate as to have the happiness that you should be good enough to vouchsafe me the honour to honour me with the favour of your presence…'

To the passionate frustration of Jourdain's practical wife, he remains blithely unaware that he is being deceived on all sides. Count Dorante borrows vast sums of money from him—Jourdain sees it as a privilege to be allowed to lend to such a great man—and claims to be furthering his suit to Dorimène. The deceptions become more surreal as a mysterious visitor tells the ever-credulous Jourdain that the son of the Grand Turk (or Ottoman Emperor) has fallen in love with his daughter Lucile and wants to marry her. And by an extraordinary coincidence, he is told, the son of the Great Turk looks just like the man she wanted to marry, Cléonte. The new fiancé is, of course, identical with the old one and the climactic deception enables the lovers to marry while keeping Jourdain preoccupied with the grand (or preposterous) ceremony in which the invented title "Mamamouchi" is solemnly conferred on him.

The four performances at Chambord (and those which followed at St.-Germain-en-Laye) were spectacular affairs, involving richly costumed actors, musicians and, in the *intermèdes* which punctuated and amplified

the action, dancers. The cost was increased by the need to transport most of the performers and equipment from Paris. Altogether the royal accounts list expenses of 49,405 *livres*. Ninety-three pairs of silk hose were needed and eleven dozen pairs of gloves. Molière, as Jourdain, wore an extravagant hat with gold and green feathers. Lully, as the alleged Mufti who presides, chanting in mock-Turkish and general Mediterranean *lingua franca*, wore 300 *livres* worth of suitably oriental garb. And there were fireworks and fountain shows in the grounds.

Perhaps at times the humour seems superficial, hallowed by three hundred years of repetition. But there is a fairly subtle, and often amusing, element of self-referentiality. Molière, author of such verse plays as *Le Misanthrope*, is forced by Jourdain's essentially prosaic nature to speak prose—conventional, besides, for a stage bourgeois. Similarly it is all the funnier to have a notable actor—Molière, originally—playing a man who cannot act convincingly as a "gentilhomme" and cannot see through the acts around him. Indeed, as one of the deceiving "Turks" comments, it is as if Jourdain has learnt his role of dupe by heart—as the actor actually has. There is also self-reference for Lully: Jourdain can pay for, although he cannot appreciate, the best available music by the royal composer and favourite, the coming man who would soon dominate and develop the new art of French opera. When Jourdain does sing a song it is a parody of the work of Perrin, Lully's unsuccessful rival. Lully's music for the entry of the Turks, in spite of its local purpose of gulling and mocking Jourdain, is one of his most exciting, inventive and famous pieces—many people today first heard it in Alain Corneau's film *Tous les matins du monde*. Its extraordinary bravura is licensed by the absurdity of the situation; Jourdain will be deceived with some panache, with the aid of music good enough for the court composer and his discerning, un-Jourdain-like, audience.

BLOIS

Edith Wharton's *Motor-Flight through France* (1908) brought her to Blois at sunset, which "burnishes the great curves of the Loire and lays a plum-coloured bloom on the slate-roofs over-lapping, scale-like, the slope below the castle." The quality of the "roof-view" suggested why she spent so much time in France: "the blue sweep of gables and ridge-lines billowing up here and there into a church tower with its *clocheton* mailed in slate, or breaking to let through a glimpse of a carved façade, or the blossoming depths

Blois: "the full poetry of old roofs"

of a hanging garden: but perhaps only the eye subdued to tin house-tops and iron chimney-pots can feel the full poetry of old roofs."

At ground level there are riverside walks and some interesting churches. The cathedral has a numinous early crypt with some traces of wall-painting. Flaubert found that "the streets of Blois are empty; grass grows between the paving-stones; on each side stretch long grey walls." Within the mysteriously quiet houses the future novelist cannot but imagine a "deep intimate history": "the unspoken love", perhaps, "of some pious old maid or virtuous woman", "some pale beauty with long nails, an aristocratic lady… who is married to a churl, a miser, a jealous man, and who is dying of consumption." Did Balzac take such people from Touraine, Flaubert wonders, or is it just that Balzac's books make him imagine such scenes as he wanders through Blois? The town is now less empty. Already by 1907, one of Wharton's fellow motorists complained, "Blois is tourist-ridden" and would-be sketchers are likely to be "crowded out by 'bounders' in bowler hats and others of the genus tripper" (Francis Miltoun, *The Automobilist Abroad*).

What most of the bounders and the rest of us have come for is the château. This was the fortress of the Counts of Blois, the great rivals of the Counts of Anjou for regional power, and then, between the fifteenth and seventeenth centuries, a favoured palace of the Kings of France. There are three substantial main wings, built by Louis XII, François I, and Louis XIII's brother, the restless and rebellious Gaston, Duke of Orléans. At the front of Louis XII's wing of brick and stone (1498-1503) the king rides, in a statue of 1857, "under a splendid canopy, stiffly astride of a stiffly draped charger" (Henry James). François' contribution (c.1515-20) is in stone with Italianate decoration and a much-admired spiral staircase whose carving Balzac compared to Chinese ivory and Flaubert to "the high ruffs of the great ladies" who once went up it. On the ground floor of this wing is a museum devoted mainly to sculptural fragments, figures and groups removed from higher parts of the building. They are changed by their new context, some of them dwarfing the viewer. There are huge-mouthed gargoyles, François' vigorous salamanders and Louis' porcupine, carved façades and pinnacles, a whole chimney-piece. Upstairs are the main state apartments, their décor creatively and brightly "restored" in the nineteenth century by Félix Duban. Catherine de' Medici's *cabinet* or *studiolo* contains 237 wooden panels; legend has it that she kept poisons in the cupboards behind the panels.

Gaston d'Orléans, like Catherine, was involved in many an intrigue. As royal brother and, for many years, heir apparent, he kept his head while some less fortunate fellow-plotters lost theirs. But there has generally been less interest in his classicizing wing, built by François Mansart in the 1630s. For Henry James "Gaston's wing" has nothing to say; "taken in contrast to its flowering, laughing, living neighbour"—the François I—"it marks the difference between inspiration and calculation."

"EVEN TALLER NOW THAT HE'S DEAD": THE DEATH OF THE DUC DE GUISE

In 1588 the French Wars of Religion were in one of their periodically more virulent phases. King Henri III had fled Paris, which was in the hands of the formidably powerful, Spanish-supported Catholic or Holy League. The Estates General, full of League sympathizers, was summoned to meet at Blois, in the oldest surviving part of the château, the thirteenth-century Salle des États. Here Henri decided, at the end of the year, to reassert his authority by removing the leaders of the League, the Duc de Guise and his brother the cardinal. Some of the king's followers encouraged him to believe that if he did not kill the Guises they would kill him.

The duke received repeated warnings that there would be an attempt on his life. In response to one letter he is supposed to have declared boldly, or written on the letter, "They wouldn't dare." In the 1908 silent film *La Mort du Duc de Guise*, by André Calmettes and Charles Le Bargy—usefully shown, with mainly nineteenth-century paintings of the same events, in the Salle des Guise—Albert Lambert's duke, a tall, white-suited gallant, drinks his wine and writes on the letter with superb casualness. Arriving at the château before first light, the real duke came to the council chamber—a royal summons to which was the only easy way to separate him from his guards—and waited there with his brother and their ally the Archbishop of Lyon. Meanwhile the killers had assembled in an upper room. Guise, who had not eaten, sent his secretary for his *drageoir* or ornamented box containing Damascus raisins. The secretary did not return—people were not being allowed in and out of the building. Instead a valet de chambre brought some plums (Brignoles plums, some accounts specify). In one version a servant with the box did now appear. Guise ate some fruit, the meeting began, and then word was brought that Henri wanted him to join him in the room known as the *cabinet vieux*. He went in with his cloak across one arm. Immediately the door was closed behind him and he was so hemmed in by armed men that, encumbered too by the cloak, he could not draw his sword. But he certainly put up a fight. Apparently he knocked several of them down. According to the source which says he had his box, he managed to break someone's jaw with it.

In the film it is a titanic struggle: they push him from room to room, long unable to overpower this strong, courageous man who seems to be much bigger than them. He is evidently intended to contrast with Charles Le Bargy's absurd Henri, who is hyper-suspicious, full of ape-like movements, forever stooping, gesticulating and peering out of the window. He finds it very difficult to believe that his enemy is dead, as do the killers; traditionally Henri said "He looks even taller now that he's dead." In versions including the painting by Barthélémy Charles Durupt (1833) the king does have the courage to push the corpse with his foot; the action seems contemptible partly because, as usual, he is surrounded by extravagantly garbed favourites. Durupt puts near him a vacuous figure in large ruff and plumes and earrings, holding a cup and ball. Henri III loved favourites and dressing up, but this aspect of his reign has often been stressed in order to make his successor, Henri IV, look all the more wholesome, history's predestined and proper king.

Cardinal Guise, detained by force in the council chamber, heard the struggle and his brother's cries. He was imprisoned for what must have been many anxious hours before the killers came for him too. Most of the royal followers, happy enough to bring down the duke, had refused to lay hands on a churchman, but a notorious thug called Captain Du Guast was willing to do the deed. He and the four soldiers who assisted him were well-rewarded. They usher him from his cell in Albert de Medine's mid-nineteenth-century painting in the Galerie du Roi. Below it is a bloodier sixteenth-century treatment on parchment and wood: the Cardinal flails one arm, the other covering his eyes, while three of the murderers thrust their halberds into him and another stabs him in the head or neck with a dagger.

"Enfin je suis roi!" (At last I am king!) So Henri, various sources say, kept telling his favourites and counsellors and mother Catherine de' Medici, who died at Blois less than a fortnight later. But the removal of the Guises did not destroy their powerful League; it helped pro-League pamphleteers to portray the king as a remorseless tyrant, stirred up fresh fights and was a contributory factor in Henri's own assassination outside Paris in July 1589.

Among the busts of the Galerie de la Reine a rather colourless Charles IX and Henri III are followed by a more saturnine Henri IV—a *bon viveur* perhaps, with a touch of the bearded satyr, experienced, expansive, trustworthy. His dynasty continues in a painting, in the same room, of a broad-skirted Marie de' Medici and their son, the skirted, blue-sashed, miniature-rapier-bearing Dauphin (later Louis XIII), aged two.

"Some tie invisible": Wordsworth and Blois

The twenty-two-year-old William Wordsworth came to France in December 1791, ostensibly (so he persuaded his uncle) to improve his French but mainly in order to see the Revolution at first hand. Having seen Paris he settled in Orléans, but there met and rapidly fell in love with Annette Vallon (1766-1841), a visitor from Blois, and moved on to her home town in February 1792. In Blois he met Armand-Michel de Beaupuy, a fervently pro-revolutionary soldier. Beaupuy figures in *The Prelude*—which does not mention Annette Vallon—as one who, although of aristocratic birth, was bound to service of the poor

> As by some tie invisible, oaths professed
> To a religious order. Man he loved
> As man; and, to the mean and the obscure,
> And all the homely in their homely works,
> Transferred a courtesy which had no air
> Of condescension; but did rather seem
> A passion and a gallantry, like that
> Which he, a soldier, in his idler day
> Had paid to woman.

They walked by the Loire and in the forests, enthusing, in these relatively bloodless early days of the Revolution, about "Man and his noble nature", his capacity for truth, love and liberty. A people had "risen up/Fresh as the morning star".

Soon, in 1793, Beaupuy would be fighting "Upon the borders of the unhappy Loire,/For liberty, against deluded men,/His fellow countrymen." Wordsworth mistakenly believed that he was killed in this struggle with royalist rebels in the Vendée. In fact he went on to become a general of the Republic in its war against all comers and was killed in battle with the Austrians in 1796. Wordsworth and Annette had moved back to Orléans in the autumn of 1792 and their daughter was born there on 15 December. She was christened in the cathedral as "Anne-Caroline Wordswodsth". Perhaps her father would have tried to correct the spelling, but by now, short of funds, he had returned to England. Probably at this stage he intended to marry his lover. That this did not happen resulted from events, separation, and perhaps the difference in the couple's political and religious views—she was a Catholic and anti-revolutionary. The increasing bloodiness of the Revolution and then the long war between England and France helped keep them apart until the Peace of Amiens in 1802. That year, with Wordsworth's soon-to-be wife Mary Hutchinson's knowledge, he and his sister Dorothy spent a month in Calais with Annette and Caroline. Annette never married, but seems to have passed in France for the wife or widow of a mysterious Englishman.

Correspondence continued and Wordsworth provided financial help to his daughter after (and probably before) her marriage in 1816. He and several generations of his family worked skilfully to keep his involvement secret.

The affair did, however, leave its trace in *The Prelude*. The story of Julia and Vaudracour, in Book IX of the 1805 version of the poem, was allegedly first told by Beaupuy. (Having been published separately in 1820, the tale was omitted from the 1850 *Prelude*). It is a much sadder love-story than the Wordsworth-Vallon encounter, but explores the situation of lovers who similarly cannot marry, who have a child and who are at the mercy of outside forces. Since here those forces are of the *ancien régime*—an aristocratic father prevents his son's marriage purely on the grounds of the girl's social class—"Julia and Vaudracour" also contributes to the discussion of revolutionary principles. It provides simpler, clearer circumstances and motivations than those actually available in Blois in 1792: the father who can call on "the instruments of ruffian power" to enforce his authority and that of his class; the young woman who eventually agrees to enter a convent; the baby who goes on living with Vaudracour in a remote forest lodge and then, sadly but perhaps conveniently, dies.

CHÂTEAU DE CHEVERNY

Cheverny, nine miles south-east of Blois and the Loire, is surrounded by good hunting country in the forests and the Sologne. The Marquis de Vibraye's pack of hounds, a cross between fox-hounds and poitevins, can often be heard locally. They can be seen in their enclosure at the château, where feeding-time is a popular spectacle: eighty brown-and-white dogs released, ordered to wait, and then cascading and clambering and interweaving, tails up, as they seize and chomp their meat.

The marquis is a descendant of the Hurault family which has owned Cheverny for most of its history. The present symmetrical house in white, hard tufa from Bourré near Montrichard was built for them, in the 1620s-30s, by Jacques Bougier. The interior, where elements of seventeenth-century décor survive in some rooms, is unusually rich in tapestries, painted panels and gilded or bronze statues. Equally exciting for many people is the "Secrets of Moulinsart" exhibition: Hergé used the house, minus the two wings, as the Moulinsart of Tintin's Captain Haddock, which first appeared in *Red Rackham's Treasure* (1944). The original English

translation called it Puckeridge Castle. The second, in 1959, came up with Marlinspike, more appropriate to the colourfully nautical owner.

The dining room is mainly a nineteenth-century tribute to the seventeenth century, from which it retains Jean Mosnier's (or Monier's) painted panels illustrating *Don Quixote*. An armoured, unhorsed Quixote lies stunned after his encounter with the windmill; Sancho dashes towards him, hand outstretched. In another scene, tall, thin, his moustache twirled to the last degree of risibly elegant symmetry, the Don stands, gesturing with one hand, lance upright in the other. White visor aptly covering his eyes, he charges sheep. Mosnier's more conventional Death of Adonis stands between gilded statues of Venus and Mercury in the Salle d'Armes.

The most striking of the château's many tapestries is the Gobelins "Abduction of Helen" (1621) in the Salle d'Armes. At the centre in blue, white and gold Helen is pulled into the boat by Paris and his Trojans. Fierce fighting continues on shore—either a skirmish as the Spartans try to get back their queen, or the Trojan War itself. Beyond a bridge crammed with troops are other ships: again perhaps Trojan, perhaps Spartan, but inevitably reminding one of "the face that launched a thousand ships". Similarly the distant city may be Sparta or Troy. The lovers' moment and the warriors' ten years are shown simultaneously: the heavy consequence of the moment of lightness. Real weapons are displayed nearby—halberds, swords, arquebuses—and a leather-covered chest belonging to Henri IV, who spent much of his life on campaign. Here too are the miniature breastplate and helmet in which the four-year-old would-be Henri V, the Comte de Chambord, must have imagined himself campaigning.

The Chambre du Roi is almost overloaded with visual images: Odysseus' adventures in early seventeenth-century tapestries, the story of Theagenes and Chariclea, Mosnier's Perseus and Andromeda, the golden heads and golden swirls of the chimneypiece, intricate floral patterns, Aubusson tapestry fruits. Among the visual delights upstairs are the portraits in the Grand Salon, including a Cosimo de' Medici attributed to Titian. The winsome dark woman between gold-flecked female figures on the chimneypiece is Marie Johanne de la Carre Saumery, Comtesse de Cheverny, by Pierre Mignard (1612-95). The Gallery has portraits by François Clouet (c.1510-72) of Philippe Hurault, Seigneur de Cheverny—in bold beard and ruff, the image of a not-easily-daunted seigneur—and his wife and brother.

In the village church gold lettering on black memorials pays tribute to various antique Hurault Seigneurs and Comtes of Cheverny. Next to them, in red letters, the thirty-seven war-dead of 1914-18 are listed. They include Gustave, Louis and Raymond Cazin and two members—or at least people with the same surname—of each of the Bigot, Cot and Herbelin families. Outside the church a war memorial for 1939-45 adds four more names, including Armand Cazin.

"MANY FAIR NOBLEMEN'S HOUSES"

"The country about" Chambord is, notes John Evelyn, "full of corn and wine, with many fair noblemen's houses". It still is. Troussay, near Cheverny, is a Renaissance manor-house restored in the mid-nineteenth century by the local historian and numismatist Louis de la Saussaye. Villesavin, by the River Beuvron, was owned by Jean Le Breton, superintendent of works at Chambord, and probably built, in the 1520s-30s, by some of the men who worked there. Fougères-sur-Bièvre is a fifteenth-century fortress with an elegant courtyard and superb examples of late medieval carpentry in the roof-frames.

The sixteenth- and seventeenth-century Château de Beauregard, on the Beuvron downstream of Villesavin, is notable for the 327 portrait-panels of its long Galerie des Illustres. Jean Mosnier and his assistants worked, it seems, mainly from earlier portraits. Important people from the reign of Philip VI (1328-50) to that of Louis XIII (1610-43) are represented, including the kings, their courtiers and their foreign contemporaries. Among the foreigners are Paul III and other popes, Henry VIII, Anne Boleyn and Cardinal Wolsey, the Emperor Charles V, Columbus and Vespucci. Catherine de' Medici is grouped with her sons François II and Charles IX rather than her husband Henri II—her successful rival for Henri's attention, Diane de Poitiers, is directly beneath him, looking down demurely. Most convincing and most immediate to the painters is the Louis XIII group, massed with their white collars or ruffs, carefully cut beards, and moustaches as elegant as the hilts of their (unseen) rapiers. Louis himself, the reigning monarch when the work began, is granted a much larger portrait on horseback. Beneath the portraits are panels by Jean and Pierre Mosnier and a floor of Delft tiles, seventeenth-century again, with scenes of a marching army.

The "neighbourhood of Blois" and the smaller châteaux is one still, as in *The Prelude*, of "wide forests": the Forêts de Blois, de Boulogne (leading into the Parc de Chambord), de Russy. Here Wordsworth and his mentor Beaupuy would wander in earnest talk amidst "Inwoven roots and moss smooth as the sea,/A solemn region." At least in retrospect, his response to the forests reflects mixed feelings about the Revolution. He found himself—or projects himself in the poem as so doing—dreaming of hermits, of Angelica in Ariosto's *Orlando Furioso* "thundering through the woods/Upon her palfrey," of knights jousting beneath the trees, regardless of the company of the "revered", fervent and more focused Beaupuy. Fresh from this awareness of an older world, when they came upon roofless, deserted convents Wordsworth lamented "a wrong so harsh" in spite of his companion's republican anticlericalism. And again he experienced "many gleams" of "chivalrous delight" when Beaupuy pointed to the castles—to Romorantin "home of ancient kings", to "the imperial edifice of Blois" or to Beauregard.

Nevertheless, Wordsworth says, his hatred of the absolute rule for which the châteaux stood was stronger than his nostalgia. One day in the forest they met a "hunger-bitten girl" creeping along with one arm attached to a heifer which picked "from the lane/Its sustenance" while she used both her hands to knit "in a heartless mood/Of solitude." At this sight Beaupuy "In agitation said, ''Tis against *that*/Which we are fighting.'" It seemed, from the strength of his reaction, that "a spirit was abroad" which would soon end poverty, reward "The industrious, and the lowly child of toil" and defeat inequality and injustice. This was not to prove as simple as it sounded, but "Bliss was it in that dawn to be alive."

CHÂTEAU DE CHÉMERY: DON'T SAY "BON COURAGE"

Restoration has been in progress at Chémery, about eighteen miles south of Blois near the small river Renne, since the architect Axel Fontaine bought the château in 1981. There is an exciting sense of the provisional and the potential; elements of picturesque decay co-exist with evidence of recent activity. Re-tiling continues; walls are being rebuilt and wooden beams replaced. In the courtyard is "Le Théâtre de Verdure", whose benches, some more repaired than others, suggest opportunities for intimate performance or conversation. From 1729 until 1981 the château was a farm; the theatrical space stands where the slurry-pit once was.

The buildings, mainly of the fifteenth and sixteenth century, contain an eclectic mixture of historical costume prints, plants, furniture, looms and spinning-wheels. The atmosphere is very relaxed compared with that of the more famous, more spruce and regulated châteaux. No dignitaries seem to have been assassinated or entertained here, although something dramatic presumably happened to a man whose skeleton was found walled up behind a fireplace in 1850. One tradition wants him to have been caught *in flagrante delicto* with some lady of the house.

Visitors to Chémery are given an information sheet. Towards the end facts give way to proud injunction: "Don't say to us *Bon courage*. We have it. Don't say to us 'There's a lot of work to be done.' We know there is. Take part in the restoration yourself" by donating to the foundation. Perhaps the largest donations come from those well-wishers who are about to shake their heads, smile and depart with a cheery cry of "Il y a du travail!" only to glimpse with embarrassment the pamphlet's stern commands.

CHAUMONT-SUR-LOIRE: THE CHÂTEAU

A fortress was built high on the left bank of the Loire at Chaumont in the tenth century. It was developed later into the stronghold of the Amboise

family: powerful local lords or, by the time of Louis XI (ruled 1461-83), over-mighty subjects. When Pierre d'Amboise took part in the unsuccessful rebellion of the "League of Public Good" early in the reign, Louis razed Chaumont. But Pierre quickly managed to make his peace with the king and was allowed to begin building the present château on the same site in 1468. It was completed by his grandson in 1510.

In 1550 Chaumont was acquired by Queen Catherine de' Medici. There is a small portrait of her in black dress, black cap and white ruff in the room named after her. Thanks probably to hindsight rather than the portraitist's perception, her expression seems part baleful, part shifty. Her most famous involvement with Chaumont was the way she disposed of it. After the sudden death of her husband Henri II in a tournament in 1559 she forced Henri's long-term mistress, Diane de Poitiers, to exchange it with her for the more magnificent Chenonceau. Although Diane did not take up residence at Chaumont, preferring to retire to her château of Anet, she continued work on the entrance and east wing. In the nineteenth century her monogram on a chimney-piece— the letter delta combined with three circles—was confidently interpreted as a cabbalistic sign and the room therefore named after Ruggieri, Catherine de' Medici's astrologer.

Much of the present appearance and lay-out of Chaumont dates from the time of Marie-Charlotte Say, Princesse de Broglie, the sugar-refinery heiress who owned it from 1875 until, no longer wealthy, she made it over to the state in 1938. She and her husband furnished the house and restored the "appartements historiques" upstairs. They installed the tiled seventeenth-century majolica floor, bought in Sicily, in the Salle du Conseil: pastoral and hunting scenes, plants and decorative swags, in green, blue and yellow. The room, with its mid-nineteenth-century blue painted walls and fleur-de-lys, has been restored recently.

A series of coincidences have made women unusually important in the history of Chaumont. Catherine, Diane and the Princess owned it, and Mme. de Staël stayed here. In the Catherine de' Medici room there is a late fifteenth-century Tournai tapestry of scenes from the myths of Pegasus and of Perseus. Perseus has just cut off Medusa's head with a large scythe, almost too big for him to manage. "It's shocking," I heard a mother instruct her daughter: "une présentation de la femme qu'il ne faut pas." She was talking about the whole business of presenting women as gorgons, rather than Perseus' violent conduct only. But "elle est encore belle," thought the daughter. She—or the tapestry—is still beautiful.

VIGNY'S CHAUMONT: THE STALWART BASSOMPIERRE

Alfred de Vigny's historical novel *Cinq-Mars* (1826) opens at Chaumont. Family and guests are at dinner before the protagonist, the young Marquis de Cinq-Mars, sets off to enter royal service. The old Maréchal de Bassompierre talks repeatedly and at length about the good old days of the sociable and generous Henri IV. Then noble service was voluntary, personal and valued—as not under Cardinal Richelieu's centralizing regime. The reign of Louis XIII (1610-43), much of it dominated by the cardinal, was, Vigny later says, a weak interlude "between the splendours of Henri IV and of Louis the Great" (XIV); the weakness of the crown and the resulting rivalries for power, however, helped make it a favourite setting for fiction and drama including *Cinq-Mars*, Dumas' *Three Musketeers* and Rostand's *Cyrano de Bergerac*.

The marshal bids fair to become a figure of fun. His hobby-horse bores or embarrasses his aristocratic fellow-diners. Young Cinq-Mars may be sympathetic to his views, but has other things to think about, including love, and is gazing out of the window—still a profitable activity at Chaumont—at the Loire below. Bright sun renders the sands golden, the trees and lawns emerald, and on the then-busy river he sees the great lateen sails of the merchants' boats. Forcing his attention back at last to Bassompierre, Cinq-Mars exchanges smiles with some of the guests. But the tone changes when, after the departure of the young marquis, the marshal is alone in his room. With the window open, melancholy in the extreme heat, he continues to think about the glories of the past reign and the infamies and misfortunes of the present. He watches as lights wander about the château and are extinguished one by one. He settles sadly in his chair but is soon leaping up, sword drawn, as the door is flung open. M. de Launay must, apologetically, arrest him on the orders of the king; thirty of the cardinal's musketeers are waiting below. Bassompierre behaves with an old-fashioned dignity, courtesy and courage which no-one will laugh at now. It is in his master Henri IV's name that he surrenders his sword to the agent of Henri's son. With a firm look he commands Launay, who hangs his head in shame, to follow him downstairs. Soon he is refusing to be rescued by Cinq-Mars, who has remained nearby, waiting for a parting tryst with his beloved Duchess Marie Gonzaga. In the rest of the novel the doomed Cinq-Mars remains a dangerously more impetuous figure than the loyal marshal.

CHAUMONT GARDEN FESTIVAL: "BEAT VEGETATION"

The important and inventive International Garden Festival happens annually between April and October in the park of Chaumont. Each year about thirty plots are landscaped and planted to illustrate and explore a new theme: memory, water, mobiles, ricochets, order and disorder, shared gardens. Although most of the exhibits are shown for only one year, there is some continuity. There are often water-features—reflective pools, hydraulic engines, water-gongs and machines generating jungle mist. Complementing, framing or contrasting with the plants are stone, glass, metal, pottery, wood, paper, slate and rubber. In 2007 an old Volkswagen Dormobile was part of "Beat Vegetation"—glancing at Kerouac's *On the Road* and the Beat Generation. It had wandered the world and brought back "atmospheres, colours, plants and some surprising formations of pots"— some of them on the roof of the van. There were suggestions of African markets and Indian temples. Seriousness and game are for ever mingling. Also in 2007, machines in Hafsa Devauvre's and Sacha Goutnova's "Asteroids" fired bubbles, children yelled delightedly, and a grandmother cried repeatedly "Les bulles! Les bull*es*!"

The gardens which I remember most from Chaumont since I first went to the festival in 1996 include Jenny Jones's "A garden can't exist without us" (2000). Here you could sit at a long silvery table covered with a "feast" of salad, fruits and vegetables. As people sat on either side of the table—friends, strangers—in different combinations, they became part of the interactive design. A similar effect was possible when people looked at each other through the red frames of "Jouez… comme il vous plaira!" by Céline Dodelin, Matthieu Lanher and François Wattellier (2006). Everything here was theatre. "Jouez", like "play", can mean "act"; "Comme il vous plaira" is *As You Like It*, and the plants included roses called "Christopher Marlowe" and "Sweet Juliet". Buddleia attracted butterflies, which "stand for the ephemerality of theatre". And you could scramble and totter about in "I know it's not real but I'm only two years old", the 2005 entry by a group of "landscape-architects" from the Green Concept company of Lyon. The idea here was to take us back to early childhood by scaling the setting up by 2.2—enormous steps, gigantic washing on the line and large raised plants to go with them: sunflowers, giant dahlias, marguerites, cabbages, rhubarb and marrows. Also in 2005 Fabrice Moireau and team presented "La Mémoire des canettes", in which battered, rusty drinks cans were sculpted and arranged to take on a strange, jokey or moving personality. In "Le Jardin des arbres bleus" (Christine O'Loughlin, Catherine Villefranque and Michel Euvé, 2007) bright blue humanoid branches seemed to walk amid agapanthus, salvias and euphorbias. There have also been some striking simpler, less conceptual, gardens. In 1996, for instance, the Quasar Institute of Rome presented "Jardin des lavandes", mixing the greys, purples and blues of lavender and verbena. A record of each festival is available at chaumont-jardins.com.

Chapter Five

FOUR CHÂTEAUX IN TOURAINE

FROM AMBOISE TO VOUVRAY

The Loire and its tributaries the Cher and the Indre begin slowly to con-
verge in a rich landscape of forest and farmland: Alfred de Vigny's fecund
and industrious Touraine with "valleys full of handsome white houses in
their groves of trees, slopes made yellow by the vine or whitened by cherry-
blossom, old walls covered in coming honeysuckle," rose-gardens, towers,
troglodytic dwellings. Travellers trying to follow the Loire are likely,
instead, to digress south from Amboise, through the Forêt d'Amboise, to
Chenonceau on the Cher and, south again, to Loches, its beautiful oak-
forest, and the Indre.

The rocky spur above Amboise and the Loire is an obvious place to
put a fortress. There was a Gallic *oppidum* here, and the present château is
still a dominant presence; Gustave Flaubert, with some youthful exaggeration, said that it made the town look, by comparison, like "a heap of little
pebbles". The Loire continues to further rocky scenes. Balzac, in *La Femme
de trente ans*, describes the remarkable view from its confluence with the
River Cisse at Vouvray: the Cisse winding like a silvery snake through the

emerald spring grass, the islands in the Loire "like the jewels in a necklace". In the distance, through the trees on the islands, the city of Tours appears to rise, like Venice, from the waters. Vouvray village nestles among rocks, and between Vouvray and Tours vine-growers somehow contrive to live in the "frightening crevices" of the pitted hill:

> in more than one place there exist three storeys of houses, dug into the rock and connected by dangerous stone-hewn staircases. At the top of a roof a little girl in a red petticoat runs to her garden. Smoke from a chimney drifts up between the shoots and new branch of a vine. Farmers plough perpendicular fields. An old woman, sitting on a fragment of fallen rock, turns her spinning-wheel under a flowering almond-tree and looks at the travellers as they pass by, smiling at their alarm.

AMBOISE

> We were staying, once, he and I, at Amboise, the little village with its grey slate roofs and steep streets and gaunt, grim gateway, where the quiet cottages nestle like white pigeons into the sombre clefts of the great bastioned rock, and the stately Renaissance houses stand silent and apart... And above the village, and beyond the bend of the river, we used to go in the afternoon, and sketch from one of the big barges that bring the wine in autumn and the wood in winter down to the sea, or lie in the long grass and make plans *pour la gloire, et pour ennuyer les philistins*, or wander along the low, sedgy banks, "matching our reeds in sportive rivalry," as comrades used in the old Sicilian days.

Oscar Wilde constructs an aesthetic Amboise in the "Envoi" to his friend Rennell Rodd's *Rose Leaf and Apple Leaf* (1882).

Less idyllic memories are associated with the château. In March 1560 a Protestant conspiracy to remove the young king, François II, from the clutches of the all-powerful Guise family, went terribly wrong. The chief conspirator, Jean du Barry, Seigneur de La Renaudie, was betrayed by a lawyer in Paris whom he had tried to persuade to join him. (The Prince de Condé, who was probably the real power behind the conspiracy, managed to avoid being implicated.) Unaware that the plot had been revealed, La Renaudie continued to mobilize men for an attack on

Amboise, to which the peripatetic court had removed from Blois. Meanwhile the château, strongly positioned above the town and river, was made even more fortress-like. The first Edict of Amboise was also issued, attempting to weaken the rebel cause by offering an amnesty to those Huguenots who were already in prison and who were neither pastors nor involved in conspiracy. More brutal methods were then ordered. Royal soldiers easily repelled the expected assault on the château. La Renaudie and some of his followers were ambushed in the nearby woods. He, more fortunate than many of his colleagues, was killed. His corpse was hanged from the bridge and then quartered so that it could be displayed at each entrance to the town. Many of the prisoners were drowned in the Loire. Others, about a hundred of them, were saved for a great exemplary show at the château, watched by the court including the king and queen (Mary Stuart) and masterminded by her uncle, the Duc de Guise. Before large crowds some of the aristocratic conspirators were beheaded, while most of the victims were hanged from the windows, the balcony or the battlements. The bodies were left to decay.

A boy of eight witnessed the horrific scene a few weeks later. The future poet and Protestant soldier Agrippa d'Aubigné (1552-1630) was travelling with his father, Jean, who had escaped after taking part in the attack on the château. Agrippa remembered the rotting bodies and his father's reaction when he saw a display of his friends' heads: "They have decapitated France, the butchers." He laid his hand on his son's head and told him that he must be prepared to risk everything to avenge these honourable men. If not, "you will have my curse." His course in life was set. There was an obvious classical parallel in the story, used by d'Aubigné at the beginning of his *Les Tragiques* (published 1616 but written mainly in the late 1570s), of the oath Hamilcar Barca makes the child Hannibal swear to pursue revenge on the Romans.

The killings had, of course, achieved little beyond stirring up Protestants like the d'Aubignés to further acts of resistance. Thirty-five years of on-and-off civil war were about to begin. Near the end of the first bout, in February 1563, the Duc de Guise was assassinated by a Protestant survivor of the Amboise affair. (Guise's son and successor would be assassinated at Blois in 1588.) In March 1563 another edict was promulgated from Amboise by the new boy-king Charles IX, his mother and members of the council. This granted a degree of religious toleration in the hope of buying peace. But followers of Guise were soon swearing to avenge him and "exterminate" all Protestants, and war would soon resume.

Much of the château which Charles VIII, Louis XII and François I expanded and embellished in the fifteenth and sixteenth centuries was demolished in the early nineteenth century. Charles had attempted to create the first Italianate palace in France with the aid of Italian architects, painters and gardeners who came home with him after his expedition of 1494-5, but little evidence of their work remains. The king himself came to misfortune here in 1498—he died, we are told, some hours after walking into a door lintel. But some medieval buildings do survive, among them the Logis du Roi with its royal apartments and, next to it, the round Tour des Minimes, up whose spiral ramp horses could ascend and from whose roof there is a spectacular view of the Loire. We also have the small cruciform Chapelle St.-Hubert, built for Charles VIII in 1491. Guidebooks habitually call it a "gem". It is "one of the most exquisite morsels of profusely florid Gothic in France," declares Murray's *Handbook* (1843) in appropriately florid tones. More precise study of the interior, with its delicately carved foliage, follows: "the leaves, showing all their fibres, [are]

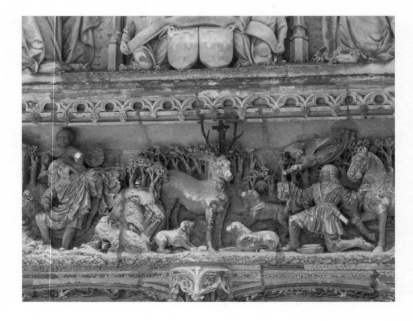

crisped and curled round the edges like kale." The external lintel shows the vision of St. Hubert. Hubert, an ungodly hunter, is converted to higher concerns when confronted by a stag between whose antlers appears a crucifix. Since 1869 the chapel has been the burial-place of the probable remains of Leonardo da Vinci, who died at Le Clos-Lucé in 1519 and was originally buried in a church near the château.

'ABD AL-QĀDIR AT AMBOISE: "THE WILD HAWK OF THE DESERT IS CAUGHT AND CAGED AT LAST"
King Louis-Philippe's Amboise was, as befitted a monarch who wanted to distance himself from the unpopular splendours of his predecessors, "simply furnished as a country gentleman's house". According to Murray's *Handbook*, what may once have been prison cells and oubliettes have been converted into "comfortable kitchens, larders, pantries, and cellars; while the upper rooms, papered, polished, and filled with cast-off furniture from the Palais Royal, preserve no traces of antiquity."

Such modern comforts provided little or no consolation to the people who were held prisoner here, even if not in dungeons or oubliettes, between 1848 and 1852. 'Abd al-Qādir (1808-83), known in Europe as Abd El-Kader, was the emir who led resistance against the French colonizers of Algeria for fifteen years before surrendering, in 1847, on the solemn promise that he and his family and retainers would be allowed to leave for the Levant. A fighter of considerable skill and verve, he had persistently evaded capture. The promise was made by General La Moricière and the Duc d'Aumale, son of Louis-Philippe, but disregarded by the French government. 'Abd al-Qādir and his followers were shipped to Toulon and locked up there. There was agitation for his release both in France and abroad; W. M. Thackeray published a poem lamenting that "the wild hawk of the desert is caught and caged at last." But the downfall of the monarchy in 1848 allowed the new Republic to stall on honouring promises made under the old regime. 'Abd al-Qādir, with a group of seventy-seven people including his three wives, mother, sons, daughter, other relations and servants, was imprisoned first at Pau and then, from November 1848, at Amboise. Communication with the world outside the castle was strictly controlled. There seemed to be little prospect of release. Many of the prisoners began to suffer illness and depression. Several members of the emir's family had died in Pau. The followers who died at

Amboise are now commemorated by stone slabs from Aleppo in Rachid Koraïchi's oriental garden (2005).

'Abd al-Qādir maintained his dignity. He refused offers of compromise: property, an influential position in society, a good life of hunting and farming, if he agreed simply to stay in France. No amount of riches poured "into the skirt of my *burnous*", he told Marshal Bugeaud, could equal his liberty; even unto death "I will not give you back your word." He lived mostly in his rooms, joined the family for prayers, tested his sons on their lessons and wrote books including the philosophical *Hints for the Wise and Instructions for the Ignorant*. He saw himself as a man of prayer and meditation who had been forced accidentally into the life of a warrior. The Marquess of Londonderry, who was allowed after some delay to visit the prisoner in 1851, described the "dreary, dismal old château"—Murray's polishing and papering, no doubt, had worn thin by now—and its occupant:

> His *burnous* is as white as the driven snow—his beard as black as jet—his projecting huge eyebrows of the same hue, with teeth like ivory, and most expressive dark eyes, showing peculiarly the white liquid tinge surrounding the pupils. His stature is tall and commanding; his gesture, softness and amiability of expression almost inexplicable.

Perhaps there is a little of the European stereotype of the noble Arab here, but he seems to have struck everyone who met him as both dignified and charismatic.

'Abd al-Qādir asked Londonderry, who was an old friend of the President of the Republic, Prince Louis-Napoleon Bonaparte, to press for his release. Eventually, in October 1852, soon before he assumed power as Emperor Napoleon III, the prince came in person to Amboise to tell the emir he was free. He gave him a letter which, while maintaining that it was God's will for the French to rule Algeria, insisted that he had long felt distress at his captivity since it reminded him of his predecessors' failure to honour their word to "an unfortunate enemy". The future emperor also saluted his courage, stoicism and "uprightness". They embraced. There were tears of joy. 'Abd al-Qādir's mother blessed the liberator and he consented to take a bowl of couscous before he left. It was all, of course, excellent propaganda for the new regime.

'Abd al-Qādir seems to have felt remarkably little resentment towards France. He spent most of the next thirty years in Syria, apart from a year at the holy places of Arabia and a visit to Paris and London. Once, in Damascus in 1860, he returned to active intervention in public life. When the city's Maronite Christians were being massacred he made his house a safe haven for them, went out with his loyal Algerians to rescue people, and reasoned with the mob that religious persecution was unIslamic. He is said to have saved 12,000 lives.

LE CLOS-LUCÉ: LEONARDO DA VINCI

Not the least achievement of François I, the new young king, victorious in Italy, was to persuade Leonardo da Vinci to come to France as royal painter, architect and engineer in 1516. By this time the mere presence of Leonardo brought prestige to his hosts. Such was his reputation that Vasari's later verdict would already have had its supporters: usually people have various different talents, "but occasionally, in a way which transcends nature, a single person is marvellously endowed by heaven with beauty, grace and talent in such abundance that he leaves other men far behind, all his actions seem inspired, and indeed everything he does clearly comes from God rather than from human art" (George Bull's translation). In Milan he had obliged François, Vasari says, by making him a mechanical lion which took a few steps and then opened to reveal lilies—the royal flower, the fleur-de-lys. In fact the lion seems to have been made originally for Louis XII, but went on to greet François on at least one later occasion. The king was much more impressed, however, by Leonardo's *Last Supper* at Santa Maria delle Grazie; only the fact that it was painted on a wall prevented its removal to France. But the master himself did go, and took with him several paintings, including the *Mona Lisa*, which are still in France. François gave him a large salary and a manor-house later called Le Clos-Lucé, near the royal château of Amboise.

"Clearly," says Vasari, "it was because of his profound knowledge of painting that Leonardo started so many things without finishing them; for he was convinced that his hands, for all their skill, could never perfectly express the subtle and wonderful ideas of his imagination." Many other unrealized, if fascinating and sometimes feasible, projects fill his notebooks. The designs for forty machines have been fulfilled at Le Clos-Lucé, including a swing-bridge, a paddle-boat and a machine-gun.

Leonardo also sketched Amboise, probably designed court entertainments for the château and, according to one theory, planned the new Château de Chambord. Certainly he worked on some imaginative ideas for a new town at Romorantin, in the Sologne, in 1517-18. Two manuscripts with his plans survive; the relevant material is reproduced in Carlo Pedretti's *Leonardo da Vinci: the Royal Palace at Romorantin* (1972) and the British Library online gallery (www.bl.uk: 'the Leonardo Notebook', p.23). It was to be a commodious city, on a classical rectangular plan. Leonardo prescribes "fountains in every piazza". He notes that he intends to redirect the River Sauldre and move the inhabitants of Villefranche to Romorantin. They would take with them, dismantled, their wooden houses. The most detailed provision, however, is for the new palace. The halls for dancing and any similarly vigorous movement of large groups "must be on the ground floor for I have already seen such places collapse, causing many deaths." Important, too, were the palace privies or *neciessari*, which must be reached through a sequence of rooms, have doors which would close themselves by means of a counter-weight, and be ventilated "through the thickness of the walls in such a way that they will exhale through the roofs." The scheme died with Leonardo in 1519.

According to Vasari, the king so honoured the great man that he often visited him during his last illness. They talked and Leonardo "protested that he had offended God and mankind by not working at his art as he should have done." He died, says Vasari, in François' arms. This is not possible—the king is known not to have been in Amboise at the time—but the tale has proved popular. Ingres imagined the scene in a painting of 1818, now at the Petit-Palais museum in Paris: the large, splendidly clad François gazes down at the profusely white-bearded old man, supporting his head, almost inhaling his last breath. Some of his courtiers share, or are duly amazed by, the royal grief. A stout, rather supercilious churchman at right seems, perhaps, less certain how to react.

THE PAGODA OF CHANTELOUP

South of Amboise the tall "pagoda" is all that survives of the once splendid Château de Chanteloup. Its owner was Étienne François, Duc de Choiseul-Stainville (1719-85), Louis XV's successful general, diplomat and minister variously for war, foreign affairs and the navy—and governor of Touraine, and national superintendent of couriers and post. In the

1760s he held several of these positions concurrently. But he owed his prominence partly to the favour of the royal mistress, Mme. de Pompadour, who died in 1764. Her successor, Mme. du Barry, was less persuaded of the duke's merits; she and other enemies helped to bring him down. He was sacked on 24 December 1770 in a curt note from the king, and ordered to withdraw to Chanteloup until further notice.

The duke accepted his exile with some equanimity, or was very good at giving this impression. He took the opportunity further to embellish Chanteloup, already much altered and extended since he became its owner in 1761. Surviving pictures, accounts and inventories record pavilions, grand courtyards, fine furniture, chandeliers and paintings, gardens, grottoes and a famous wine-cellar. The house became, somewhat to the annoyance of the aging Louis XV, a fashionable social and intellectual centre. Choiseul's whole intention in building the pagoda was, as the duchess put it in a letter to Mme. du Deffand in 1778, "to make it a monument of his gratitude by inscribing there the names of all his friends and all those who, during his exile, showed him signs of affection, of good will, of attention... A building which cost 40,000 écus, with no other object than to decorate a garden, would have been a monument of madness." (The names were removed during the Revolution.) The pagoda could therefore be seen as a 145-foot high sign either of defiance of the king or of acceptance, in classical tradition, of the good, "simple" country life led among loyal friends. Either way, posterity was provided with a superb view from the duke's tower, across his forests to the vast sweep of the Loire, upstream towards Blois and downstream towards Tours.

Following the king's death in 1774 the duke and duchess were allowed to return to Paris but continued to spend some of the year at Chanteloup. Choiseul died in 1785. During and after the Revolution the paintings and furniture began to be dispersed; a good number of paintings, including several Bouchers, were sent to Tours and can be seen at the Musée des Beaux-Arts. After a period of neglect the château was demolished in 1823-5.

The reformist agricultural writer Arthur Young visited the place not long after Choiseul's death. Taking in the view from the pagoda, he reflected on the ruinous amount of money the duke put into keeping his forest well-stocked for his and his noble friends' hunting expeditions. Great lords, says Young, are too fond of hunting, "instead of marking their residence by the accompaniment of neat and well cultivated farms, clean cottages, and happy peasants." Perhaps they would not do much "gilding domes, or bidding aspiring columns [or pagodas] rise," but their homes would be comfortable and happy "and their harvest, instead of the flesh of boars, would be in the voice of cheerful gratitude." But at least the duke was a good enough farmer to build "a noble cow-house". He imported 120 Swiss cows and "visited them with his company every day."

CHÂTEAU DE CHENONCEAU: "A CERTAIN SPRINGING LIGHTNESS"

"The great curiosity of Chenonceaux," says Henry James (adding the *x* now granted only to the village, not the château), is its "long, straight gallery of two storeys" crossing the Cher. "It forms on each floor a charming corridor, which, within, is illuminated from either side by the flickering river-light." The royal financier Thomas Bohier had built, between 1515 and the early 1520s, a Renaissance château over the river on the foundations of a former mill. (The fifteenth-century keep of an earlier castle was preserved.) The work seems to have been supervised by Bohier's

wife, Catherine Briçonnet, beginning the line of important women who lived here. Family debts forced Chenonceau into royal hands in 1535, and in 1547 the new king, Henri II, gave it to his long established mistress, Diane de Poitiers. Diane is represented, in the François I room, by Primaticcio's portrait "in the costume of her namesake, the goddess, with a dog in a leash, a bow at her back, and wearing a taffeta petticoat, embroidered with golden fleur-de-lys" (Murray's *Handbook*, 1843). In less fantastical mode, she had Philibert Delorme build a bridge linking the château with the opposite bank of the Cher.

After Henri's widow, Catherine de' Medici, had forced the no-longer powerful Diane to exchange Chenonceau for Chaumont, she had the gallery installed on the bridge in the 1570s. It is "richly articulated with an almost Mannerist love of complexity", says John McNeill's *Blue Guide*, and Catherine and her sons Charles IX and Henri III held spectacular entertainments here. Yet the atmosphere is more relaxed than grand: for James, Chenonceau "has the villa-quality,—the look of being intended for life in common. This look is not at all contradicted by the wing across the Cher, which suggests intimate pleasures, as the French say,—walks in pairs, on rainy days; games and dances on autumn nights; together with as much as may be of moonlighted dialogue (or silence) in the course of evenings more genial still, in the well-marked recesses of windows." Characteristic of Chenonceau is "a certain springing lightness".

When Jean-Jacques Rousseau stayed at Chenonceau, for parts of 1745, 1746 and 1747, the dominant female presence was Louise-Marie-Madeleine, Mme. Dupin (1706-99). She was the second wife of the tax-farmer Claude Dupin, who had bought the château and other property in the area for 130,000 livres in 1733. Rousseau was employed partly as her secretary, partly as her stepson's. He took dictation, made relevant extracts and gave general assistance on the works she wrote, but did not publish, including a book on women. She was a believer in equality: "un vrai philosophe", says her stepson's grand-daughter, Aurore Dupin, better known as George Sand. Her reputation for justness, good works and amiability, together with her great age, seem to have persuaded local revolutionaries to leave her and her house unscathed. A few paintings were confiscated, but according to Sand, "she sacrificed them, with good grace, to the exigencies of the time." A mark of unusual distinction, as Sand notes, is that Rousseau does not attack Mme. Dupin in his *Confessions*.

Less flatteringly, all she would say about him, in her old age, was that he was "un vilain coquin"—a knave. Her tomb is in woodland on the left bank of the Cher.

The stepson was Louis-Claude Dupin de Francueil (1715-87). Rousseau worked with him on chemistry, which they had studied together in Paris, and natural history. Their laboratory was in the outbuilding which now houses a waxworks museum; some of their equipment, including an armillary sphere, is in the Hôtel Gouïn museum in Tours. Together they "somehow set to work scribbling about this science, whose elements we barely grasped" (*Confessions*, Book VII). The resulting 1,206 sheets of the unpublished *Institutions chimiques* were rediscovered only in the early twentieth century. At the same time Rousseau enjoyed less academic pursuits. He grew, proverbially, "as fat as a monk". Music and acting were going on, so he composed several musical trios and wrote in a fortnight his rather slow-moving sentimental comedy *L'Engagement téméraire* (published 1781). Its only merit, said the author, was "beaucoup de gaîté". Among shorter pieces he wrote *L'Allée de Sylvie*, which took its title "from a path in the park beside the Cher". It consists of reflections beneath shady trees and "the silvered stream" on passion, ambition and virtue. But "while I was getting fat at Chenonceau," the passage in the *Confessions* continues, "my poor Thérèse was getting fat in Paris in quite another way." Notoriously Rousseau consigned his children by Thérèse Levasseur to a foundling hospital.

LOCHES: PRISONERS AND POISONS

Henry James saw the "gray old city" of Loches in appropriately grey weather. He and his party moved briskly with "our train on our minds". Nevertheless James is one of the best guides to the "cluster of curious things" to be seen here: Loches

> rises above the valley of the Indre, the charming stream set in meadows and sedges, which wanders through the province of Berry and through many of the novels of Madame George Sand; lifting from the summit of a hill, which it covers to the base, a confusion of terraces, ramparts, towers, and spires… I hardly know what is best there: the strange and impressive little collegial church, with its romanesque atrium or narthex, its doorways covered with primitive sculpture of the richest kind…; or

the huge square keep, of the eleventh century,—the most cliff-like tower I remember, whose immeasurable thickness I did not penetrate; or the subterranean mysteries of two other less striking but not less historic dungeons, into which a terribly imperative little cicerone introduced us, with the aid of downward ladders, ropes, torches, warnings, extended hands, and many fearful anecdotes,—all in impervious darkness.

Today the dungeons are more accessible, the darkness usually more pervious. Some of the "fearful anecdotes" have been modified, although there are still some horrors, including, in the "Salle de la question", a metal bar to which those being questioned were attached by the ankles before enduring torture of fire, water or boot. A persistent tradition said that Cardinal Balue was imprisoned in a cage which could be suspended from the roof of the deep, domed, echoing dungeon named after him. He had intrigued against Louis XI. Since Balue had himself invented such cages, the king decided that poetic justice should be done. The idea would not have been uncharacteristic of Louis, but in fact the cage was not the cardinal's invention, he may not have been put in one, and he was probably not imprisoned at Loches. Nevertheless such things did happen at the time: the chronicler Philippe de Commines records that he was caged for eight months by Louis' son, Charles VIII.

A prisoner who was certainly held at Loches was the deposed Duke of Milan, Lodovico Sforza, known as "il Moro" (probably a reference to his dark complexion). He came here, in 1504-8, at the end of a remarkable career. He had seized power as regent for his young nephew, Duke Giangaleazzo, in 1480, and became duke himself in 1494. He spent lavishly on court shows, religious benefaction, and art and architecture—he employed both Bramante and Leonardo da Vinci. But the high taxes which paid for this magnificence made Lodovico unpopular at home and his foreign policy was ill-judged. In 1493 he had encouraged Charles VIII's destabilizing Italian expedition. But subsequently he was involved in anti-French alliances; and the new king, Louis XII, as a direct descendant of the earlier Visconti rulers of Milan, had an added reason or excuse to oppose Sforza. He was forced into exile in 1499 and again, before his capture by the French, in 1500. From 1504 Sforza was held at Loches, probably in the chamber known as Le Martinet. His fate provided Montaigne with an example for his essay "That Men Should Not Judge of Our Happiness Till

After Our Death": he "whom all Italy had so long truckled under, was seen to die a wretched prisoner."

Legend rather exaggerated the wretchedness. Finally, it was said, Sforza was released only to collapse and die when he moved from dark cell to bright outside. But in fact the present bare chamber was then well appointed and he was allowed company including his Fool. He was even permitted the princely distraction of hunting, under supervision, in the Forêt de Loches. Louis needed simply to keep him out of circulation. The wall and ceiling-paintings, which tradition says are by Sforza, suggest both creativity and frustration. They are crude, of course, compared with the Leonardos the prisoner could once admire. The main surviving elements are large red stars (once redder) and a much larger helmet and lances, perhaps a reminder of past tournaments and dreams of martial glory. The inscriptions (now worn away) included "Celui qui n'est pas contan"—"He who is unhappy".

Agnès Sorel (c.1422-50), mistress of Charles VII, is the other historical character most famously connected with Loches, which was one of Charles' favourite residences. As well as bearing him four daughters she exercised a fair degree of political influence. She died near Jumièges, in Normandy, but was buried at Loches in the church of St. Ours. Her tomb was vandalized and her remains scattered during the Revolution. After restoration work on the effigy a few years later it, and part of the remains, were placed in the château. They were eventually brought back to St.-Ours in 2005.

"She has always, I know not with what justice, enjoyed a fairer fame than most ladies who have occupied her position," says the diplomatic James, "and this fairness is expressed in the delicate statue that surmounts her tomb. It represents her lying there in lovely demureness, her hands folded with the best modesty, a little kneeling angel at either side of her head, and her feet, hidden in the folds of her decent robe, resting upon a pair of couchant lambs, innocent reminders of her name" (Latin *agnus*, French *agneau*). We now know that her physical appearance corresponded well with the effigy and with the painted figures she inspired, notably the Virgin in Jean Fouquet's *Melun Diptych* now in Antwerp. In 2004, before she was reinstalled in St.-Ours, a team in Lille led by Dr. Philippe Charlier subjected her to "palaeopathological" investigation. The state railway company, the SNCF, provided the royal mistress with free TGV transport between Tours and Lille. As a gesture somewhere between due solemnity and bureaucratic process, advertising and joke, they issued her a ticket. She was shown to be naturally blonde, with smooth hair which was worn drawn back—as in the pictures. Her complexion was pale. She usually enjoyed good health. She died as a result of mercury poisoning, perhaps an accidental overdose since mercury was used for medical purposes and in cosmetics. But possibly, as has often been suspected, Agnès Sorel was murdered. She had enemies, naturally for someone in her position, most obviously the Dauphin, later Louis XI.

Chapter Six

BALZAC'S LOIRE

FROM TOURS TO LANGEAIS

The city of Tours was built on an island between the Loire and one of its most important tributaries, the Cher, still about fifteen miles before their confluence. For centuries pilgrims sailed up one river or the other to worship at the shrine of St. Martin. By the nineteenth century they came more often by train. Travel on the Loire could be difficult in summer, when, Murray's *Handbook* reports, "only 3 or 4 of the arches of the bridge bestride the shrunken stream, while the rest traverse wide, ugly beds of bare gravel."

Modern industrial Tours has spread north of the Loire and south of the Cher, but the long island continues westward into greener places. Nearly opposite the end of the island, across the Cher, is the Château de Villandry with the colourful *parterres* of its formal gardens, reconstructed from sixteenth-century plans; from the highest parts of the château there is a striking view across the gardens and to the confluence of the rivers.

The Cher at Tours can seem, as Douglas Goldring says, "a placid stream which dawdles along in no hurry to join the Loire." It has flowed up through Bourges, past the stout keep of Montrichard, and under the light-filled gallery at Chenonceau. But at last, just after Villandry and roughly opposite Cinq-Mars-la-Pile, it will be absorbed in the Loire. Another mighty tributary, the Indre, has some miles further to run. Some of its water forms the lake at the small, sparkling château of Azay-le-Rideau, and it passes north of Saché: both significant places for Honoré de Balzac, who was born in Tours.

In this area rivers are often close together. Balzac, like Félix de Vandenesse, the narrator of *Le Lys dans la vallée*, was accustomed to seeing Loire, Cher and Indre in the course of a day's walking. Young Félix, in the excitement of first love, walks out from Tours, across the bridge over the Cher and on towards the Indre. His "boundless love... found expression, in [his] fancy, in that long ribbon of water streaming in the sunlight between two green banks; in these rows of poplars adorning with their quivering lace this vale of love; in the oak woods thrusting beyond the vineyards upon slopes which the river rounds in every varying curves, and in those blurred horizons that merged in the far distance" (Lucienne Hill's translation).

TOURS AND TOURAINE: "DOMESTIC SECURITY"

Geography—near enough to Paris but not too close—and its traditional image as the fertile, peaceful symbolic heartland of France made Touraine a natural destination for exiles and travellers from the capital and elsewhere. Tours served briefly as the capital of France during two periods of crisis. In 1870, when Paris was besieged by the Prussians, Léon Gambetta, Minister for the Interior in the new republican government, escaped by balloon en route for Tours, where he was to organize the attempted French fight-back. The aim was that he would be wafted all the way, but a contrary wind complicated the plan. In the end it took a carriage and two changes of train to get Gambetta to Tours.

In June 1940 the government evacuated there for two days before, as in 1870, being forced further south to Bordeaux. Thousands of refugees fleeing Paris had thought they would be safe if only they could reach the Loire or the Cher. In Irène Némirovsky's *Suite Française* (written 1941-2, published 2004), the company director M. Corbin motors off for Tours, to which his bank is to relocate, with his mistress. His employees the Michauds, who were supposed to travel with him, find the railway station jammed and unusable and have to set off, like so many others, on foot.

As befits a "heartland", Touraine has a reputation for correctness in language. For Vigny in *Cinq-Mars* the *Tourangeaux* speak "the purest French, not slow, not fast, unaccented". Major Thompson, Pierre Daninos' Englishman in France, with his white moustache, dark suit and striped tie, goes to Touraine mainly because he has heard about its "beau langage". When he returns to Paris people are quite mystified by the regional expressions he has succeeded in learning. But he seems to have spent as much energy on the fine wine of Touraine as on its fine speech: "my very British complexion of red mottled with blue was, thanks to the Vouvray I consumed, more highly coloured than ever" (*Les Carnets du major W. Marmaduke Thompson: découverte de la France et des français*, 1954).

British men and women came, in search of good speech and good mottling Vouvray, long before the major. Instruction in dancing, deportment, fencing, mathematics, drawing and most other subjects was widely available to foreign visitors to Tours in the seventeenth and eighteenth centuries. John Stoye's study of travellers in the seventeenth century concludes, indeed, that "Touraine and Anjou deserve more attention than Winchester or Eton for the history of education among the higher ranks of English society" at this time. Still in the twentieth century, according to Ralph Dutton and Lord Holden in *The Land of France* (1939), "There is an air of safety and domestic security about the town which, apart from the purity of the local accent, make it a particularly suitable place for the young English student to learn the language." Balzac's novels suggest that the air of security can sometimes be deceptive.

MARTINOPOLIS: ST. MARTIN OF TOURS AND THE BASILICA

Martin, a fourth-century Roman soldier from Pannonia, was at the gates of Amiens when he performed the deed ("the Charity of St Martin") which came to define him. It was a terribly cold winter, says Sulpicius Severus in the best-known early life. At the gate was a "poor, unclothed man" who was begging for help from the passers-by. No pity was forthcoming until Martin arrived, saw that something must be done, and divided his military cloak in two with his sword. He only gave one half of the cloak, say some later versions, because the other was, technically, army property. That night, according to Sulpicius, the soldier had a vision of Christ wearing half the cloak, for the Lord had said that whatever you have done "to these the least of my brethren, you have done it to me" (*Matthew* 25.40).

Soon afterwards Martin was baptized. Having left the army he went to work for Bishop Hilary of Poitiers, near where, at Ligugé, he founded a monastery said to be the first in Gaul. His connection with Tours began when its bishopric fell vacant in 372. Martin had no desire to leave the monastic life and become a bishop, we are told, but a deputation from Tours effectively kidnapped him. Some clergy, including several other bishops, opposed his elevation, "saying that he was a contemptible person", pitiful in appearance, his clothes dirty and his hair a mess (Sulpicius). Later commentators add that he was not much of a theologian. The people, however, wanted him. He had an impressive record of performing miracles and converting pagans. Sulpicius is pleased to say that episcopal dignity did not change the holy man of Ligugé. He founded, and lived like a hermit at, the monastery of Marmoutier, built partly into cliffs near the Loire—a place then, says Sulpicius, "as solitary as a desert". In subsequent centuries Marmoutier expanded, became powerful, was sacked by Vikings in 853 (over a hundred monks were massacred) and recovered to flourish for another nine hundred years. The buildings were sold off during the Revolution and most of them were demolished soon afterwards, but the thirteenth-century portal of the abbey church survives. The nuns of Sacré-Coeur bought the land in 1847 and built a new convent.

After many a miracle and many a successful struggle with the Devil (and the secular authorities) Bishop Martin died at Candes, at the confluence of the Loire and the Vienne, in 397. There were huge economic and political advantages—and spiritual, no doubt—for a church and town which could acquire the body or relics of a saint or saint-to-be. And so there was "a great altercation", says Gregory of Tours in his *History of the Franks*, between the people from Poitiers and from Tours who were present at the death. Did he belong in the land of his early ministry or of his later, longer episcopacy? There had been more miracles in Poitou, but at least some in Touraine. St. Gregory, himself a notable sixth-century Bishop of Tours and promoter of Martin's cult there, tells with relish the tale of the removal of the body by the Tourangeaux. Sleep conveniently—or providentially—overtook the *Poitevins*. Martin was smuggled out through a window and taken by boat along the Vienne to the Loire and so home to Tours. Gregory is triumphant about his team's success: the Poitevins, woken only by their rivals' loud singing as they sailed up the Loire, went back to their city "sore confounded" (in O. M. Dalton's translation).

The tomb of the saint—he was canonized within a few years of his death—became a place of pilgrimage. The first stone church on the site was consecrated in 471 and a monastery established. One of its most culturally active periods was when Alcuin of York, Charlemagne's adviser and teacher, was abbot (796-804). Like Marmoutier, St. Martin's was sacked by Vikings, several times burned down and repeatedly rebuilt. So important was the area around St. Martin's, superseding the old walled city and cathedral, that in the eleventh century it was known as "Martinopolis". The mighty thirteenth-century pilgrimage-church had five aisles, five towers and a splendid shrine for the saint. But recovery was slow after 1562, when the monastery was pillaged by Huguenots at the beginning of the Wars of Religion. The saint's tomb was smashed. Retaliatory massacres by the city's Catholics soon followed.

After the French Revolution the abbey church became for a time a parish church but was soon in a state of collapse. For a while it was a stable and then it was decided, in 1802, to demolish most of the buildings. All over France churches, chapels and monasteries became sheds, shacks, stables, housing and barracks—or fell into final ruin. In Tours the thirteenth-century church of St. Julien was used as a staging-post. Contemporary engravings show a stagecoach comfortably parked beneath the arches. The loss of the basilica, however, was especially keenly felt in St. Martin's city. Mademoiselle Gamard assures Balzac's credulous Abbé Birotteau, in *Le Curé de Tours,* that the demolition workers all died (the Curse of Tutankhamun effect) within six months of finishing the job.

Two substantial towers, the eleventh-century Tour Charlemagne and twelfth-century Tour de l'Horloge, were almost all that remained. The first is said to have acquired its name because Luitgard, wife of the Emperor Charlemagne, was buried here several centuries earlier. The second was part of the main façade of the basilica. A new church was planned only after the discovery of what was left of the tomb and relics of St. Martin in a cellar in 1860. The new tomb (incorporating some of the earlier stone) and reliquary became the focal-point of the crypt. The new basilica itself was built, partly on the site of the old, between 1887 and 1924. The style is "neo-Byzantine"—"heavy-handed revivalism", according to John McNeill's *Blue Guide*. The architect was Victor Laloux (1850-1937), who also designed the station and town hall in Tours and the Gare—now Musée—d'Orsay in Paris.

BALZAC AND TOURS

Honoré de Balzac, "in the maturity of his vision, took in more of human life than any one, since Shakespeare, who has attempted to tell us stories about it." Henry James therefore finds himself "a little shocked", in *A Little Tour in France*, to discover that the novelist was born "in a house 'in a row'" and not even a very old house; "if the tenement selected for this honour could not be ancient and embrowned, it should at least have been detached"—with an implied link to Balzac as detached observer. But, as Graham Robb points out in his biography of Balzac (1994), "it seems fitting... that a life devoted to exploring the private worlds of his contemporaries should have begun within hearing of the neighbours."

The three-storey "tenement" where Balzac was born in 1799 was destroyed in Second World War bombing. Further along the street, the building which became the family house from 1803 survives at what is now 53 Rue Nationale. In any case, Balzac saw very little of the house since he was farmed out to a nurse at St.-Cyr, on the other side of the Loire, for his first few years. Félix de Vandenesse, the narrator of *Le Lys dans la vallée* (1836), says simply that he was "forgotten by [his] family for three years". From 1804 Balzac was at school at Pension Le Guay, where he felt no more welcome. Today the school building is the Hôtel du Théâtre. A version of his experience there also features in *Le Lys*, where Félix longs for the "famous *rillettes* and *rillons* [preserved pork] of Tours" which the other children bring for lunch. They have nothing but contempt for the cheese or dried fruit they find in his lunch-basket. After Pension Le Guay, Balzac boarded for six years at the Collège de Vendôme (see pp.133-5). Following his removal from there, in a state of apparent mental "coma" in 1813, he spent the rest of his teens mainly in Tours and Paris.

Le Lys, probably now departing somewhat further from the author's actual experiences, tells the story of what happens to Félix at the grand ball to welcome the Duc d'Angoulême, nephew of the restored Louis XVIII, to Tours. He is to represent the family in the absence of his father and his favoured elder brother. (Balzac's own elder brother died before his birth, a fact to which he attributed his mother's coldness towards him.) Formally dressed for the first time as a respectable man of his class, and confused by the noise and heat, Félix wanders about because he lacks the courage and experience to join in the dancing. He sits in a corner and there is enraptured by a woman sitting nearby. He is particularly taken with her silky white shoulders and he can see, through the covering gauze, the "perfectly round globes" of her breasts "lying snugly" in lace. He also likes the shiny, sleek hair and velvety neck. Overcome—he is, after all, fifteen—he "dives" at her back and covers her shoulders with kisses. Her anger is disarmed by his tears and he is overjoyed to be addressed by her as "Monsieur". At once he falls wildly in love.

Determined to search the local châteaux until he finds the beloved, Félix follows the route from Tours to Saché which Balzac often took, and looks down at the emerald valley of the Indre, of which he is sure—whence the title—the unknown woman is the lily. While staying at the Château de Frapesle, based on Valesne near Saché, he is introduced to her at the Château de Clochegourde, which is partly Vonne, a house with terraced gardens above the Indre near Pont-de-Ruan. So begins his long, intense but platonic relationship with Mme. de Mortsauf, inspired to some extent by Balzac's relationship (not always platonic) with Mme. de Berny.

Tours: St.-Gatien Cathedral
"It is a very beautiful church of the second order of importance, with a charming mouse-coloured complexion and a pair of fantastic towers." Henry James, as often in *A Little Tour in France*, tempers sober informativeness with personal, slightly ironic reaction. St.-Gatien took, he continues,

> a long time to build. Begun in 1170, it was finished only in the first half of the sixteenth century; but the ages and the weather have interfused so well the tone of the different parts, that it presents, at first at least, no striking incongruities, and looks even exceptionally harmonious and complete. There are many grander cathedrals, but there are probably few more pleasing; and this effect of delicacy and grace is at its best toward the close of a quiet afternoon, when the densely decorated towers... lift their curious lanterns into the slanting light, and offer a multitudinous perch to troops of circling pigeons.

James moves into the interior, which "has a stately slimness with which no fault is to be found, and which in the choir, rich in early glass and surrounded by a broad passage, becomes very bold and noble." The glass survives mostly from the thirteenth century. Its dominant colours

include deep blue, red and golden yellow. Among the lives of the saints narrated is that, in the apsidal chapel of SS. Julien and Ferréol, of St. Martin (c.1300). One of the most striking and compact scenes, on the right, shows two monks transporting the mitred, red-coped body of the saint in a yellow boat with billowing white sail. As often in such circumstances, the holy cargo enables the monks to pray instead of steering the boat. Among the scenes of the left-hand window Martin halves his cloak and resists temptation in the form of a mischievous yellow-headed devil who tries to make him fall down some steps—an angel flies in to save the falling saint. Doors miraculously open, forcing the hitherto unreceptive emperor to receive him.

In the 1830s the tomb of the two young sons of King Charles VIII and Anne of Brittany, completed in 1503, was installed in a chapel off the south transept. Heartrendingly small figures in royal finery, the work of the sculptor Michel Colombe or his studio, lie with small angels before and behind. The highly decorated Italianate base by Girolamo da Fiesole includes *putti* and, in honour of the brief status of Charles-Orland and Charles as Dauphin, dolphins. In the same chapel there are fragments of an early fourteenth-century tomb and wall-paintings; a restored tempera St. Martin divides his blue cloak. His "young, almost child-like" face, as the nearby label points out, "expresses great gentleness".

BALZAC'S *LE CURÉ DE TOURS*

Two clergymen move, in very different manner, about the aisles of St.-Gatien. "When the tall canon walked with solemn pace, looking sternly downwards, he excited respect: his bent face harmonised with the yellow arches of the cathedral. But the good vicar wandered about with no kind of gravity—trotted, ambled, seemed to roll." *Le Curé de Tours* concerns the long, well-dissimulated hatred of the Abbé Troubert for the innocent, unobservant, bumbling Abbé Birotteau. Balzac studies, in his habitual detail, the inexorable process of Birotteau's downfall. In bourgeois provincial life it is the small details, the author insists, which are necessary to understanding: bourgeois passions are often just as violent as those of the mighty, but often less obvious. At the beginning of the novel Birotteau has achieved his cherished desire to rent the apartment lived in by his late dear friend Abbé Chapeloud. "Perhaps he would not have wanted to resuscitate him, but he mourned him": the longing to enjoy the same cosseted, comfortable life at Mlle. Gamard's house, the mahogany furniture, the damask curtains, is too strong. The house is pictured as attached to the wall of the cathedral, close to the Renaissance cloister known as "La Psalette"—the name means "a place for singing psalms".

Vicar Birotteau, with his "good heart, narrow ideas and limited intelligence", slowly begins to perceive that his landlady is no longer treating him well. On her instructions the maid keeps him waiting outside in the rain and his fire is not made up. Mlle. Gamard speaks to him with asperity. He is incapable of understanding the apparently trivial cause of her offence. She had hoped that when he moved in he would bring to her house some of his socially prestigious acquaintances: prestigious, at least, within the narrow, whist-playing bounds of provincial society. He fails to imitate Chapeloud's interest in Mlle. Gamard, or his fellow resident Troubert's mixture of politeness and reserve. And he has no idea that Troubert is allied to their hostess in the desire to drive him out.

Birotteau, shaken by Mlle. Gamard's attitude, goes to stay at a friend's country estate. When a lawyer arrives and suggests that he clearly no longer intends to lodge with Gamard, he is frightened and confused into signing a document by which he agrees to leave. His life seems to be unravelling "like a stocking". At first friends rally round to help Birotteau. But Troubert turns out to have powerful contacts and the vicar's supporters are forced rapidly to abandon him. Legal niceties and human spitefulness combine to deprive Birotteau of his furniture; Troubert, now happily ensconced in Birotteau's old rooms, makes sure that he will be allowed to take nothing away, not even the portrait of his old friend Chapeloud which he particularly asks for.

Troubert becomes Vicar-General while Birotteau is banished across the Loire to serve as Curé of St.-Symphorien. The "village, the transpontine suburb rather, of St.-Symphorien", is described enthusiastically in Frederick Wedmore's 1890 life of Balzac, "with its shops of cooper and of basket-maker, its business of the wine-cask and of vintage-time". But for Birotteau it is a place of isolation with an agonizing view across the river to his former haunts. Troubert's shrewd and implacable pursuit of his enemies continues. Birotteau is suspended from his post on trumped-up charges and we last see him in a chair, pale and ill, by the Quai St.-Symphorien—along which Troubert, now Bishop of Troyes, is proceeding by post-chaise to Paris. "The Bishop cast a contemptuous, pitying glance at his victim," then forgot him and went on.

There is no religious devotion in *Le Curé*. People act out of ambition, politics and egotism. Even Birotteau is not, on the whole, treated sentimentally: he is a victim as much of his own imperceptiveness and self-absorption as of Troubert and Gamard. It is a world without much consolation: the dark underside of apparent provincial tranquillity.

TOURS: MUSÉE DES BEAUX-ARTS

The museum, in the seventeenth- and eighteenth-century former palace of the archbishops, looks onto the cathedral in one direction and an enormous cedar of Lebanon, planted in 1804, in the other. The collection of paintings is strong on Italian primitives, French seventeenth- and eighteenth-century artists and Orientalists. The best-known pieces are Mantegna's panels from the altarpiece at San Zeno in Verona. In the first Jesus prays on the rocky Mount of Olives with Judas already leading armed men towards him in the background. In the second Jesus rises, surrounded by bright, angel-filled rays of light, from the tomb. The intervening Crucifixion is in the Louvre.

A version (c.1598) of François Clouet's *Diane au bain* gives Diana the features of Gabrielle d'Estrées, mistress of Henri IV. A nymph holds a red silky robe behind her, more to offset her near-nakedness than to dry her (perhaps, besides, unnecessary for a goddess). A faun relaxes on the grass. Much flesh is elegantly arranged. In the background hounds gorge on a stag but apparently no Actaeon-style warning is intended for the horseman trotting in at top left. He is a proud upright figure with a golden hunting-horn at his side and a golden bridle to his horse: Henri IV in classical apparel.

Some juxtapositions in art-galleries are arbitrary but irresistible. Next to the Diana is a portrait, attributed to Arnold van Bronckhurst, of a sixteenth-century statesman unlikely to approve of naked Dianas. Certainly he would not have approved of naked Gabrielles. William Cecil, Lord Burghley, appears in his black-capped, ruffed, sober sagacity, wearing a large chain of office to which are attached St. George and the dragon. The same room contains other work by Flemish masters including Joos van Cleve. Elsewhere works by Dutch artists include a young man by Ter Borch and a slightly melancholy, tentative young woman with friendly brown eyes and huge white ruff by van der Helst. Flanked by these por-traits is Rembrandt's small chiaroscuro *Flight into Egypt* (1627): the Holy Family mystically lit against a dark background. Nearby is a van Goyen shoreline in delicate browns and greys.

Olivier Debré (1920-99) contributes some of the most noticeable ab-stract work. The museum shows his paintings (1976-81) inspired by the shifting colours of the Loire, with titles like "Rouge de Loire Touraine", "Longue blanche de Loire"—cool tones, an impression of textured white-ness—and "Ocre taches [splashes, streaks] jaunes de Loire".

BALZAC AT THE BEAUX-ARTS: AS PERSISTENT AS PETER THE GREAT

Balzac's portrait by Louis Boulanger is a running theme of his letters of 1836-8 to Eveline Hanska, the Polish countess he would later marry. Boulanger shows the novelist in visionary mood, dressed in the monk's habit which he often wore when writing. Balzac claimed to Mme. Hanska in October 1836 that he could have written two books in the time he spent having to stand and be painted. Given the author's ferocious work-rate he may almost have been right: the sessions went on for about a month.

Earlier in October Balzac had declared his approval. Boulanger had captured the "persistence which is fundamental to my character: the persistence of a Coligny, of a Peter the Great—the intrepid faith in the future". But, anxious to project the desired image to Mme. Hanska in distant Ukraine, he went on brooding over the picture. The eyes are well done but have caught the "expression psychique générale" of the worker, the writer, not "the loving soul of the individual", the tenderness of the fool whose sympathy for others is always landing him in financial difficulties (letter of 2 June 1837). He looks a little too proud (19 July 1837). The picture fails to show "the delicacy [*finesse*] hidden beneath the roundness of form" (10 February 1838); he was already swelling towards his later corpulence. By 1849, writing now from Ukraine to his sister Laure, he sounds more disappointed: the colours of this hideous "daub" have not lasted. It makes him ashamed for France and has been relegated to an obscure library in Mme. Hanska's great house at Wierzchownia. (The daub is thought to have been another, now lost version of the Boulanger, not the one in Tours.) Théophile Gautier, reviewing the piece for *La Presse* in March 1837 when it was shown at the Louvre, perhaps came nearer to defining its ambiguity: its extraordinary mixture, or "bizarre harmony", of "the monk and the *soudar*" or roughneck soldier, "of reflectiveness and good humour, of determination and high spirits".

The museum also has Jean-Alfred Gérard-Séguin's 1841 version of Balzac in black jacket, silver waistcoat and pink cravat. He looks stouter, more of an establishment figure, but his eyes still gleam. The sitter liked it less than the Boulanger: "it renders only the outer man"—a creature quite without poetry—he warned Mme. Hanska in January 1843. "You have not been misled," he goes on, "I have grown much fatter from lack of exercise." Walking, thanks to the unspeakable Parisian mud, is impossible. "I'll take some exercise in Germany, in the spring."

PLESSIS-LÈS-TOURS: "THE UNIVERSAL SPIDER"

Before Quentin Durward even comes within sight of King Louis XI's castle of Plessis-lès-Tours, now on the western outskirts of the city, he is warned to keep to the path. Everywhere else is defended by "snares and traps, armed with scythe-blades" which can chop off an arm or a leg. There are foot-piercing calthrops and deep pits. The impetuous, open-hearted young Quentin, the eponymous hero of Sir Walter Scott's novel (1823), tells his guide that if he were King of France he would defend himself not with traps but with such good government that "no man should come near my dwelling with a bad intent; and for those who came there in peace and goodwill, why, the more of them the merrier we should be." But further horrors are yet to be revealed. When he reaches the château, limbs intact, he discovers the three outer walls and triple moat, the portcullis and drawbridge, the iron palisades and murderous spikes. From the watch-towers the king's guard of Scottish "archers"—actually arquebusiers—can shoot visitors with ease. The keep is black and almost windowless. The "whole external front looked much more like that of a prison than of a palace." Recent additions further reflect Louis' love of concealment: "the darkest-coloured brick and freestone were employed, and soot mingled with the lime, so as to give the whole Castle the same uniform tinge of extreme and rude antiquity." A hanged man swings on the single tree at the front.

Certainly Plessis, which Louis XI bought in 1463 and largely rebuilt after 1469, was well protected. But it was also a commodious royal residence, well-known for its park (and therefore sometimes called Plessis-du-Parc); in 1644 John Evelyn found it still "an agreeable solitude... It has many pretty gardens, full of nightingales." Louis had kept exotic birds and hounds, and hunted keenly in the nearby islands and forests—foxes, wolves, boar, even reindeer specially imported from Sweden. He kept a troupe of musicians. Bright decoration of the spacious rooms included fifty figures of angels in gold and blue. But tradition made it Scott's more sinister place. Louis' castle had to be a suitable lair for a king known for his skill and ruthlessness in intrigue—the "universal spider" of the contemporary chronicler Philippe de Commines—cruelty to prisoners, superstition, obsessive fear of assassination and perverse preference for low-born advisers. Much of this picture is exaggerated or inaccurate: a highly coloured version of a modern, centralizing ruler who at the same time remained "medieval" in his devotion to saints and relics.

The terrible Louis XI of tradition serves Scott's purposes well. Grim Plessis and its owner's plots are opposed to Quentin's open Scottish hills and his love of honour and fair-dealing—his old-fashioned dedication to chivalry. Scott's Louis, unlike the noble youth, can be something of a joker. When the disguised king and his inseparable henchman Tristan l'Ermite show Quentin the outside of the château, he naively takes them for a rich merchant and a grazier. Earlier (mistaking him for an enemy) they had failed to warn him that he was about to cross a deep stretch of the Cher. Having pacified the soaking hero, who is of course a strong swimmer, Louis provides him with a good breakfast at an inn in the village of Plessis. This gives the spider a chance to watch his prey—he is thinking of employing him—and to enjoy his straightforward hearty youthful appetite. Like many a later book it also lets the northern reader drool over French food:

> There was a *pâté de Périgord*, over which a gastronome would have wished to live and die, like Homer's lotus-eaters, forgetful of kin, native country, and all social obligations whatever. Its vast walls of magnificent crust seemed raised like the bulwarks of some rich metropolitan city, an emblem of the wealth which they are designed to protect. There was a delicate ragout... There was, besides, a delicate ham, which had once supported a noble wild boar in the neighbouring wood of Montrichart. There was the most exquisite white bread, made into little round loaves called *boules* (whence the bakers took their French name of *boulangers*), of which the crust was so inviting, that, even with water alone, it would have been a delicacy. But the water was not alone, for there was a flask of leather... which contained about a quart of exquisite *Vin de Beaulne*.

Plessis-lès-Tours was mostly destroyed in the late 1790s. One brick and stone building with tower survives near La Riche. In the 1880s Henry James saw it "reduced to suburban insignificance", a building like a small factory with "a yard encumbered with rubbish and a defiant dog". Later it served as an "institut vaccinogène" and then as a museum of local crafts. It is now "Le Plessis, théâtres", home of the experimental theatre company of José Cano Lopez.

THE PRIEURÉ DE ST.-COSME: PIERRE DE RONSARD

In *Le Voyage de Tours* (1560) Pierre de Ronsard imagines himself and his fellow poet Antoine de Baïf—"Perot" and "Thoinet", Pete and Tony—travelling to a rustic wedding. Nearing their destination, about a mile north of Plessis-lès-Tours, they see "the bell-tower of Saint-Cosme near Tours, where the good nuptials were taking place in a meadow" on the beautiful island. (It is no longer an island—a stream was filled in during the eighteenth century.) The poem, which is probably an exercise in literary invention as much as the record of an actual expedition, is full of celebration, lovers, "mille belles fleurs" on the river-bank. Five years after the poem, however, Ronsard returned in the more grave-sounding capacity of Prior of St.-Cosme. Since entering minor orders in 1543 he had collected several such positions. He was not required to spend much time at the churches and abbeys in question. He was, however, present at the priory to receive the royal visit of Charles IX and Catherine de' Medici in November 1565. He presented them with both fruit from his orchard and with sonnets.

Flowers rather than fruit dominate the priory grounds today. Plants have been matched with appropriate quotations from the poet, one of whose best known pieces begins "Mignonne, allons voir si la rose…" (It is a *carpe diem* poem: the beloved should take the speaker's advice and gather rosebuds while she may.) As well as roses the gardens include white and pink gaura, begonias, vines and several varieties of sage. Some of the buildings also survive. Ronsard-related books and pictures are displayed and there is a model of the more extensive priory of his day with its neat rows of trees and criss-crossing paths.

On 26 December 1585 at St.-Cosme the dying Ronsard, after a period of unconsciousness, revived sufficiently to compose two short poems. "For his Tomb" begins proudly "Here lies Ronsard who, bold from his earliest youth, diverted the Muses from Helicon to France." But, he goes on, "his Muse was of little avail against the sting of Death." The second poem, "To his Soul", echoes the Emperor Hadrian's address to his "animula vagula blandula" or "little soul, little wandering, pale thing". The "Amelette Ronsardelette/Mignonnelette doucelette" is bound for the cold kingdom of the dead. It was always simple, bore no guilt "for murder, poison, or malice" and despised the honours and treasures so sought by "the crowd". "Ne trouble mon repos, je dors," he tells the soul in the last line, aptly separating it from the body with which it is about to part company. It is a neat but spontaneous-sounding ending, phrased as if he has simply broken off to address the people around him. He heard mass on the afternoon of the 27th and died early on the morning of the 28th.

SACHÉ: "BALZAC WITH BRACES"
Balzac was a frequent guest at the château in Saché, near the Indre and about twelve miles south-west of Tours. It is, says John McNeill, "a hand-

some, though unremarkable" early sixteenth-century building with attractive grounds. The owner, Jean de Margonne, was a family friend—in
fact, as Balzac was aware, he had been his mother's lover and was the father
of his brother Henry. Balzac came here at least twelve times between 1823
and 1848. In his second-floor room, wearing his monk's robe and drinking coffee through the night, he worked on novels including *Louis Lambert*
(1832) and *Le Père Goriot* (1834-5). He enjoyed Margonne's company but
occasionally found "château life" irksome, as he wrote to his friend Zulma
Carraud in July 1832: particularly the company and the fixed hours for
dressing and dining. "It would seem strange, to people in the provinces,
were one to miss one's dinner in order to pursue an idea." He was already
becoming something of a tourist attraction, whose absence from dinner
might disappoint. But on the whole he was allowed his freedom. He was
happy at Saché "like a monk in a monastery". There "the sky is blue, the
oaks so beautiful, the calm so vast." Félix de Vandenesse in *Le Lys dans la
vallée* finds the château a place of pleasing melancholy, "full of harmonies
too grave for the superficial, dear to suffering poets. Later, too, I liked its
silence, the tall, ancient trees, and that mysterious indefinable quality
which fills its solitary valley." The area also appealed to Alexander Calder
(1898-1976), maker of mobiles and wire-sculpture, who had a house and
studio in Saché from 1953.

Saché preserves the early nineteenth-century décor of several rooms
including Balzac's and the salon. It also houses a notable collection of
Balzac memorabilia, portraits and caricatures, manuscripts and facsimiles,
engravings and figurines. The novelist projects himself forcefully, with a
nod towards posterity, in a photograph of the daguerreotype of 1842. This
captures the often mentioned "fire" in his eyes. According to his sister the
pupils were brown, speckled with gold. He cuts a different, rounder figure
in Benjamin Roubaud's caricature of contemporary worthies, "Le Grand
chemin de la postérité": florid face, shiny hat, bulging waistcoat. And he
carries one of his famous walking-sticks—he owned specimens topped variously in turquoise, silver and ivory with decorative monkeys and lions. In
some pictures the cane swells into something more like a parliamentary
mace, in some he wields it like a shillelagh or hurls it like a caber-sized
javelin. Also present at Saché are the characters of *La Comédie humaine*.
There are nineteenth-century engravings of Eugénie Grandet, of Père
Goriot's vacuous daughters and (by Daumier) of the wrinkled, long-suf-

fering Goriot. Statuettes or busts, many by Pierre de Rippert, represent Vautrin, the ubiquitous, ambitious and enigmatic criminal, in green jacket and grey top-hat; Colonel Chabert; and the rival clergymen in *Le Curé de Tours*—Abbé Birotteau rotund, hands on stomach, smiling innocently, and Abbé Troubert gaunt, skull-capped and sinister.

One of Rodin's plaster studies for his statue of Balzac is the subject of a permanent exhibition in the former kitchens. Rodin read everything he could about Balzac, interviewed people who remembered him and repeatedly visited Touraine. His initial models included the daguerreotype and Estager, a 35-year-old carter from Azay-le-Rideau, who was said to be a Balzac look-alike. But increasingly Rodin sought a less realistic effect. He wanted to do justice, he wrote, to Balzac's "unremitting labour, the difficulties of his life, the unceasing battle he had to fight, his splendid courage". The naked study at Saché already shows something of the forcefulness of the eventual bulky, robed figure, dominated by the great head, looking up and out, which has become a familiar image of the author. This was put on display in 1898 and a bronze cast of the statue was finally erected in Paris in 1939. *Le Figaro* for 17 May 1898, echoing Rodin's own view, saw "this face which took on all the masques of the *comédie humaine*, not a human face, nor mine, nor yours, nor even Balzac's; but the one he had when he looked at everything he had seen. Think of it: to have *seen* the *comédie humaine*!" He had seen into the depths of every passion, every soul. A statue of a man like Balzac should do justice to this. The only alternative is the realism of the daguerreotype: "Balzac with braces!"

AZAY-LE-RIDEAU

Félix de Vandenesse, in Balzac's *Le Lys dans la vallée*, admires the château of Azay-le-Rideau as "a faceted diamond set in the Indre, mounted on wooden piles concealed by flowers". Richard Wade's *Companion Guide* compares it, a little more prosaically, to "a gigantic luxury houseboat made of stone". Henry James observed the "silvery whiteness of complexion". For Hubert Fenwick in *The Châteaux of France* (1975) it is "the fairy queen's palace to a 'T'".

The building which has elicited such general enthusiasm was conceived and executed mostly in a few years after 1518. The name of the architect is unknown but he was carrying out the wishes of the court financier Gilles Berthelot and his wife Philippe (or Philippa) Lesbahy. In 1527 the house was confiscated by François I and given to his soldier Antoine Raffin. Its distinctiveness results from its successful absorption of Italian influence. Fenwick explains:

> Though the silhouette is Gothic and romantic, every detail is Italian
> and sophisticated, but complementary to the tall French roofs with their
> gay copings and finials, decorative chimneystacks and wealth of delicate
> carving around the dormer windows. All is make-believe; the turrets
> contain no guardrooms and the *chemin de ronde* no sentry walk...; the
> round corner towers do not reach to the ground, but are supported by
> richly moulded corbelling with bands of little roundels; classical pilasters
> line the mullioned windows; and most fanciful is the double entrance
> and stairway...; at the top [of which] is a double dormer window gable,
> all lacy and playful with free-standing sculpture and Florentine motifs.

As if to contrast with all this airiness, Balzac in his *Contes drolatiques* tells the tale of a robust *curé* of Azay who keeps a concubine, is a good fighter, a hearty eater and drinker, and generally beloved. He is always, in

J. Lewis May's translation, "blessing and bussing". He is a typical of the world of the *Contes*, bawdy, full of bodily functions, and made to seem the more anarchic by Balzac's eccentric, semi-archaic spelling. "He was the first priest to say in the course of a sermon that the Devil was not as black as he was painted." He was happy, of course, to help a parishioner rein-terpret the dietary regulations of the church: he "turned partridges into fish, saying that the perch of the Indre were the partridges of the river, and similarly partridges were the perch of the air."

LANGEAIS AND CINQ-MARS

Glimpsed from the train, the fifteenth-century Château de Langeais, on the north bank of the Loire, looks wonderfully compact. The *donjon*, however, stands visibly separate, the relic of an earlier age. This somewhat forbidding building is probably the work of the ever-warlike Foulques Nerra, Count of Anjou between 987 and 1040.

In the newly finished great hall of the later château took place, in De-cember 1491, the politically highly significant wedding of King Charles VIII of France and the fourteen-year-old Anne, Duchess of Brittany. She had succeeded her father as ruler of Brittany in 1488. In an attempt to keep the duchy out of the hands of its more powerful neighbour, Anne was married by proxy, in December 1490, to the Emperor Maximilian. But French victory in the resulting war coerced her into marrying Charles instead; a papal dispensation for the first union was soon obtained. The once rather dull waxwork figures of the participants in the ceremony at Langeais have now been enlivened—and some wit injected—by illustra-tive film using the same models. The commentary stresses the urgency of preventing Maximilian from encircling France. So determined was Charles to keep the royal hold on Brittany that he had Anne bound, by contract, to marry his successor if he died before her and without male offspring. One wonders, looking at the model of the future Louis XII among the wedding-guests, what kind of calculations he was making. The sons of Charles and Anne died in infancy and Anne married Louis, as per contract, in 1499.

The interior of the château owes its present rich appearance—its tap-estries, decorated floors, ceilings, fireplaces, statues, beds and chests—to the businessman and art collector Jacques Siegfried (1840-1909), owner from 1886. He worked hard to restore the rooms to at least a semblance of their fifteenth- and sixteenth-century decoration and furnishing before giving Langeais to the Institut de France in 1904. Notable among Siegfried's purchases are the tapestries of about 1525-40 (probably Aubusson) in the Salle des Preux. They represent, in green, yellow, brown, blue and white, seven of the Nine Worthies or *Preux*: King David, Joshua, Godefroy de Bouillon, Arthur, Caesar, Alexander and Hector, all of them sword-wielding, strong, bearded, fully armed horsemen. Judas Maccabaeus and Charlemagne would have completed the set in this particular tradition. Other lists include Pompey "the big" of *Love's Labour's Lost*.

East of Langeais at Cinq-Mars-la-Pile is the partly ruined château associated with Henri d'Effiat, Marquis de Cinq-Mars (see pp.94-5) and a Roman tower or "pile". The surprising name—J. M. W. Turner noted it as "5 Marses" when he sketched here in 1826—is a corruption of St.-Médard. The function of the 95-foot high brick pile remains uncertain, but probably it was a cenotaph or a beacon. The Duke of La Rochefoucault, in the early 1780s, reports the local tradition that it was built by the fairies. Rabelais' contemporaries also found it impressive: Gargantua rides to Paris on a massive mare, sent from Africa, whose tail was "just about as big as the Pile Saint-Mars, near Langeais, and as square."

Vendôme

The River Loir—le Loir, distinguished from la Loire—winds, roughly parallel to and north of the Loire, through much green countryside. Eventually it will flow south into the Sarthe, which joins the Maine, which in turn joins the Loire near Angers.

At Vendôme the Loir splits into several branches, making it a town of islands, always near flowing water. It is known especially for its large Gothic church, formerly part of the abbey of La Trinité, and for its association with Honoré de Balzac. He arrived here, 32 miles north-east of his native Tours, at the age of eight in 1807. For six years he was a pupil at the Collège des Oratoriens. Particularly in his early years there, he tended not to do his schoolwork and spent many hours in detention in the "alcove", where he was left largely to his own devices—to miscellaneous reading and dreaming. He describes the college near the beginning of *Louis Lambert*:

> Situated in the middle of the town, its buildings bathed by the little river Loir, the college forms a vast, securely closed outer wall behind

which are enclosed the establishments necessary to this sort of institution: a chapel, a theatre, an infirmary, a bakehouse, gardens, waterways.

Pupils came from all over France and the colonies, so parents did not often visit. In reality as in the novel "the rules, besides, forbid holidays away from the college." ("No vacations, no extras", promises the advertisement for Dotheboys Hall in the nearly contemporary *Nicholas Nickleby*.) They were at least allowed to spend some time at a country house belonging to the principal of the college. According to *Louis Lambert*, discipline was harsh, but several of Balzac's school friends thought this an exaggeration.

Consolations included the right to keep pigeons—as pets and for food—and a shop which sold "boxes, stilts, tools… mass-books (rarely sold), pen-knives, paper, pens, pencils, ink of every colour, balls, marbles; in short everything childhood longs for." But objects cannot substitute for family interest and affection. At a school evidently based on the college at Vendôme, Félix de Vandenesse in *Le Lys dans la vallée* wins two prizes; his parents are the only ones not to come to prize-giving or dine out with their son, and he burns his winner's wreaths. Louis Lambert, however, lives at one remove from school life. The novel in which he is the main character concerns the madness of a man of genius who searches for the absolute. As a boy his separation from reality earns him the anger and the blows of his teachers. He searches to know why green is such a common colour; why are there so few straight lines in nature, so few curves in the work of men? A whole esoteric philosophy—with some of which Balzac sympathized—develops from his reflections on his vision, the night before a rare school outing there, of the Château de Rochambeau and its surroundings. In Lambert's vision the Loir winds and Rochambeau has turrets. Philippe Bruneau, whose duty it is to tell us the topographical truth in his *Guide Balzac* (1997), points out that the Loir is straight at this point, there are no turrets and, imposing though the position of the château sounds in Louis' description, it is just a few yards above the river. Lambert will go mad. Balzac was only taken away from the college in 1813 in a state of nervous collapse.

Vendôme is also the setting for the more fantastic events of Balzac's story "La Grande Bretèche". A *bretèche*, known in English as a bartizan, is an overhanging turret; Balzacians have identified the "old brown house" in the story with one in Rue Guesnault. The narrator, Dr. Bianchon, who is visiting Vendôme to attend a wealthy patient, is curious about the decaying, closed-up house whose overgrown gardens he likes to wander in. Weeds and untended fruit-trees are rampant. Lizards, snakes and frogs are everywhere. The doors and shutters are closed, the locks rusted, the gutters broken. There is a sense of mystery, of enigma; an atmosphere of "the cloister, without the monks", "the peace of the cemetery, without the dead who speak to you in their language of epitaphs".

Eventually the narrator is told the story of the Grande Bretèche by a succession of witnesses. A Spanish prisoner-of-war had been accommodated at the inn; one day he disappeared and it was generally accepted that he had escaped. In fact his fate was more sinister. He was the countess' lover, walled-up in the closet of her room on the orders of her husband, who had heard the closet-door close when he arrived unexpectedly at the house. The lover could not reveal his presence without dishonouring the lady; she could not admit that he was there; and her husband avoided an open breach with her by not opening the door. He simply stayed in the house for twenty days. Balzac's usual insistence on detail—the crumbling buildings and wild gardens, the comic tics and tricks of speech of the witnesses—makes what might be an improbable Gothic tale something much more chilling.

Chapter Seven

GIANTS AND PRINCES

FROM USSÉ TO MONTSOREAU

For its last few miles the Indre runs mostly parallel to the Loire, separated only by streams and narrow, sandy strips of land. Just after the confluence is the spherical containment vessel of the Chinon-Avoine nuclear power-station: *la boule*, as it soon became known. Work began at this, the first nuclear station in France, in 1957, and production in 1963. Further reactors were added subsequently. Gabrielle Hecht in *The Radiance of France* has studied the response of local people. Villagers at Avoine were angered by the initial decision to call the installation by the name of the nearest main town, Chinon, but otherwise seem to have been well disposed. The plant brought new prosperity to the area—workers needed housing, food and services—and even generated tourism. In Avoine you could buy post-cards showing the *boule*. A "view of vines near the power station" featured on Chinon wine-labels. In 1986 the original power station became a Musée de l'Atome. Even so long after the sphere was built it stands in strange, futuristic contrast with the surrounding fields and waters.

Immediately after Chinon-Avoine a bridge crosses the Loire to Port-

Boulet and then the chalky plateau of Bourgueil and its vineyards. Their wealthy owner was, until the Revolution, the Benedictine abbey at Bourgueil. Today the red wines of Chinon and Bourgueil are often bracketed together. Roger Voss in *Wines of the Loire* (1995) tries to separate them: generally "the wines of Chinon have a greater softness and roundness, while those of Bourgueil have a more rustic quality, greater tannins and perhaps more finesse." Some say the former smells of strawberries or raspberries, the latter of violets. In each case the gravelly, sandy soil nearest the rivers produces wines which are drunk "young" and the higher clay and limestone contribute to those which age better.

After Port-Boulet the river continues to its confluence with the Vienne, much wider and more impressive than that of Loire and Indre, at Candes-St.-Martin. Here, on the site of a chapel founded by St. Martin, is the large twelfth- and thirteenth-century Collegiate Church dedicated to him. The area around the river has many other medieval connections. The tombs of the Plantagenets are at the abbey of Fontevraud, in wooded country to the south of Candes. The Vienne has recently passed through the Plantagenet and later stronghold of Chinon, with its long pale castle strung out above the river. And on an island in the Vienne at Chinon in 1321 occurred one of the most horrific incidents in the bloody history of medieval France, when 160 Jews, accused of poisoning the wells of Chinon, were burned alive on the instructions of King Philippe V. The island has become part of the larger Île de Tours which partly supports the modern bridge across the Loire.

From the castle at Chinon there is a view of the Clos de l'Echo vineyards, another reminder of the local importance of the wine industry. Ancient stone quarries in the town were long ago converted into extensive cellars, the *caves peintes*. François Rabelais' giant, Pantagruel, says that he has drunk "many a glass of good cool wine" there. The drinking fraternity of Les Bons Entonneurs Rabelaisiens de Chinon meets at the cellars to maintain his practice.

USSÉ: "LA BELLE AU BOIS DORMANT"
Ussé, a white tufa château by the River Indre, "combines the imposing air of a fortress with the elegance of a graceful residence," says Richard Wade in his *Companion Guide to the Loire*. "Its drawbridge, its towers and the wall machicolated practically all the way round are like the magnificent

Ussé: "made to impress"

dress uniform of a soldier, made to impress but not for the wear and tear
of battle." It is therefore not surprising that the château has become associated with Charles Perrault's (and Tchaikovsky's) fairy-tale of Sleeping
Beauty. In "La Belle au bois dormant", first published with other "Mother
Goose" tales in 1697, if the wicked fairy Carabosse had her way the castle
would crumble and the princess die: falling victim to an unfair, contingent,
"wear and tear" world. But the good fairy, although she cannot completely
countermand the spell, can ensure a "magnificent dress uniform" of an
ending with a court and castle perfectly preserved after a hundred years of
suspended animation.

It is at one of her family "maisons de plaisance" that the girl pricks
herself in Perrault. The place is big enough to have a keep and, in a room
at the top, an old woman who does not know that fifteen years earlier the
king prohibited sewing with, and possession of, spindles. The princess runs
about the château, climbs "from room to room" and is eager to know how
to use a distaff and spindle. Her vitality is in evident contrast with her im-
minent century-long collapse. But while she sleeps, apparently, she has
pleasant dreams which make her, when the time comes, less tongue-tied
than her lover; and the moment she wakes everything will spring back into
action. Meat continues roasting on the spits, drink in the guards' cups is
still palatable, old instruments play like new for the wedding. In a room
of state which can easily be imagined at Ussé, the princess had slept "on a

bed embroidered with gold and silver. She was so beautiful that she looked like an angel: for her fainting had not made her complexion any the less healthy. Her cheeks were rosy and her lips like coral; true, her eyes were closed, but you could hear her breathing softly, which showed she was not dead."

Owners of the château have been less keen to identify it with the castle where, in the rarely mentioned second part of the tale, the prince's mother does her best to eat his bride—Sleeping Beauty—and children. The prince has now become king. When he goes away, as kings will, to wage war, he makes the Queen Mother regent. With the lack of foresight common among people in fairy-tales, he has entrusted his country, wife and children to a woman who happens to be "de race ogresse" and as such possesses "les inclinations des ogres". She tells her steward that she must eat her grand-daughter. He takes pity on the child and hides her, serving his mistress a lamb instead. When she orders grandson she gets goat-kid. Finally a doe is substituted for the young queen. The ogress is satisfied with her meals, but one day she recognizes the children's voices as she is prowling about the castle looking for more food. She condemns the mother, the children, the steward, his wife and his servant to be cast into a great vat of toads (always poisonous in folklore), vipers and other kinds of snake. Just in time, of course, the king comes home and expresses some surprise at his mother's proceedings. (She had planned to tell him that his family had been devoured by wolves.) Furious, she leaps in with the "vile creatures" and is at once, and justly, eaten. The king laments her fate: "she was his mother; but he soon consoled himself with his beautiful wife and his children."

CHINON AND THE PLANTAGENETS

People stroll in the streets of Chinon. There are cafés, plane-trees, poplars, a statue of the jovial Rabelais and pleasant walks by the Vienne. The castle, however, looks rather less carefree. "The remains are of vast extent, but too much demolished, and too white in colour, to be very picturesque," notes Murray's *Handbook* in 1843. But, as the vastness of the château (really three linked châteaux) suggests, a great deal happened here. Some of it has been regarded as picturesque.

In 1044 Chinon passed from the Counts of Blois to the Counts of Anjou. In 1151 the eighteen-year-old Count Henry inherited it from his

father, Geoffrey V, who was known as "Plantagenet", tradition says, because he wore a sprig of broom or "planta genista" in his hat or helmet. By inheritance, conquest and marriage Henry soon became the ruler of an empire including most of northern and western France as well as England, where he succeeded as Henry II in 1154. But Chinon remained one of his favourite residences. He built much of what can still be seen, and died here, defeated by his sons and the King of France, in July 1189.

Henry lived in such a way as to spawn legends. He was famous for his energy, explosive temper, intellect, generosity, love of hunting and grasp of legal and administrative affairs. He could not abide resting, says the chronicler Walter Map, and "had no hesitation in disturbing near half Christendom". His wife Eleanor, Duchess of Aquitaine and ex-Queen of France, was at least equally remarkable. She bore ten children, waged war against Henry—who imprisoned her—and was a patron of poetry, music and religious life. In her seventies, when her son Richard I had become king, she withdrew to the abbey of Fontevraud, but re-entered politics very actively after his death in 1199, working to ensure her youngest son John's succession to the throne. Perhaps inevitably, one of the most forceful women of the Middle Ages attracted a misogynist "black legend" to herself. According to this she was not merely a warrior and intriguer but a perpetrator of murders and enjoyer of incestuous affairs. "The jealous Eleanor," Jules Michelet assures us (*Histoire de France*, 1869), "passionate and vindictive—a woman of the South—nurtured the rebelliousness and impatience of her sons, put them up to parricide... Eleanor herself took for a lover Henry II's very father, and the sons she had by Henry were at great risk of being the brothers of their father." Chronology does not bear this out; even less probable is her alleged liaison, while on crusade, with the future Sultan Saladin. He was ten years old at the time.

CHRISTMAS AT THE CHÂTEAU DE CHINON: "WELL—WHAT SHALL WE HANG?"

James Goldman, in his play *The Lion in Winter* (1966; filmed in 1968 and 2003), simplifies the "political manoeuvring" of the 1170s and 1180s by "combining a meeting of the French and English kings in 1183 and a Royal Court held at Windsor in the following year into a Christmas Court that never was" at Chinon. Goldman goes on, in his preliminary note to the play, patiently to explain that the "anachronisms in speech, thought, habit, customs and so on" are deliberate. But the characters' passion for scheming against each other, and their extreme loves and hates, are true to history.

Goldman's Henry, at once proud and self-pitying, dwells at one point on how his life "will read better than it lived". He was "a king at twenty-one, the ablest soldier of his time", a great leader of men who "cared for justice when he could and ruled, for thirty years, a State as great as Charlemagne's. He married, out of love, a woman out of legend. Not in Alexandria or Rome or Camelot has there been such a queen" (much though he tilts with her during the play). But there was a problem: "King Henry had no sons. He had three whiskered things, but he disowned them." The sons are the warlike Richard Coeur de Lion, the unloved schemer Geoffrey, Duke of Brittany, and John, a spotty teenager described by Richard as "a walking pustule". John is Henry's favourite and Richard is Eleanor's. (The family Christmas has been made possible by her temporary release from imprisonment.) Also present is the young King Philippe-Auguste of France, who intends, whether by alliance or opposition or marriage-treaty, to take over the Plantagenet lands. In reality he eventually succeeded in this during John's reign, capturing Chinon and the seemingly impregnable Loches in 1205.

The Lion in Winter revels in its one-liners. Henry inaugurates Christmas: "Well—what shall we hang? The holly or each other?" It is difficult to dissociate Eleanor's sharp, wry wit from Katharine Hepburn, who played her to Peter O'Toole's Henry in the 1968 film. She recalls the marvellous teeth of Henry's late mistress, Rosamund Clifford: "She smiled to excess, but chewed with real distinction." (Rosemary Harris created the role of Eleanor in the theatre. Glenn Close took the part in the film of 2003.) At Chinon high medieval politics are combined with the traditional elements of the modern family Christmas: tensions, overheard remarks, disputed memories and jealousies. "Well, what family doesn't have its ups and downs?" Eleanor comments after tormenting Henry with a claim to have had sex with his father.

JOAN OF ARC AT CHINON

In 1429 Charles VII of France was at Chinon less as a lion than, as one of G. B. Shaw's characters puts it, "like a rat in a corner, except that he won't fight". Many people called him dauphin, not king. Northern France was under English or Burgundian rule and the child King of England, Henry VI, was also, according to the provisions of the treaty of Troyes, King of France. And then a peasant girl of about seventeen, known as "la Pucelle" (the maiden) and later by the surname d'Arc, sought an audience with Charles. Their encounter, which took place on the first floor of the Logis Royal, rapidly became the stuff of legend. It was structured, or came to seem structured, as folktale. We are told that Charles, wanting to test the girl who claimed to be sent by God—there were many such girls in the fifteenth century—hid behind his courtiers when she was ushered in. One of them stood at the front, trying to look kingly. In Shaw's *Saint Joan* it is Gilles de Rais, the future "Bluebeard" (see pp.197-9), who takes Charles' place; his "sporting the extravagance of a little curled beard dyed blue at a clean-shaven court" is a rather evident clue as to his real identity. Joan was apparently a little nonplussed at first, and must have been subject, in her male attire, to some stares. "My dear! Her hair!" cry Shaw's court ladies. But soon she recognized her man.

Joan and Charles talked privately. She gave him some form of "sign": an angel presented him with a crown, she later told her interrogators. Charles was persuaded; dull enough usually, he looked "radieux" according to one witness. In *Henry VI*, Part One, it is a practical test which convinces him: if she can "buckle" with him in single combat and win, her "words are true". Charles in the play is not the weakling of some traditions, but he is soon overcome by this "Amazon" who fights with the biblical "sword of Deborah". More precisely, as she has just told him, she is armed with her "keen-edg'd sword,/Deck'd with five flower-de-luces on each side,/The which at Touraine, in Saint Katherine's churchyard,/Out of a great deal of old iron I chose forth." Her knowledge that such a sword would be found at Ste.-Catherine de Fierbois was one of the miraculous signs of her divine credentials; the "old iron" of the play and Holinshed's chronicle suggests a more sceptical response.

After further questioning by theologians of the University of Poitiers (omitted in the swifter-moving *Henry VI*), she rode off at the head of an army which relieved the siege of Orléans and turned the tide of the war. How much difference she personally made, the nature of her "voices", and why Charles abandoned her to her fate when she was captured, have been much debated since. Near the beginning of Shaw's play Robert de Baudricourt tries telling Joan that her voices come from her imagination. Her reply keeps the enigma intact: "Of course. That is how the messages of God come to us."

The Musée Jeanne d'Arc in the Château de Chinon collects prints, faïence, statuettes, tapestry, postcards, medals and children's books inspired by Joan. In a large terracotta medal of 1896 by Edouard Avisseau she has a dreamily visionary look. In a bronze group of 1838 by Jean-François Gechter she is more active as, her horse rearing above him, she unhorses an English knight. Elsewhere she is strong, boyish, girlish, her hair is long, short, hidden by bonnet or helmet. Marina Warner in *Joan of Arc: the Image of Female Heroism* (1981) looks at the historically incorrect long hair as a legacy of the romantic warrior maidens of sixteenth- and seventeenth-century Italian literature—Ariosto's Bradamante, Tasso's Clorinda. More directly relevant to Chinon is a lively 1965 model, in glazed clay, of the "scène de la Reconnaissance" (Joan recognizing the king) by local nursery-school children. An elderly visitor to the museum sounded less easily enthused. "Jeanne, Jeanne," she sighed. Perhaps she had seen enough of the saint for one lifetime.

RICHELIEU: "MOST RICHLY FURNISHED"
South of Chinon, long after its days as a royal centre, Cardinal Richelieu built himself a palace fit for a king. John Evelyn relates that he was "allured to build" so far out of the way "by the name of the place, and an old house

there belonging to his ancestors". In 1631 work began, following the designs of Jacques Lemercier, on the "princely pile" recorded by Evelyn in 1644:

> The rooms are stately, most richly furnished with tissue, damask, arras, and velvet, pictures, statues, vases, and all sorts of antiquities, especially the Caesars in oriental alabaster. The long gallery is painted with the famous acts of the founder; the roof with the life of Julius Caesar; at the end of it is a cupola or singing theatre, supported by very stately pillars of black marble… The gardens without are very large, and the parterres of excellent embroidery, set with many statues of brass and marble; the groves, meadows and walks are a real paradise.

In fact the cardinal did not openly display paintings of his own "famous acts" in the long gallery. They were, at least in theory, the achievements of Louis XIII, Evelyn's editor E. S. DeBeer points out. The collection of paintings also included work by Titian, Caravaggio, Rubens, Claude and Poussin. On either side of the entrance were Michelangelo's "Dying Slave" and "Rebellious Slave", meant for the tomb of Pope Julius II and now in the Louvre.

Richelieu died in 1642, before he could spend much time at his palace. Its remoteness from Versailles—a problem even for more established châteaux—was a factor in its subsequent decline. The art collection was split up, partly in the 1720s and partly during the French Revolution. Most of the buildings were demolished in 1805. The great park survives, and in it a domed pavilion, orangery and wine-cellar. There is a small museum in the Hôtel de Ville; virtual visits, making clear the splendour and the vast extent of the château, are available between June and September at 28 Grande Rue.

The Hôtel de Ville and Grande Rue are part of the town, more enduring than the château, which the cardinal also had constructed. Its precise rectangular plan, substantial, symmetrical *hôtels particuliers* and piazza-like squares cater to his love of order and suggest that this is a great city rather than a town which now has a population of about 2,200. There were 3,000 in 1709, 2,649 at the census of 1851, 2,433 at that of 1982. In the market square are the church of Notre-Dame and the fine chestnut-wood market building, both built by Jacques Lemercier's brother, Pierre, in the 1630s. Worship and trade continued while the cardinal's dream of an elite academy which would perpetuate his memory soon faded. At the academy, says Evelyn, "besides the exercise of the horse, arms, dancing etc. all the sciences are taught in the vulgar French by professors stipendiated by the great Cardinal, who by this, the cheap living there, and divers privileges, not only designed the improvement of the vulgar language, but to draw people and strangers to the town." But already, two years after Richelieu's death, it was "thinly inhabited".

Four miles north of Richelieu, at Champigny-sur-Veude, the cardinal demolished part of the château which had formerly belonged to Louis XIII's dangerously dissident brother, Gaston d'Orléans. The early sixteenth-century chapel, however, is magnificently intact. Its stained glass, particularly rich in reds and blues, is arranged in three unusually clear and coherent registers. At the top are scenes from the Passion of Christ, in the middle the life of St. Louis (including crusader battles and remarkably detailed ships), and at the bottom the kneeling descendants of the saint—mainly the Dukes of Bourbon and Counts of Montpensier whose family owned Champigny for much of its history.

Rabelais and La Devinière

François Rabelais was probably born at La Devinière, a farm owned by his father at Seuilly, near Chinon, some time between 1483 and 1494. The fine stone buildings are now a Rabelais museum.

Rabelais was a monk who left the cloister in 1526 to become a doctor and priest: the respectable, gravely hatted figure who appears in some of the visual representations displayed at La Devinière. Certainly his works, beginning with *Pantagruel* (1532) and its "prequel" *Gargantua* (1534), show the fruits of wide and often learned reading in theology, medicine, classical literature and history. But, as the illustrations here remind us, these books are also full of outrageous jests, explosive scatology, puns, glorious exaggeration, insults, practical jokes, over-imbibing and over-eating. Gustave Doré's versions in particular do justice to the gigantic task of sustaining the giants Gargantua and Pantagruel with food and drink. (Pantagruel, even when very young, requires the milk of 4,600 cows.) The books combine the intellectual and the earthy and so it seems fitting that at La Devinière there are not only rooms suitable for determined reading and writing but cool troglodytic cellars, cut into the tufa, where wine was stored and animals stalled.

Feeding Gargantua: as seen by Gustave Doré

Rabelais had some problems with censorship, particularly in his later years—a less liberal climate was developing in the period just before the French Wars of Religion. The change is reflected in the darker, more obviously satirical tone of the third and fourth books (*Le Tiers Livre*, 1546, and *Le Quart Livre*, 1548-52). Here Panurge, variously roguish, crafty, cowardly and self-centred—if often entertainingly so—provides a less optimistic emphasis. But Rabelais had some powerful protectors including cardinals, and no amount of censure from the Sorbonne could make his work unpopular. There were more than a hundred editions during the sixteenth century alone. Later he would be especially influential outside France, in the work of Swift, Sterne and Joyce.

The action of *Gargantua* takes place mainly in the villages around La Devinière. These are elevated, for comic, satirical or allegorical purposes, to towns, forts, even kingdoms. In a "willow-grove" at La Devinière Gargantua's parents and their boon companions consume suitably gigantic portions of tripe followed by gallons of wine. One drinker remains discerning enough to recognize the "gentil vin blanc" of La Devinière. "Upon my conscience," he cries in Sir Thomas Urquhart's translation of 1653, "it is a kind of taffatas wine… well wrought, and of good wool."

Drink features also in the prologue to *Gargantua*, which is addressed to "Beuveurs tresillustres et vous Verolez tresprecieux". ("Beuveurs" are modern "buveurs" or drinkers and "Verolez" or "vérolés" are people who have had the pox, Urquhart's "pockified blades"). But the prologue—like Rabelais' work more generally—is not simple roistering stuff. It suggests that readers must look for a "higher sense"—search out the marrow in the bone. And it should be noted that there is no evidence that Rabelais himself was a *beuveur*. The drinking-scene at La Devinière celebrates language as much as wine.

The war of the *fouaciers* of Lerné—a parody of the battles of chivalric tales—is an instance of the combination of entertainment and seriousness. *Fouaces* are a type of flat-bread bun and Lerné a village near Seuilly. The bakers refuse to sell their produce to Grandgousier's (Gargantua's father's) subjects. Hostilities break out and the King of Lerné, the tyrannical Picrochole, or "Bitter Bile", orders his men to attack the abbey of Seuilly and pillage the town and vineyards. Most of the monks chant useless prayers, but the enemy have reckoned without the vigorous Frère Jean— "young, gallant, frisk, lusty… adventurous, resolute… and to conclude summarily in a word, a right monk". He is so desperate to save the vines and the wine that he starts laying about him with "the staff of the cross, which was made of the heart of the sorb-apple-tree." With it he brains, impales or disjoints 13,622-odd enemies. "The cartoon-like violence can scarcely be taken tragically," observes Michael J. Heath in a 1996 study of Rabelais. But the vigorous, cross-wielding Jean, in contrast with his feeble brethren, may stand for the reformed Catholicism which Rabelais supported, partly under the influence of Erasmus.

The war spreads—to places which are in reality just a few miles from Seuilly—giving rise to Grandgousier's letter to Gargantua expressing a peaceable desire "not to provoke but to appease; not to attack but to defend; not to conquer but to protect my loyal subjects and hereditary lands." But diplomacy fails to "moderate [Picrochole's] tyrannical rage" and so Gargantua has to fight. Having won the war, however, he does not abandon his father's (or Erasmus') idealism. He rewards Jean by providing him with a new abbey. Thélème, on the banks of the Loire, will be run as the monk chooses and in marked contrast with the abbey at Seuilly. Sir Thomas More's *Utopia* (1516) was an influence. Gargantua himself ordains ways in which the new institution will be "contrary" to others: no enclosing walls, no clocks or sundials since people should not waste time "regulating themselves by the sound of a bell and not by the rules of good sense and intelligence". The order will accept only beautiful and good-natured men and women—and both sexes must be present. They can leave whenever they choose; Rabelais obtained papal dispensation, in 1535, for having left his monastery without permission. Usually the religious take vows of chastity, poverty and obedience; at Thélème they can marry, be rich and live in liberty.

The abbey is a magnificent building, endowed with 9,332 separate apartments. Does the gigantism suggest the impossibility of the ideal? There are libraries of Greek, Latin, Hebrew, French, Italian and Spanish works. There are pleasure gardens, an orchard, a maze, a tilt-yard, a deer-park, targets for archery and stables. On the great gate are inscribed verses declaring who is and is not welcome. The unwelcome include, in the vigorous words of the original, "hypocrites, bigotz,/Vieulx matagotz, marmiteux, borsouflez"; the little less vigorous Urquhart lists among others

vile bigots, hypocrites,
Externally devoted apes, base snites,
Puft up, wry-necked beasts...
... base pinching usurers,
Pelf-lickers, everlasting gatherers,
Gold-graspers, coin-grippers.

The purer-hearted folk who may come in will rise, eat and work as and when they choose, obeying only one rule: "Fay ce que vouldras", "Do what thou wilt." This is often taken, out of context, as a libertarian watchword; but what the good people of Thélème will naturally want is the good of others, of the community.

Gargantua ends with teasing allusion to its own meaning or the lack of it. Gargantua and Jean have completely different interpretations, divine and comically secular, of the "Prophetical Riddle" which is discovered in the foundations of the abbey. Is it about "the progress and carrying-on of the divine truth" or "a set at tennis in dark and obscure terms" where "the globe terrestrial is the tennis-ball"?

FONTEVRAUD

In April 1931 Virginia Woolf noted in her diary "Saw beautiful bare old convent church... The tombs of Plantagenets: like Edith Sitwell: straight, narrow, side by side: re-painted, blue & red." The effigies, several times moved and restored, are of Henry II, Eleanor of Aquitaine, their son Richard I "Coeur de Lion", and their son John's widow, Isabelle of Angoulême. The two kings (c.1200) look rather uninspiring, indeed dead. Kathleen Nolan, in *Eleanor of Aquitaine: Lord and Lady* (2003), explains that this "flattened, arid style" was intended to recreate the royal lying-in-state, which itself was designed to recall the coronation. The aim was to assert dynastic authority rather than personality. There is little indication of the Plantagenet passions. Richard's formal posture suggests nothing much lion-hearted, nothing noble. Perhaps the inhuman appearance is apt, if we accept Edward Gibbon's verdict on Richard as crusader: "if heroism be confined to brutal and ferocious valour, Richard Plantagenet will stand high among the heroes of the age."

The wooden figure of the less powerful Isabelle, installed in 1256, over fifty years after John lost Anjou and Touraine to France, is also fairly

nondescript. (The three other figures are in tufa.) But Eleanor's effigy is different. As Nolan says, it is more alive, "more robustly three-dimensional... and lacks [the kings'] mannered, angular drapery folds." She goes on to argue that the book Eleanor holds is a statement of a power other than dynastic: a "sign of her autonomy and self-identification, perhaps even evoking her own literary patronage". Also, of course, the book suggests religious devotion, especially aptly at Fontevraud. She had used the abbey and monastic community as a place of retreat and had endowed it, in her later years, with rights, money, gold and silver crosses, chalices, vases and silks. After her lifetime of secular power and involvement she asserts a distinctive image still, but with a humbler, devotional colouring.

The community of Fontevraud was founded in about 1100 by Robert d'Arbrissel, an itinerant preacher with many disciples. Unusually, the community was at first mixed: monks and nuns together. Later they were divided into four separate, unmixed groups. But by the founder's will overall authority belonged to the abbess. The royal connection continued long after the time of the Plantagenets. Many of the abbesses were "filles de France"—royal daughters or relations including a succession of Bourbons. "The Abbesses had themselves painted in frescoes—fat, sensual, highnosed faces," says Woolf. (Some of them were added as praying figures to the sixteenth-century paintings of the Life of Christ in the Salle Capitulaire.) But since Napoleonic times the abbey had been a prison. Leonard Woolf was told he need not take off his hat and they heard "prison bells ringing for [the inmates'] dinner".

Among the prisoners at Fontevraud was Jean Genet—or "Plantagenet", suggests an unhelpful warder in the novel he set partly here, *Le Miracle de la rose* (1946). Genet (1910-86) had committed a string of thefts; *Le Miracle* draws on his experiences as a youth detained at Mettray, the "agricultural penal colony" near Tours, in the late 1920s, and as a man at Fontevraud in the early 1940s. It is a prison of "white corridors, very clean, violently well-lit, smelling of enamel"; a place of terrible silence, of unique "distress and desolation". The narrator "will not attempt to identify the nature of its power" over its inmates—"whether it has something to do with its past, its abbesses who were *filles de France*, or the way it looks, its walls, its ivy, or the convicts passing through on their way to Cayenne, or prisoners who are more wicked than elsewhere, or its name, it doesn't matter." But what have the most powerful effect are the condemned cells and especially the condemned murderer, Harcamone, based on the real Maurice Pilorge whom Genet had known in another prison. Harcamone's self-control and lack of remorse transcend, for Genet, everyday morality. In a miraculous vision his heart becomes an enormous rose.

MONTSOREAU: BUSSY'S LAST STAND

The fifteenth- and sixteenth-century castle of Montsoreau, overlooking the broad Loire just beyond its confluence with the Vienne at Candes-St.-Martin, is associated with Françoise de Maridort, her husband the Comte de Montsoreau, and her lover Louis de Clermont, Seigneur de Bussy. In August 1579 the count forced his wife to invite Bussy to a rendez-vous and then, with the assistance of a large group of retainers, ambushed and killed him. (This took place on the north side of the Loire in the now lost château of La Coutancière.) In life Bussy, better known as Bussy d'Amboise (1549-79), was already well known as a turbulent, swaggering lover and fighter. The spectacular heroism of his death conferred mythic status on him. His story was endlessly re-told and elaborated, most famously in George Chapman's *Bussy D'Ambois* (c.1604) and Alexandre Dumas' *La Dame de Montsoreau* (1846-7, co-written with Auguste Maquet and originally using the spelling "Monsoreau").

In Dumas' version Françoise de Maridort becomes Diane de Méridor, a virtuous young woman trapped into an unhappy marriage. The loyal Bussy is, from the beginning, a force to be reckoned with. He is "a handsome, proud young man, who walked with high head, insolent eye and disdainfully curling lip," and dressed simply in black velvet: a complete contrast with the decadent court of Henri III. When the king and his jester, Chicot, try to confuse him by claiming to be each other, Bussy bites back: he asks Chicot's pardon for not having addressed him with due respect, but "there are some kings who look so like fools that you will, I hope, excuse me for having mistaken your fool for a king." He will show the same bold spirit in his fight for Diane. His last battle is the great set-piece of the final section of the novel. He kills fourteen out of twenty assailants, dodging and ducking pistol-shots, rushing the enemy, fighting until his sword becomes a broken, twisted fragment. His friend Rémy, already in the heap of dead, revives long enough to pass him a fresh sword. After that too is gone he fights on with a three-legged stool and turns a dagger against its owner. Montsoreau, meanwhile, lurks behind his men and shoots at Bussy but, in this version, is eventually killed by him. Bussy himself is trapped, finally, because his blood-soaked boots make him slip. As a new troupe of attackers arrives, he falls onto the points of their swords. He is despatched at close range with an arquebus while the real villain, the Duke of Anjou, stands mockingly by.

Chapter Eight

SAND, TUFA AND SLATE

FROM SAUMUR TO MAUVES-SUR-LOIRE

From Touraine the Loire moves into the old county of Anjou, roughly equivalent to the modern *département* of Maine-et-Loire. Saumur, the first substantial town, extends on either side of the river, spanning the Île Offard. Angers, the capital of Anjou, is built not on the Loire but "in a fine amphitheatre made by a bend" of its short tributary, the Maine (*Bradshaw's Illustrated Travellers' Hand Book to France*, 1856). Between the city and the confluence the river passes close to the Lac de Maine, an artificial lake established on its flood-plain in the 1970s, and its Parc de Loisirs.

As the Loire flows west temperatures rise: in Anjou palms, fig-trees and mulberries flourish as well as vines, roses and sunflowers. "La douceur angevine", the softness or sweetness of Anjou, is much referred to in brochures and books about the area. The phrase was first used by Joachim Du Bellay (1522-60) in a poem, sonnet 31 of his *Regrets*, contrasting France and Rome. Du Bellay was in Rome in the mid-1550s in the entourage of his cousin Cardinal Du Bellay. His preference for France, which he proclaims "mother of arts, of arms, of laws", reflects the aim of the Pléiade group, which included his friend Ronsard, of creating a newly authoritative, reinvigorated French verse on classical models. But there seems also to be a genuine longing for Anjou and specifically Du Bellay's village of Liré, just south of the Loire, and the "poor house" of his ancestors. Fine slate pleases him more than hard Roman marble, his taste is more for "the Gallic Loire than the Latin Tiber,/My little Liré than the Palatine Hill,/And more than sea air the softness of Anjou."

This is the land also of the suitably named Mme. Rose, in Maurice Fourré's *La Nuit du Rose-Hôtel* (1950). She has run a hotel in Paris, near Montparnasse station, for thirty years. But her heart is elsewhere: Montparnasse is the station for Anjou. As a good *Angevine* she is always smiling, as her grandfather did when he emerged, on hot evenings, from his cool troglodytic wine-cellar at Les Rosiers-sur-Loire, downstream of Saumur. She comes from a place of flowers, harmony and sparkling wit and is conditioned by it still after all her years in Paris. The "shaded arbours" are always with her, the garlands of honeysuckle and roses, the pale tufa and dark slate, the "bons compagnons" at table with their wine-glasses beaming silver in the sun.

Sands, islands and marshes are frequent between the confluence of Maine and Loire and St.-Florent-le-Vieil. Between Rochefort and Challonnes the Corniche angevine provides grand views, reaching out, as John McNeill says, "across the vineyards to the silent, marshy islands of the Loire [or its channel, the Louet], tussocked with grass and fringed with scrubby poplars." There are panoramic views also from St.-Florent, soon after which the Loire enters the département of Loire-Atlantique. It passes the town of Ancenis, now a lively enough community but in the 1930s, according to Lucien Bodard's novel *La Chasse à l'ours* (*Bear Hunt*, 1985), a place of "contented stagnation" where nothing happened apart from the odd procession and the annual flooding of the Loire.

After yet more small islands the river reaches the high cliffs of Clermont and Mauves-sur-Loire. J. M. W. Turner produced a series of gouaches and watercolours based on his sketches here in 1826. (Most of them now belong to the Ashmolean Museum in Oxford.) The sails of river-boats glow red-orange in the sunrise, the cliffs are bluish turquoise in the distance, there is a faint image of the Château de Clermont on a far crag. Of course, real rivers rarely look quite as evanescent as Turner's versions, but he is true to the spirit of the place on some days at least. Leitch Ritchie, in the text accompanying *Wanderings by the Loire – Turner's*

Annual Tour, declares that "Here Turner was in his element; he rioted in beauty and power; and if to the cold in soul and imagination his paintings may seem defective in mathematical accuracy, they will be identified at a single glance with the originals by all who can *feel* genius, and who are capable of seeing in nature something beyond its outward and tangible forms." Mauves also has a more practical appeal. The water is so abundant in perch, roach and bream that special trains for anglers used to come here from Nantes.

SAUMUR: *EUGÉNIE GRANDET*
The white, slim towered château of Saumur, raised above the town with its sheer defensive walls, looks all that a French medieval château should. It features on the page for September in the *Très riches heures du Duc de Berry* (c.1413-16). Sacheverell Sitwell describes its (somewhat idealized) appearance there in *The Hunters and the Hunted* (1947): "It springs from a grassy bank high into the empty sky. Vineyards stretch right up to the foundations of its towers, and it is the grape-gathering. A two-wheeled ox-cart is pushed into the vines, and its pair of tubs or barrels are filling with the grapes, while donkeys with loaded paniers are waiting in the path." The towers are "magnificent in their corbelling... while the tall chimney-stacks and conical, pointed roofs make a spectacle of fantastic complexity and elaboration, and we can see the white stone lilies of France upon the battlements of the towers and the gilded fleurs-de-lis below the weather-vanes." The building now houses museums of the horse and of decorative arts. There are also distractingly wonderful views of the Loire.

The château was a palace and stronghold of the Dukes of Anjou, the Kings of France, and the Protestant leader Duplessis-Mornay, governor of Saumur between 1589 and 1621. Later its importance declined; the population of the town decreased dramatically when many Protestants left after the revocation of the Edict of Nantes in 1685. Saumur became, as Murray's *Handbook* (1843) puts it, "torpid". In Paul Morand's tale *Milady* (1936) there is a vignette of the retired officers of Saumur, the arthritic "ex-beaux cavaliers" whose broken bones were once a laughing matter, quietly doing nothing "in the shade of the poplars and willows of the Loire".

The most famous version of life in this quiet, restricted place, however, is in Balzac's *Eugénie Grandet* (1833). "One finds, in certain provincial towns, houses whose sight inspires just as much melancholy as that provoked by the darkest of cloisters, the bleakest of moors, and the saddest of ruins." This is a claustrophobic Saumur; the splendour of the high white castle and the Loire with its bridges and vast sand-banks seems simply not to exist for the characters.

Attempts to identify the house of M. Grandet with an actual building in Saumur have met with little success. But in the smaller streets of Saumur, on the way to the church of Notre-Dame-de-Nantilly, for instance, it is still easy to imagine the quiet, even deathly atmosphere in which Balzac's characters move. The house, where most of the action takes place, is on a steep street leading up to the château, unlike which it is described in minute detail. The "pale, cold, silent" dwelling by the ruined ramparts suggests the spiritual poverty within. And the minuteness with which the place and its owner are described reinforces the attention to detail which has enabled the former master-cooper Grandet gradually to build a great fortune, beginning by buying up confiscated farms and vineyards at the Revolution. He is good at pretending to be poor or stupid, concealing his commercial instincts and grasp of the law, and avoiding unambiguous commitment. He has a range of four possible responses to questioning: "I don't know, I cannot, I don't want to, we'll see about that." At home expenses are kept rigidly to the minimum—fires not lit until November, wife and daughter too much in the habit of skimping to know any different, work inside and outside the house done by one strong, fanatically loyal servant, "la Grande Nanon", for next to nothing. Once, when she helped with an especially difficult harvest, he gave her his old watch. He offers his bereaved nephew a glass of wine because, as the narrator observes, "wine costs nothing in Saumur; there they offer wine like cups of tea in the Indies." The mixture of serious and comic continues, much later, at Grandet's death, when he makes a materialist's last "frightful gesture" to seize the silver-gilt crucifix the priest tries to hold to his lips.

Grandet threatens—he would be happy to do it—to take over the novel. He "is not simply an object of moral condemnation," says Graham Robb, "nor even just an example of destructive economic practices; he embodies a vital force, an *idée fixe*, and this is where Balzac rises above the sentimental novelists of the day." But when his daughter does eventually dare to oppose him, he realizes that she is "more Grandet than I am Grandet". Eugénie shares his willpower, in her case driven by love (misplaced, as it turns out) for the cousin who arrives in the dark house one evening from the unimaginably different world of Paris. He is a dandy with a magnificent collection of waistcoats and a whole "cargo" of other "futilités parisiennes". In Paris a great lady, "his Annette", is his mistress. Provincial life, which he scrutinizes through a monocle, astonishes him. When he finds that he has lost everything, however, he is happy to accept Eugénie's carefully hoarded cash, swear eternal love, and depart.

THE CADETS OF SAUMUR

In June 1940 German troops blitzkrieged their way to the Loire. On the 17th Marshal Pétain called on French forces to lay down their arms. But at Saumur the commandant of the Cavalry School, Colonel Daniel Michon, decided without hesitation to fight on. Under his control were 780 cavalry cadets and officer-instructors. They were reinforced by men from various army units who had found their way to Saumur, including Algerian riflemen and troops who had been evacuated at Dunkirk but made their way back to France. The total size of Michon's force was about 2,000 men.

The Cavalry School, descended from an institution which first came to the town in the late eighteenth century, was famous for its equestrian prowess. Since the 1820s, interrupted only by war, the annual Carrousel has been held in the Place du Chardonnet. By 1940 the school also provided training for modern, mechanized warfare; the horses were sent south just before the battle. The students, apparently first called "cadets" by the German general who praised their courage in 1940, were mostly in their late teens. Many had aristocratic blood or connections. They had yet to fight, but subscribed to a strong traditional code of military honour. Pétain's attitude was, as Roy Macnab says in *For Honour Alone: the Cadets of Saumur* (1988), "a mockery of everything that Saumur had taught its cadets: to surrender without fighting was unthinkable." The name "cadets" stuck, as Macnab notes, partly because of its association with the heroic-sounding days of three hundred years earlier, and particularly with the Gascony Cadets who, in Edmond Rostand's *Cyrano de Bergerac* (1897), give their lives at Arras.

Between midnight on 18 June and the early hours of the 21st Michon's forces, armed mainly with old-fashioned machine-guns, held back 18,000 well-equipped Germans. The French combatants were stretched along 25 miles of the Loire in vineyards, by the remains of the bridges they blew up as the enemy arrived, on the island between Les Rosiers and Gennes, on the Île Offard at Saumur and at the Cavalry School. The Mayor of Saumur, having unsuccessfully begged Michon not to fight, helped civilians find shelter in troglodytic cellars and caves. The ensuing bombardment badly damaged the churches of St. Pierre and St. Nicolas.

Legends were in the making. A stained glass window in the church at Milly-le-Meugon, south of Gennes, commemorates the vigil of Captain Foltz's squadron, who prayed here in small groups in the early hours of 19 June. Lieutenant Jacques Desplats and many of his men died after heroically defending the island at Gennes. And when a cadet said to another officer-instructor, the future General de Galbert, "*Mon Lieutenant*, you are sending me to my death," he replied calmly "Je vous fais cet honneur, Monsieur." In fact the cadet, like Galbert, survived. Many such examples are usefully gathered by Macnab and by Patrick de Gmeline in *Les Cadets de Saumur Juin 1940: Document*, published in 1993.

Angers and Lyon had been occupied but Saumur held on. Eventually the German commanders decided temporarily to bypass the town. Michon's men fought final engagements with them at Aunis Farm and Port-Boulet. The commandant wanted to die like a hero of old, facing the enemy with his pistol, in full-dress uniform, at the gates of the School. He was persuaded, however, that it was pointless to sacrifice the lives of more young men and that he should now obey the order to cease hostilities. Michon successfully led one group towards Fontevraud and beyond the demarcation line of what had just become Vichy France. The rest of the defenders were captured but well treated—at least partly because the men who did battle with them were from the German 1st Cavalry Division and shared a similar upper-class background and martial ethic. Many had attended the Cavalry School at Hanover, the German equivalent of Saumur, and some had competed against their fellow cavalrymen in equestrian events only the previous year. The prisoners were soon released rather than interned like most defeated French soldiers; they marched off to German salutes.

German troops entered Saumur on the morning of 21 June 1940. Before they were expelled on 30 August 1944 there was further serious bombardment, this time by the Allies. In the meantime the town was a centre of the Resistance. The cadets and the resisters fought for France in what many regarded as its symbolic heartland.

The Dolmen of Bagneux: "this dismal relic of the darkest antiquity"

The "Grand Dolmen" of Bagneux, near Saumur, was excavated in 1775. Elizabeth Strutt, author of *Six Weeks on the Loire with a Peep into La Vendée* (1833), was shown the way here by a local peasant or smallholder. He was, she says, so pleased with the tip her party gave him that "he insisted on running to a neighbouring cottage for a ladder, in order that I might ascend to the top of this gloomy temple of the most abominable of all superstitions." (Human sacrifice was believed, mainly on the strength of a reference in Caesar's *Gallic Wars* VI. xvi, to be one of the Druids' principal activities. Megaliths looked good places to do the killing.) Apparently some English gentlemen who once made the ascent were in less solemn mood. They "gave a dinner on top of the cave, and amused themselves by pelting the passers by with eggs and fruit." "'Funny people, these English,' said the guide, and we could not deny the charge."

Determined, no doubt, to show that not all English people were so superficial, the visitors entered

> this dismal relic of the darkest antiquity... shuddering to think of the horrors that had been performed within its gloomy walls; if rude masses of granite, put together without cement or insertion of any kind, may be dignified with an epithet of anything belonging to architecture. An immense oblong piece of granite... serves as a foundation, no doubt polluted with libations of the blood of human victims... Two immense masses serve as a roof to exclude the light of the sun, which otherwise might be supposed to sicken at the scenes it would have had to look upon. The end of the cave is shut up by a single stone, and the mouth nearly closed by another. Such is a Druid's cave, rude, barbarous and dark.

It was all very unsettling. That such a place should even survive was rather worrying: "whilst the noblest works of art have been levelled in the dust, whilst Palmyra is silent in the desert, and Rome buried in the remains of her own grandeur, these dismal stones remain, exactly as they were two thousand years ago" and—now she admits to less certainty about the sacrificial business—"only the doctrines of those who reared them [are] involved in obscurity, dimly guessed at by the cruelties with which tradition has invested them." The stones' staying-power threatened all sense of orderly progression, of civilized control.

ANGERS: THE CHÂTEAU

From across the River Maine there is a fine view of the towered, black and white castle of Angers and, further back, the cathedral. In the Middle Ages the castle was even closer to the river than now, well placed to receive goods and supplies from the Loire only two and a half miles downstream. It was a desirable site; in Shakespeare's *King John* (c.1595) both the French and the English are determined to take Angers, threatening to put its citizens to the sword, or the "iron indignation" of their cannon, if they do not let them in. There is much posturing on both sides and much work for trumpeters. Eventually, however, a peaceful settlement is worked out. The French dauphin will marry King John's niece, Blanche of Castile, and everybody can now go into Angers for a wedding instead of a massacre.

In reality the wedding did not take place in the city. But Blanche, who in 1226 became regent for her young son Louis IX (St. Louis), was certainly important in its history. She and Louis were responsible for rebuilding the castle after Angers became part of the royal domain in 1230. Most conspicuously, they added the seventeen towers of dark schist banded with pale limestone. The towers, crowned by "pepper-pot" roofs, once rose, as John McNeill points out, over thirty feet above the walls; they "created the type of silhouette Viollet-le-Duc attempted to recapture at Carcassonne… and intimidated the surrounding area with what amounts to a serial exhibition of *donjons*" or keeps. From the outside, settled in its deep dry moat, the castle still looks coherent enough, but some people find it ugly. Henry James saw "no beauty, no grace, no detail, nothing that charms or detains you; it is simply very old and very big," a "perfect specimen of a superannuated stronghold", grim and black as befits a town so famous for slate that it used to be known as "Black Angers". An alternative name, more tactful or more responsive to the effects of sunlight, was "la Ville Bleue".

The castle acquired its "superannuated" aspect during the sixteenth-century Wars of Religion, when Henri III, anxious to prevent it being used as a Protestant stronghold, ordered the reduction of its towers. The captain of the castle, Donadieu de Puycharic, carried out the letter of his instruc-

tions but at the same time modernized the fortress, adapting the towers for the use of new defensive artillery. Subsequently Puycharic was promoted to the rank of Seneschal of Anjou by Henri IV. His well-preserved tomb effigy, attributed to Gervais Delabarre, is now in the Musée des Beaux-Arts. He kneels in armour and chain of office, a poised figure with curled moustache, shapely beard, and, before him, gauntlets and plumed and visored helmet: traditional chivalric garb for a man who lived in days of cannon and bloody civil strife.

Inside, James could find little to do but to walk the ramparts; the castle was used as a "magazine of ammunition, and the yard contains a multitude of ugly buildings." Today, thanks to patient restoration work, there are some more interesting elements including a vineyard, a reconstructed medieval garden and a chapel and lodgings for the fifteenth-century court. Most of the surviving buildings have associations with René of Anjou (1409-80). René, Duke of Anjou from 1434, nearly ruled many lands, including the kingdom of Naples and Sicily, where he was supplanted by Alfonso of Aragon in 1442. He kept the title "king" but spent much of his life alternating between the main dominions that were prepared to have him, Anjou and Provence. He travelled between the two, by Loire and Rhône, with courtiers, chaplains, minstrels, fools, tapestries and jewel-boxes. At the castle of Angers, one of his more frequent residences between the 1440s and 1460s, he left some personnel and an active menagerie of "lyons, lyépards et autres bestes sauvaiges" including dromedaries, wolves, ostriches, peacocks and a porcupine. Possibly less impressive was the "strange sheep" for presenting which a man obtained four florins in 1449. The lions, which usually did not live long in captivity, had their own *logis* by the moat. The wild boars, who flourished contrastingly well, consumed too much corn and so all but the original two were moved out to "our forest of Bellepoule" in 1464. Also interesting to visitors was René's favourite Moor, Falcon, who wore exotic "Saracen robes".

René had many other interests, and indeed has often been remembered for these more than for his rather unfortunate political career. He wrote, probably first in the 1450s, the romance *Le Livre du cuers d'amours espris* (1477), the story of a lover's heart. He participated in courtly shows and jousts and composed a treatise "on the form and the device of a tournament" (c.1444). Legend made him also an accomplished painter and a keen gardener. A popular later view is summed up by Sir Walter Scott in *Anne of Geierstein* (1829), where the monarch's main function is to provide comic relief:

> René was a prince of very moderate parts, endowed with a love of the fine arts, which he carried to extremity, and a degree of good humour, which never permitted him to repine at good fortune, but rendered its possessor happy, when a prince of keener feelings would have died of despair. This insouciant, light-tempered, gay and thoughtless disposition conducted René, free from all the passions which embitter life, and too often shorten it, to a hale and mirthful old age.

"Le bon roi René" was remembered in Anjou, but with less warmth than in Provence. When the nephew who had briefly succeeded him died without heir in 1481 the duchy of Anjou simply reverted to the French crown, which had bestowed it on René's grandfather. But for Provence it meant the end, effectively, of existence as a separate country. Anjou continued to be regarded, almost as much as Touraine, as part of the French heartland. It seems suitable, therefore, that Pierre-Jean David d'Angers' statues of René in Aix-en-Provence and Angers are so different. The "little black bronze" near the castle is not quite as "weak" as a disappointed Henry James declares. But the girlish hair, small crown and skirted tunic contrast with the combined dignity and geniality of the Aix statue—a model for which can be seen in Angers at the Musée David d'Angers, by the entrance desk. There René is older, square-jawed as in the most famous representations of his own day, more real. The museum also has the models for the statuettes of other rulers of Anjou which surround the little black bronze. The heroic Roland looks like someone hiding in a suit of armour whose visor keeps coming down. Foulques Nerra looks dashingly, and Foulques V sternly, Victorian.

A more convincing memorial to René was, for three centuries, his tomb in the Cathedral of St. Maurice. He died in Provence, where he spent his last years, in 1480. His widow, Jeanne de Laval, brought his body back to Angers. Tradition has it that she had to smuggle it out of Aix in a barrel—the locals wanted to keep their beloved count. In reality it had been arranged that they would at least keep his entrails. Work on the tomb had begun thirty years earlier. It was destroyed in the Revolution; a few delicate white marble fragments of the canopy have been preserved in the Musée des Beaux-Arts.

APOCALYPSE TAPESTRY: "THE GREAT WINE PRESS OF THE WRATH OF GOD"

The seventy-six scenes of the Tenture de l'Apocalypse (Apocalypse Tapestry) are kept at the château in a large, low-lit, L-shaped gallery. Their number and their scale (330 feet long in total, 15 feet high) are appropriate to the huge story of the end of time. Jean Bondol, painter to King Charles V of France, designed the tapestries for Duke Louis I of Anjou, René's grandfather, in 1377. Nicolas Bataille supervised the work, which was largely completed by 1380. Bondol worked from a thirteenth-century manuscript of the Apocalypse or Book of Revelation but gave the figures a distinctive fourteenth-century flavour: "The heads are tilted, the shading is graduated, the perspective architecture is suitably fantastical, and the expressions of torment have been sharpened," observes John McNeill.

The general impression of the tapestries is of a colourful, disconcerting, intense, movement-filled world of many-headed monsters, crowned heads, thrusting and impaling lances and collapsing and glorious cities. Babylon crumbles, its towers and steeples snapped, or is infested by large demons, its splendour laid waste "in one hour" (*Revelation* 18.17). In no. 54 a city looks as yet undamaged, with its towers, flags and open portcullis, but the large horse's head protruding from it suggests that all is not well: this is the city of *Rev.* 14.20, outside which the grapes of wrath are trodden and blood flows "out of the winepress, even unto the horse bridles" for a space of two hundred miles. Further on, the New Jerusalem stays contrastingly bright and glorious. At the left of most of the scenes St. John is to be seen in a variety of postures. Usually he either writes his scrolls—the angel of the Lord tells him to write what he sees, which becomes *Revelation*—or watches with wonder or attention. Sometimes he holds his metal-clasped book, sometimes he takes dictation (no. 68). In no. 65 John's niche is empty: an angel carries him "in the spirit" (*Rev.* 17.3) to contemplate the Great Whore riding the seven-headed beast (sidesaddle) and holding "a golden cup... full of abominations and filthiness of her fornication" (17.4). In the previous scene he was led forward to see her seated on the waters, girdled, combing her long hair and looking at herself in a hand-mirror.

There are other arrestingly odd apocalyptic scenes. In no. 69 frogs issue from the mouths of the Devil and his representatives—the many-headed beast and the many-headed dragon standing on its back. More reassuring is the sleep of the Just, peaceful bearded figures with pillows, four in one bed and three in another. The horsemen of *Rev.* 9.16-19, however, will destroy a third of humankind. As prescribed there, the horses have lions' heads and their tails end as biting serpents. But the pictorial emphasis is on the riders, who look more like contemporary men-at-arms, seasoned killers from the Hundred Years' War, than creatures of apocalyptic dream. Because the text has the horribly-endowed "horses" do the killing, most of the horsemen keep their weapons upright. This lends them a terrifying casualness; some of them seem to be chatting as they ride on over the dead and dying. One, his face impervious, carries a huge, vicious, hooked scimitar, mirrored by his elaborately curly helmet or head-dress (a touch of fantasy rare in this scene). Another does put his lance to use, driving it into the next victim, who looks back at him as he falls. Perhaps the most sinister, however, is the man with two long, narrow plumes: the brim of his tin-hat-like helmet presents us from seeing his eyes.

THE CATHEDRAL AND THE *SACRE D'ANGERS*

The Cathédrale St.-Maurice is, Henry James somewhat grudgingly admits, "a sufficiently honourable church"; it is a familiar landmark, whose "high west front, adorned with a very primitive Gothic portal, supports two elegant tapering spires, between which, unfortunately, an ugly modern pavilion has been inserted." Inside, the most striking elements include the thirteenth-century glass in the choir and the huge, overflowing neo-gothic pulpit by Abbé René Choyer in the nave. It rises in towers, pinnacles and canopies and illustrates at least forty biblical scenes, replete with luxuriant vegetation, buildings, rocks, devils and sheep.

For centuries the cathedral, placed emphatically on its hill above the Maine, was at the centre of religious and public life in the city. In King René's day a great festival took place on 28 January. At its centre was a red porphyry, jewel-encrusted, ancient urn or "ydrie" believed to have been used by Jesus at the wedding in Cana to turn water into wine. René had purchased it from the convent of St. Paul in Marseille in 1449. The following year it was installed near the high altar at St.-Maurice. Each year, following a grand procession, the miracle was re-enacted and wine was distributed from the urn, perhaps solemnly, perhaps with vinous holy joy.

The ceremony of the urn seems to have fallen gradually into disuse. The vessel itself was transferred, in the nineteenth century, to the Jardin des Plantes and then to the museum. A more lastingly popular rite was the *Sacre d'Angers*, which was still flourishing in the eighteenth century. This was the annual Corpus Christi procession, involving elaborate biblical tableaux—or what the diarist Thomas Marwood called in 1701 "12 Pageants of History in large Wax Work, but too Romantick for so August a Solemnity" (quoted by John McManners in *French Ecclesiastical Society Under the Ancien Régime: a Study of Angers in the Eighteenth Century*, 1960). The pageants were displayed in the cathedral during the Corpus Christi mass and then were taken out in procession by the town guildsmen, who had paid for them. Judges, lawyers, the bishop and many and various clergy marched out with the guildsmen and the Holy Sacrament. Accompanied by the drumming and trumpeting militia they went, through streets hung with tapestry, to celebrate at other holy sites including, across the Maine, the abbey of Le Ronceray (founded in the eleventh century, dissolved in 1790). Later a sermon was preached, but at that point most of the procession disobligingly went off for lunch. It was, McManners concludes, "a ceremony in which the sacred and the secular were inextricably blended": a spectacle, a carnival with the usual "opportunities for libertinage", a parade with the usual disputes about precedence. The *Sacre* was so popular that the revolutionary festivals which replaced it—celebrations of Victory or the Supreme Being—were closely modelled on it.

By the eighteenth century one in every sixty people in Angers was a priest, monk or nun. It had become a clerical and legal city with little industry and little awareness of new political ideas. "Mediaeval Anjou with its counts and feudatories had gone like a dream, but their pious foundations remained, ruling the air by the music of their bells and the eminence of their spires, ruling the ground by their leases, rents and feudal incidents," writes McManners. There were churches and convents everywhere before the Revolution. One of the largest was the Abbaye St.-Aubin. The substantial Tour St.-Aubin is its most obvious remnant; bronze crosses on the paving of Place Michel Debré show where the pillars of the 280-foot long abbey church once stood; and remains of the cloister and chapterhouse wall, with some of its paintings and sculpture, are incorporated in the nearby Prefecture.

The collegiate church of St.-Martin also survived until the Revolution. Eventually it was taken over by the neighbouring school and then, in 1986, by the Département de Maine-et-Loire. The restored church was finally able to open to visitors in 2006. Beneath an eleventh-century nave and Gothic choir, the crypt at St.-Martin takes us back to the beginnings of Christianity in Angers and beyond. There are traces of an ancient north-south road and of several early churches with fragmentary sarcophaguses and wall-paintings. In places the effect is one of tumbled, jumbled confusion: the debris of centuries, an exciting prospect still for archaeologists.

SECULAR ANGERS: MAISON D'ADAM

The most notable secular building to survive from late medieval Angers is the Maison d'Adam of about 1500. It takes its name from the tree, in leaf and fruit, carved at the ground-floor corner and once accompanied by Adam and Eve. The remaining carvings are a compendium of religious and secular scenes and images. A man mounted on a pillar prepares to

thrust his sword up at the descending head and neck of a dragon. Angels move outward from the building. A pelican feeds its young, no doubt with its own blood, symbolizing Christ's sacrifice. A man near the top of the second storey exposes himself. There are musicians and monsters. A centaur brandishes a scimitar. Courtly lovers hold hands. In Henry James' day the basement of this "admirable house... gabled, elaborately timbered, and much restored" was "occupied by a linen-draper". Today it is a superior gift-shop, a Maison des Artisans with copies of the Apocalypse Tapestry, blown glass and figurines.

In the nineteenth century Angers expanded on both sides of the Maine and developed grand local government buildings. Wide boulevards replaced obsolete defensive walls. The city had been, Henry James wrote in his notebook in 1882, "stupidly and vulgarly modernized"; "Black Angers" was now "quite unworthy of its admirable name" and had been, "as the English say, 'done up'". The less sentimental Baedeker's *Northern France* (1889) liked the transformation of the "formerly very badly built" black town "by handsome boulevards adjoined by modern suburbs".

The Jardin des Plantes flourished. It had been founded in the eighteenth century and was landscaped in its present form in 1901-5. The Jardin du Mail retains a nineteenth-century atmosphere with its 1855 tiered fountain, 1877 bandstand, rhododendrons, palms in pots and overwhite, chastely naked classical statues. At the base of the fountain sit drenched deities and some of the water spouts from the mouths of a slightly absurd or delightful ring of frogs; their spitting-power is remarkable for their size. Beyond the Jardin du Mail is the much quieter Avenue Jeanne d'Arc, on the site where "jeu de mail" or pall mall was played in the seventeenth century—a game with mallets and balls and some similarities to croquet and golf. The long pedestrian avenue is shaded by tall plane-trees and has some elegant houses particularly at the Jardin du Mail end. Traffic noise gives way to birdsong and the meditative tread or measured jog of feet on gravel.

ANGERS: MUSÉE DES BEAUX-ARTS

Since 1801 there has been a museum in the Logis Barrault (1486-93), which was splendidly restored between 1999 and 2004. The logis was the palatial residence of the courtier and Mayor of Angers, Olivier Barrault, Vicomte de Mortain. The walls are of schist faced with white tufa. Inside is a museum of the history of Angers and, on the upper floors, the city art collection.

There is a selection of finds from the Roman city, Juliomagus: statuettes, mosaic, a second-century AD limestone lion once attached to a tomb. (The name "Angers" comes from the local tribe, the Andecavi.) The museum is especially rich, however, in medieval fragments and artefacts: stone and metal, jewel-inlaid reliquary crosses, tiles, the narrow, gilded funerary masque of Alès Lanier from the late thirteenth century. On an eleventh-century capital from the church of St. Nicolas two diabolical griffins seize a chalice; the scaly, winged creatures, tails writhed beneath them, curl around the capital. There is a thirteenth-century ivory horn or "olifant", of Byzantine workmanship, supposed to have been brought back from the Fifth Crusade. It is decorated with a lion, griffins, and a small figure who blows a similar horn while riding a beast like a camel without a hump. The most famous of oliphants occurs in the *Chanson de Roland*, where Charlemagne's paladin Roland at first proudly refuses to sound the horn for reinforcements—and later sounds it, too late.

Later displays include paintings and photographs of old Angers, and material from eighteenth- and nineteenth-century distilleries. Guignolet, one of the most popular drinks, was based on cherries and produced originally at the Convent of La Fidelité. Cointreau, which uses the peel of sweet and bitter oranges, was first distilled by Edouard Cointreau in 1875; there is a Musée Cointreau near St.-Barthélémy d'Anjou in the outskirts of Angers.

The collection of paintings at the Beaux-Arts includes a good range of work of all periods from medieval to modern. Carthage is very actively besieged in an anonymous Florentine piece of the sixteenth century. There are two Guardis: gondolas, domes, the Giudecca. There are Chardin still-lifes—fruits lustrous or downy; *fêtes galantes* by Watteau, Lancret and Fragonard; and nineteenth-century landscapes and ruins including Corot's San Marino, near Rome, in creamy light browns. In Maurice Denis' *St Georges aux rochers rouges* (1910) saint and dragon are secondary to the hot red rocks and dark blue sea of the Breton landscape.

MUSÉE DAVID D'ANGERS

"Grâce aux prisonniers!" This was the dying wish of Charles-Melchior de Bonchamps, a leader of the Vendéen royalists who had won a series of vic-

GRÂCE AUX PRISONNIERS !

tories over republican forces but was mortally wounded at Cholet in October 1793. The prisoners to whom the mercy was shown, at St.-Florent-le-Vieil on the Loire west of Angers, included Pierre-Louis David, father of the sculptor Pierre-Jean David d'Angers (1788-1856). His Bonchamps, a cast of the original erected in 1825 in the church at St.-Florent, faces into the gallery from near the entrance. He raises himself on one arm, hand outstretched, gasping out his last urgent request. The incident commemorated was one source for David's missionary sense that it was his duty, as much as his living, to represent great men (and some women) and especially his contemporaries. The fruits of this passion can be seen in many parts of France, but have been displayed to advantage in David's native city only since the early 1980s.

David added Angers to his name partly in order to distinguish himself from the still more famous Jacques-Louis David, the painter who had taken an interest in his work in Paris in 1810. Jacques-Louis was a more extreme republican than Pierre-Jean; he was unlikely to salute Vendéen generals whatever they did, and the dissociation was politic in the post-republican regimes under which David d'Angers spent most of his life. Loyalty to his native city, however, was the principal reason for taking its name. From early in his career he sent copies, models, and when possible original work, to the museum. There in 1839 a dedicated David gallery was inaugurated: an extraordinary honour during the lifetime of an artist, as he was keenly aware.

By David's death in 1856 the collection of statues, busts and medallions had grown beyond the ability of the museum to show it satisfactorily. The gallery was in the former refectory of a seminary, now the entrance hall of the Musée des Beaux-Arts. Over a century later a solution was found which did much to restore the sculptor's somewhat languishing reputation. In 1981-4 the former church of the Abbaye Toussaint was converted into the Musée David d'Angers. The architect Pierre Prunet restored its Gothic vaulting and transformed the church into a watertight but light-filled gallery, roofed in wood and glass. Bathed in light, the exhibits can be seen as if in the open air. The space also allows an effect not available to the individual monuments in town squares or churches: you can see many busts, statues and reliefs at once, and watch David's pantheon of the just assemble. Classical exemplars mingle with the younger worthies of the 1830s, their hair bouffant. Often the eye is led back to Bonchamps or to the huge Jean Bart (1845), naval commander and corsair (1650-1702), a model for the statue in Dunkerque. Hair and plume blowing, sabre waving in one hand and pistol clasped in the other, he steps across a cannon and towards victory, an image of apparently easy heroism.

David d'Angers remained true both to Bonchamps' compassion and to his father's politics. One of his most vigorously republican works is his relief for the Marseille Arc de Triomphe, "The Departure of the Volunteers of 1792". The museum has the half-size model of this and two other panels made in 1831-5. It is very much in the spirit of the *Marseillaise*, the song the volunteers famously sang; a banner proclaims "Allons enfants de la Patrie" and a row of bayonets cross it, ready, no doubt, to spill the "impure blood" of the song's refrain. Hats, muskets and swords wave or are dedicated, with women's jewellery, to France and to victory. Women are saying goodbye to the men who will march off to defend the much-beset new Republic, but the wives look just as determined as the husbands and even a small child, clinging to his mother's skirt, strikes one sabot-shod foot forward as if to march. The five-year-old David had been taken on campaign with his father in 1793. Another, older mother fortifies her drummer-boy son. There are no smiles, only the desperate determination which repeatedly beat off France's enemies in the wars of the 1790s.

The darker east end of the museum is adapted from the eighteenth-century choir of the church. Here, in glass cases, are smaller models and some David memorabilia including medals and—strangely, sadly decaying after all the clay and stone—the red, white and blue sash with gold tassels which he wore as Mayor of the Eleventh Arrondissement of Paris following the revolution of 1848. Upstairs, back in the light, are busts, usually larger than life size, of the vast range of people David either felt it his duty, or was commissioned, to record: George Washington; the young guillotined poet André Chénier; Balzac and Victor Hugo. There is a colossal Goethe, wise, pensive and wrinkled. The actress Mademoiselle Mars is shown with a smile or reply beginning to play around her lips; among the few other women represented are the English novelist and poet Amelia Opie (1769-1853) and the Irish novelist and travel-writer Sydney Owenson, Lady Morgan (1776-1859).

THE SONG OF THE WORLD

Jean Lurçat's ten tapestries of 1956-65, *Le Chant du monde*, were conceived as a response to the medieval Apocalypse Tapestry in the château. Nuclear destruction was the apocalypse Lurçat feared, but he believed that states of mind or ways of life as joyous as the New Jerusalem were still possible. The first impression is of works in rather gaudy contrast—yellow stands out especially—with their pure, pale, vaulted hall. This was for centuries the vast main ward of the Hôpital St-Jean, one of the principal buildings in La Doutre, the quarter on the right bank of the Maine whose name comes from *outre*—over, beyond—the river. Founded in 1180, it remained a hospital until 1965.

The impression of garishness tends to diminish as one engages with the individual patterns and ideas of the tapestries. *La Grande menace* addresses the nuclear threat. A vulture-like bird descends on its prey, the earth, which has an erupting volcano beneath it. But there seems to be some hope: to the right a man, with a dog beside him, pilots a craft across the blackness. The craft is a Noah's Ark equivalent, with a duck, a turtle, a rabbit, fish and plants. It looks freer, however, less prescribed or policed. Often the creatures travel partly outside, accompanying rather than contained. There are green fish beneath, although the blackness suggests space as much as sea. The owl of Pallas Athene, representing wisdom and foresight, sits above the man. *L'Homme d' Hiroshima*, bleaker, puts a skeletal figure against green columns and a mushroom cloud. His hair is a mass of flaming red. He has a flame through one eye, tears of blood falling from the other. Books and manuscripts fall into space. The Cross splinters. Stars like crumpled paper echo the hair-flames.

Since Lurçat had difficulty, he said, in imagining the end of everything, the smaller *La Fin de tout* includes a plant, broken, dead, but something, some sign of what has been lost. On the more optimistic other side of the room *La Poésie* relies more on the artist's personal mythology: Sagittarius as the procreative spirit, mysterious scenes of full-breasted women and huge leaves. *Champagne* is a more straightforward celebration. Liquid effervesces joyously from a cask with multi-coloured vine-leaves and energetic roots. White, blue and red drops begin in the cask like Keats' "beaded bubbles". They are surrounded by bright butterflies as they rise and fall. (Lurçat himself, talking about this piece, mentioned ejaculation.) The drops descend among irises— yellow, red and white on grey—fertilizing them or becoming them or creating them. The butterflies are especially delightful: child's butterflies, large of body and wing, with questing, joyous antennae.

CHÂTEAU DE SERRANT

Serrant is north of the Loire about eight miles west of Angers. It was built in the 1540s, possibly to designs by Philibert Delorme. *The Rough Guide to the Loire* has mixed feelings about the exterior: "a domineering rather than a graceful structure, its walls built in the striking Angevin combination of purply-brown schist... edged with creamy tufa, while heavy, bell-shaped slate cupolas press down on the massive corner towers." The interior has been admired for its symmetry, its vaulted staircases, its chapel by Jules Hardouin-Mansart and baroque marble monument to the Marquis de Vaubrun by Coysevox (1673). Fine too are its bathrooms of about 1890, "skilfully fitted into little closets in the thickness of the tower walls, inserted into former bed alcoves, or, in one case, disguised as a bedroom wardrobe" (Mark Girouard, *Life in the French Country House*). Serrant also has associations with eighteenth-century British history. It was bought in 1749 by François-Jacques Walsh, subsequently Comte de

Serrant, who was the brother of Antoine or Anthony Walsh (1703-63). Anthony had been given the title Earl Walsh by the exiled Jacobite court in October 1745 in recognition of his service when, earlier that year, he organized the delivery of the Young Pretender—"Bonnie Prince Charlie"—to Scotland. Walsh, who had been born in France to an Irish family, was variously a merchant, shipowner, and privateer. The prince sailed with him on the ship *Du Teillay* in July 1745 and disembarked at Lochailort in August.

A painting at Serrant shows the parting of Walsh and the Pretender. The latter, flatteringly taller than the former, wears full Highland dress. Graciously he hands Walsh documents to carry back to France. Had the prince not foundered at Culloden in 1746, Walsh's earldom would have had more practical advantages. The family continued to flourish in France, however; Serrant passed to its descendants, the La Tremoïlles and the Mérodes.

WALKING WITH VIPERS: HERVÉ BAZIN

The Anjou of roses, Renaissance châteaux and the wide, sandy Loire is not to be found in Hervé Bazin's first novel, *Vipère au poing* (1948). Here the countryside near Segré, 25 miles north-west of Angers, exhibits "nothing picturesque": low meadows, some heath, hedges, "cider apple-trees overgrown with mistletoe" and endless ponds. It is "an earthly paradise" for birds and rabbits, but not for the tubercular, cancerous inhabitants with their "drooping moustaches, taste for soups as thick as mortar, complete submission to the curé and the château", obstinacy and "a certain weakness for sloe-brandy and above all for perry". Small rivers wind through the landscape: the Argos flowing into the Verzée just before it joins the Oudon, which is a tributary of the Mayenne and so, at several removes, of the Loire.

Jean, the narrator of *Vipère*, has reason not to like the area. At the beginning of the novel, as a small child, he succeeds, Hercules-like, in strangling a viper; the look in its eyes reminds him, later, of his mother, the antagonist thanks to whom he has become, by the end, "the man who walks clasping a viper". Bazin's description of hatred between mother and son shocked some readers. The energy of the hatred suggested a strong autobiographical element; the fictional village of Soledot and pretentiously neo-Gothic "château" of La Belle Angerie resemble the real village, Marans, and house, Le Pâtis, of Bazin's childhood, and his fictional mother, like Bazin's, comes into the child's life when she returns from China on the death of the grandmother. Jean, who becomes known as Brasse-Bouillon (roughly translatable as "Trouble-Maker" or "Stirrer"), and his brother, Frédie, have been living relatively normal lives with their grandmother. But when they rush excitedly to meet their mother at Segré station, she greets them with furious slaps. Having "missed her vocation" as a prison-warder, she imposes a regime with much emphasis on early rising, lessons, prayers, food deprivation and beatings. Tutors and servants who protest are dismissed. The boys' father is simply too weak to stand up to the woman they christen "Folcoche"—mad sow, a combination of "folle" and "cochonne". Many a battle ensues, with Brasse-Bouillon in particular resisting domination however he can. (At one point she admits that he is the child most like her.) Eventually Folcoche agrees to send the boys away to the comparative sanity of school. But because of her "I no longer believe in anything, or in anyone... All faith seems to me a deception, all authority pestilential, all tenderness calculating... Man must live alone. To love is to surrender. To hate is to assert oneself. I am, I live, I attack, I destroy. I think, therefore I contradict." The last statement, of course, remakes Descartes' "I think, therefore I am".

From this negative but energizing state of mind comes the novel's satire on family, religious and educational life. Bazin's great-uncle, the traditionalist Catholic writer René Bazin (1853-1932), becomes, almost without disguise, René Rezeau, "that little man with a moustache whose main talent was for handing out prizes in Christian schools". Old Bazin wrote novels like *La Terre qui meurt* (1899), opposing rural virtues to the sins of the city and campaigning against depopulation of the countryside. What he advocates, as far as young Bazin and his narrator are concerned, is "Back to the land, back to the past, back to faith, for ever backwards!" The land of the viper is not one to be returned to.

St.-Florent-le-Vieil and Cholet: "the valley and the great river which must be crossed"

The "War of the Vendée" is the name given to the royalist insurrection of 1793 in west-central France. In fact it involved not just the Vendée but several areas south of the Loire, especially the Mauges, in whose main town, Cholet, some of the bloodiest fighting and massacres occurred. About 150,000 people died in the war and its aftermath. The initial provocation was an order by the revolutionary Convention for the raising of 300,000 troops. There was violent unrest at Cholet and St.-Florent-le-Vieil. A "Catholic and Royal" army was soon established, and won several victories against the soldiers of the Republic. For a time they held Saumur and Angers. The "Whites"—from the colour of the royal standard— enjoyed strong support not just because of the conscription issue but in reaction against a series of "reforms" by the new regime: increased taxes, persecution of the clergy in an intensely Catholic region and imposition of city dictates on agricultural communities.

The Loire itself was involved in one of the more dramatic incidents of the war, in October 1793. The story is told in the memoirs of the Marquise De La Rochejaquelein, widow of one Vendéen general and later married to the brother of another. Both generals died in the uprising.

> The heights of Saint-Florent form a sort of semi-circular *enceinte*, at the bottom of which one vast beach extends to the Loire, which is very wide

at this point. 80,000 people were crowded into this valley: soldiers, women, children, old people, the wounded, all in total confusion, flying from murder and fire. [Behind them, the republicans or Blues were burning the villages.] You could hear nothing but crying, moaning and shouting.

Amid this confused crowd, everyone was trying to find their relatives, friends or protectors. No-one knew what fate awaited them on the other bank... About twenty boats, in poor condition, plied to and fro, crammed with fugitives. Others attempted to cross on their horses. All stretched out their hands towards the other side, begging people to come to their aid. The scenes of disorder and despair, the valley and the great river which must be crossed, reminded many of pictures of the fearful day of the Last Judgement.

The young marquise, born in the palace of Versailles in 1772, was even less accustomed to such scenes—outside scripture—than most. She was, understandably, in such a state of terror and confusion that she found it difficult to remember the crossing directly and had to consult other witnesses when she wrote about it. Amazingly, very nearly all the fugitives made it across the river, mostly either in the boats or on a makeshift bridge of doors and planks. But their numbers were much reduced by the time, after more battles and skirmishes, they wanted to re-cross the river in December from Ancenis, about eight miles downstream of St.-Florent. This time the republicans were ready for them. They opened fire on the Whites' reconnaissance boat and the crossing had to be abandoned; long marches, desertions and massacres ensued.

The depth of local feeling is suggested by the renewed Vendéen upsurges of 1795, 1815 (against Napoleon's return from Elba) and 1832 (in favour of the deposed Charles X). Cholet, which was taken and lost several times by the Whites before General Turreau and his punitive "colonnes infernales" burned it down in 1794, commemorates the war in its Musée d'Art et d'Histoire. Documents, prints and weapons are displayed, and a series of paintings of the anti-republican commanders commissioned in 1816 by Louis XVIII. In the Forêt de Maulévrier, west of Cholet, where terrible massacres took place in 1794, is the "Cemetery of the Martyrs". The other best known Vendéen memorial is the tomb of Bonchamps in the church at St.-Florent.

Chapter Nine

LOIRE MARITIME

FROM NANTES TO THE ATLANTIC

Suddenly the river "takes on a blue-green colour and seems to be rolling mud or dirty sand. The sea is getting near, casting up the tide: the Loire is going to end and the Ocean begin." The future journalist and novelist Jules Vallès, travelling to Nantes as a teenager in the icy December of 1845, could already perceive the change in the river at Ancenis, about seventeen miles upstream of the city. Beyond Nantes is the estuary; now colour, light and smell become unmistakably maritime.

The estuary is a continually changing environment in which islands dissipate or become attached to the shore or are artificially removed. As in so many earlier stretches of the river, the struggle against silt is unending. Dredgers are always at work and there have been periods when only boats of limited draught could dock at Nantes: in the eighteenth century, as Nathaniel Wraxall noted, goods were "brought up in large boats from Paimboeuf [further down the estuary], at which place vessels of burden are obliged to unload." Paimboeuf itself later silted up, and in the nineteenth century was superseded by the port of St.-Nazaire. Most large ships still use St.-Nazaire, but dredging and the extension of quays in Nantes have now enabled cruise liners up to 650 feet long to come into the city.

Leaving the outskirts of Nantes, the river passes Couëron and, on each side, extensive marshland. At Couëron is the country house of the sea-captain and former plantation owner Jean Audubon, La Gerbetière. His son Jean-Jacques—better known as John James—lived here as a boy in the 1790s and early 1800s and studied nature in the marshes. Already "none but the aërial companions suited my fancy"; his first bird-drawings he remembered as "rude sketches" destined for the bonfire. "The worse my drawings were," he recalled, "the more beautiful did I see the originals." Gradually Audubon was learning the skills which he would perfect in America after 1803; *The Birds of America* began publication in 1827. The estuary is still rich in bird-life: herons, lapwings, spoonbills, terns, among much else. Heavy industry threatens this diversity, although the only sign of it at Couëron is the disused 96-foot shot-tower by the Loire, put up in the 1870s.

Ever widening now, the river continues past the marshes and the red and white towers of the power station at Cordemais. After Paimboeuf its

width increases dramatically, as does its depth. Industry now dominates the right bank from Donges to St.-Nazaire: the views are of oil-tankers and refineries, containers, cranes, factories, shipyards. At Donges is the huge Total refinery, producing around 230,000 barrels of oil a day. An accident here in March 2008 poured about 3,000 barrels' worth into the Loire, a reminder of the precariousness of the bird reserves and beaches of the estuary and Atlantic coast. A few miles further on is the spectacular bridge from Mindin to St.-Nazaire, reaching a height of 200 feet: a suitably emphatic farewell to the Loire which, soon afterwards, merges with the Atlantic after its 630-mile journey.

For many people, of course, this has been a place of arrival as well as departure. Among the larger groups were the troops of the American Expeditionary Force who landed at St.-Nazaire in April 1917 on their way to fight in the First World War. They are commemorated at Grand-Traict beach in a statue by Gertrude Vanderbilt Whitney, destroyed during the German Occupation but rebuilt in the 1980s.

Just beyond the estuary on the north side are long beaches and the resorts and casinos of Pornichet and La Baule and on the south, beyond the Pointe de St.-Gildas, is Pornic (already in 1867, says J. W. C. Hughes in *Bradshaw's Illustrated Hand Book to Brittany*, "a somewhat fashionable watering place, with a casino and other *agrémens*"). Access to these places was opened up in the mid and late nineteenth century by the railways— when, as Hughes has it, "the iron horse set his foot upon [Breton] soil," trampling, incongruously but usefully, on what was "for centuries such a *terra incognita* and land of romance". But behind the resorts an older, wilder south Brittany survives, with dolmens and menhirs, the vast salt-marshes on the Guérande peninsula, and the Côte Sauvage. North of St.-Nazaire, protected by canals and dykes from the incursions of the sea, is the Parc Naturel Régional de Brière. At its centre is the peaty, rush-filled Grande Brière, inhabited by herons both grey and purple, bittern, rail and teal.

Nantes: "neither flesh nor fish"

Nantes has an advantageous position at the beginning of the Loire estuary, poised between river and sea. But for most of its history the city was more obviously dominated by water than it is today. Everywhere there were bridges and islands and inevitably people compared it with Venice. The

Loire divided into several different branches and was joined by the Erdre and the Sèvre Nantaise. In the 1770s Nathaniel Wraxall described the Erdre, close in to the city, still winding "between groves of chestnut, oak, and poplar, which cover the banks to the edge of the water, and which are only broken by vineyards, gardens, and elegant villas." But as expansion and industrialization continued, the water began to be built over wherever possible. After 1926, the Erdre in Nantes was diverted underground and most of the branches of the Loire were filled in. In many areas of the city it is now possible to forget the existence of the rivers. Alain Defossé, in *Retour à la ville* (1995), addresses the city as people born "after the mutilation" know it: "diminished: closed to the outside world, and closed in on yourself, deprived of your aquatic lungs." Gone is the old life of dockers loading and unloading, yellow trams full of workers, the boats on Quai de la Fosse which used to "disgorge hectolitres of North African wine, 18% proof," the "cigarette girls hurrying off to the tobacco factory and the *métallos* to the shipyards." Women haggled for fish at one end of the Île Feydeau while children played on a spit of sand at the other. Anglers lined the quays and there were red-sailed boats on the river. Nantes "breathed to the rhythm" of its people.

Another "mutilation" for many *Nantais* is the fact that their city and their *département* of Loire-Atlantique are no longer officially part of Brittany. In 1962 Nantes was made the administrative centre of the new region of Pays de la Loire, consisting of Loire-Atlantique, the Vendée to its south, Maine-et-Loire to the east and Mayenne and Sarthe to the north-east. The authorities hoped that this would assuage Nantais resentment for being sundered from Brittany. But anger persisted in some quarters; none of these other départements had ever been Breton. On the other hand, many people feel that the modern, active Nantes, the sixth largest city in France, with rapid communications with the rest of the country, has little in common with traditional Brittany.

Julien Gracq, who was born in Nantes, went to school here and often returned, endeavours to sum up its contradictions in *La Forme d'une ville* (1985). "Neither really Breton... nor truly of the Vendée, it isn't even of the Loire, despite the artificial creation of the 'Pays de la Loire' region, because it stops up, rather than vitalizing, a lifeless river." The advantage of this indefinite identity, for Gracq, is that Nantes is probably, with Lyon and Strasbourg, "the least provincial of the major cities of France". But the city has its particular appeal: "Neither completely of the land, nor completely of the sea: neither flesh nor fish—just what is needed to make a Siren."

HISTORY OF NANTES: THE CHÂTEAU-MUSEUM

At one time Nantes was distinctly Breton, indeed a capital—if often in rivalry with Rennes—of the independent Dukes of Brittany. Here Duchess Anne, the last independent ruler, made her second marriage to a King of France, Louis XII, in 1499. Architecturally the principal vestige of the dukes is their château. The palace of Anne and her father, Duke François II, was built in the late fifteenth century, when it still had useful direct access to the Loire. (A stout fourteenth-century tower remains from one of the earlier fortresses on the site.) Within strong defensive walls are elegant, tapering towers in shining white tufa. Italian influence is especially evident in the loggias of the Couronne d'Or tower. The general emphasis is very much vertical apart from the grand sweep of the Louis XIV staircase of the Grand Gouvernement building.

Inside the Château des Ducs de Bretagne is the extraordinary new 32-room historical museum or Château-Musée. This takes Nantes from the ancient tribe of the Namnetes to its plans for the future. It does this with the aid of inscriptions, maps, models, film, furniture, paintings, posters, documents, ships' figureheads, costumes, weapons and historic biscuits and their ingredients. Trade is a central theme in the history of Nantes. In the Middle Ages the main exports were salt, wine and cloth. Later the city dealt with about a third of the French eighteenth-century slave-trade— about 450,000 captives shipped from West Africa and on across the Atlantic to Louisiana and the West Indies. Slavers also brought back gold and ivory from Africa and sugar, cocoa and cotton from America. The museum shows shackles for hands and neck, plans of ships over-crammed with people and documents concerning the appalling treatment of slaves in the French colony of Saint Domingue. It was a highly lucrative business. Many of the "sentimental, music-loving, sadistic slavers" (Gracq, *La Forme d'une ville*), and other successful merchants, built themselves mansions on the Île Feydeau in the eighteenth century. In the 1780s the Quartier Graslin, a popular place for the wealthy to live in, was built by Mathurin Crucy on land owned by the financier Jean-Louis Graslin. Crucy's neo-classical Théâtre Graslin opened in 1788 and burned down in 1796. Its replacement, still flourishing as an opera-house, opened in 1813.

The museum has some mahogany clocks and porcelain-filled cupboards from the mansions of the rich. Paul Morand's novella *Parfaite de Saligny* (1947) fills out the picture with an account of a magnificent town house whose contents are sold off during the Revolution. The owners' wealth and social ascent came from slavery, whereas Loup de Tincé, who observes the sale from various places of concealment in the house, comes from an impoverished family of the old nobility. "Behind all this gilding and lacquer, these carpets and crystal-ware, he imagined the groaning of the blacks, the crack of whips, the sputtering of flesh under the red iron of the brand, the roaring of the Atlantic wind in the sails." Here all the suffering has been transformed into luxury in multi-faceted jewels, silks, paintings, rock-crystal vases and carafes, faïence, carriages and litters— and the room, in white satins, ivories and muslin, of the daughter of the house whom Tincé must nevertheless love. Parfaite is the "inheritor of original sin, innocent daughter of the executioner, end point of a collapsing civilization." Morand, writing in 1946, had strong feelings about guilt by association. Having served as a senior Vichy diplomat he had now withdrawn to Switzerland.

The Revolution affected Nantes more than most of the Loire towns. Royalist Vendéen forces failed in their attempt to take it at the end of June 1793. There had already been extensive killing on both sides. Between October 1793 and February 1794 the Terror was visited on captured rebels, priests and others suspected of Vendéen sympathies. The persecution was presided over by Jean-Baptiste Carrier (1756-94); over 3,500 death-sentences were passed in the département of Loire-Inférieure (now Loire-Atlantique). Some victims were guillotined, others shot, and probably at least two thousand were drowned in the Loire. "Quel torrent révolutionnaire que la Loire," enthused Carrier. The method was to row barges out into the river, remove temporarily-nailed planks, and leave the bound captives to drown. "Vertical deportation," the unpleasantly humorous Carrier is said to have called it. There seems to be no evidence, however, that he conducted "republican marriages"—tying naked men and women together, especially priests and nuns, before drowning them. In *Parfaite de Saligny* this does happen. Morand imagines the feelings of those anticipating death in the "slaty Loire". Tincé at last finds his Parfaite, whom he thought was safe, roped to him by Carrier's jeering, drunken accomplices. He experiences a "terrible joy" at the strange destiny which "joined him closely to the one who had always kept him at a distance." The thugs force their lips together in a kiss and then throw them overboard—more dramatic than waiting for a holed barge to sink. An anonymous picture in the museum has Carrier, eyes blazing with implacable hatred beneath his revolutionary red bonnet, pointing his sword at the bound, naked and vulnerable victims. Eventually, like so many republican leaders, he too was arrested. Even the Committee of Public Safety thought that the scale of his savagery was possibly counter-productive. He was guillotined in Paris in December 1794.

NANTES AFTER THE REVOLUTION: "THE INDUSTRIAL STRUGGLE FOR LIFE"

By the mid-nineteenth century, as Murray's *Handbook* reported, Nantes was "gradually changing from a commercial to a manufacturing town." Much cotton yarn was produced and there was also

a singular manufacture here of preserved dinners ready cooked (Conserves Alimentaires), prepared by the firm Colin et Compagnie, Rue de

Salorges, No. 9, which sends forth, hermetically sealed, all kinds of provisions, so as to be capable of perfect preservation in all climates, and for any length of time. 150,000 boxes of young peas and 800,000 boxes of sardines (pilchards) are embalmed in one season, and 8 oxen can be cooked at once in a single boiler. Roasting is carried on by heated air, and boiling by steam, in a kitchen roofed with glass.

In 1889 Baedeker's *Northern France* notes that "the outskirts of the town are thickly sprinkled with iron-works, ship-building yards, cotton-mills, glass-works, and other factories." In 1914 Elise Rose, in pursuit of *Cathedrals and Cloisters of Northern France*, was less happy with this state of affairs: "commercialism is rampant and the industrial struggle for life is insistent" in Nantes, where "the Loire is the drudge of the merchant and the manufacturer and belongs to the ugly, 'work-a-day' world; and it is typical of the city that the finest view of its mediaeval Castle and Cathedral is obtained from the open space in front of a biscuit factory."

Biscuits were indeed important. The ingredients, as shown at the museum, came from two directions: sugar, chocolate, coconut and vanilla from the port and dairy products, eggs and fruit from the agricultural countryside. The most successful biscuit-makers were the LU company, which took its name from the founder (1885) Jean Lefèvre and his wife Pauline Utile. The LU tower is still a famous landmark in Nantes; since 2000 it has formed part of a cultural centre which cleverly reinterprets the initials as "Lieu Unique". The petit-beurre was the flagship product. In a piece by Alphonse Mucha for the LU calendar of 1897 a girl with fair hair, surrounded by wheatsheafs and huge red poppies, offers a plate of thin vanilla wafers.

Also in the historical museum are tourist posters from the 1920s and 1930s. Some show the château or cathedral while others prefer the boats, whether old galleons or new tankers. More concentrate on the port. "Nantes: Grand Port Industriel et Colonial," proclaims Bernard Lachèvre's poster for the Chamber of Commerce (1932). It shows the thriving port with ships, docks, and the famous Pont Transbordeur or transporter bridge, designed by Ferdinand Arnodin, which functioned between 1903 and 1955. It was demolished in 1958 to make way for the Anne de Bretagne road-bridge. Surviving piers of the Pont Transbordeur were incorporated in the new river-promenade at Quai François-Mitterrand which

opened in January 2005. By the 1980s, with the closure of the shipyards, Nantes projected a less confident image. But in more recent years there has been some determined regeneration, especially on the Île de Nantes, formerly the Île Beaulieu. Often the old shipyards have been turned into new "cultural spaces"; *Le Monde* (3 December 2008) reports the view of Jean Relet, a former trade union representative, that the island is becoming a district of "bobos"—bourgeois bohemians, yuppies.

The museum ends with a contemporary high-definition film, projected onto a panoramic screen, by Pierrick Sorin. It will be replaced after two years but is worth recording here. Boat after boat of Nantais and Nantes-connected people go along the Loire and round again in different combinations. The whole history of Nantes is present, including, although the tone is mostly more happy, shackled slaves and a man, tied to a mast, about to be shot by a Gestapo officer. Painters, workers, Romans, Vikings, go round; a bewigged merchant with a pile of outsized gold coins, revolutionaries, the castle and a sand-castle. (Almost all the characters are played by the artist.) The huge mechanical elephant, based since 2007 in the former Dubigeon shipyard, struts on shore. To the accompaniment of exuberant jazz, Sorin—who plays the musicians too—seems at once to celebrate Nantes and, smilingly, to mock it. It is the ideal climax or antidote to the extensive and comprehensive museum.

Religious Nantes

In Bertrand Tavernier's comic film *La Fille de D'Artagnan* (1994) Cardinal Mazarin, played by Luigi Proietti, has just given Louis XIV his final warnings and advice before the young king is crowned and begins his personal rule. Having closed the door, the cardinal realizes what else he should have said: "I forgot the Edict of Nantes… and never to revoke the Edict of Nantes." He speaks as if, like weary generations of students in French schools, he already knows that Louis will revoke the edict twenty-five years later and that the long-term consequences will be unfortunate for the nation.

The Edict of Nantes (1598) came at the end of nearly forty years of religious conflict. Henri IV at last had enough power to negotiate a settlement allowing Protestant worship. The edict was promulgated in Nantes partly as a show of royal authority—the Duc de Mercoeur, the last leader of the Catholic League to submit to Henri, had been governor of Brittany. Protestants would be allowed to worship publicly in territory administered by great lords who were their co-religionists, and in private elsewhere. Civil rights were also granted or guaranteed, including the right to hold public office, to trade, to inherit and to attend a university. Under Louis XIII and the cardinals many of these permissions were abolished, but Protestant worship remained, with certain conditions, legal. Louis XIV, however, was suspicious enough of Protestant assemblies as an alternative power-base to his own to issue a full revocation. The Edict of Fontainebleau (1685) banned Protestant worship. The pastors were banished while their congregations were forbidden to go with them. Nevertheless, according to some estimates, about 200,000 out of 800,000 Huguenots did succeed in leaving the country, mainly for Prussia and Britain. They included many skilled workers such as weavers, lace-makers and glass-makers; arguably their removal from the French economy was one of the causes of the Revolution, a century after the revocation.

By the time Stephen Spender came to Nantes, Protestantism was tolerated once more. In his autobiography *World within World* (1951) he recounts that his grandmother wanted him, between school and university, to go abroad "to learn a useful language". Rebelling against her, he held out for France rather than Germany; she blamed the French "for everything that had miscarried in Europe since the [First World] war" and moreover "she considered the French to be immoral." (Forty years earlier Wilde's Lady Bracknell, rejecting French songs, declared that "German sounds a thoroughly respectable language, and indeed I believe is so.") But she had heard good things about the Protestants of Nantes, which was "nice and 'quite, quite different' from Paris." Fearing that he might nevertheless be waylaid en route by the "nasty French", she took him in person to the godly city. Spender stayed with the Protestant pastor, an unhappy man tormented by hay-fever, and was terribly homesick. He was put off France and came to share his kinswoman's, Auden's and Isherwood's interest in Germany.

> Nantes was a grey stone provincial town, with a third of its population always dressed in mourning for some far-removed deceased cousin. It seemed as respectable as my grandmother could have wished, but for a very strong local wine which affected drinkers so potently that they lay about the streets near the harbour, completely overcome with it. I remember my grandmother, dressed entirely in black, striding past prostrate drunkards, resolutely ignoring them, as she exclaimed in a firm

voice, "how perfectly delightful"—for now that we were at Nantes she was determined to see no ill.

NANTES: SURREAL CITY

There have been some interesting attempts to explain—not in itself a very surrealist procedure—why Nantes should have been connected in so many ways with Surrealism. The Surrealist photographer, writer and feminist Claude Cahun (Lucy Schwob) was born and grew up here. André Breton lived here for a formative year in 1915-16. It was significant also for Louis Aragon and the many other novelists, painters and poets studied in *Le Rêve d'une ville: Nantes et le surréalisme*, published on the occasion of an exhibition in the city in 1994. One of the contributors, Philippe Le Pichon, cites a description of Nantes from 1913 as a town "situated at the precise point of transition between the *Loire fluviale* and the *Loire maritime*... the Vendée, Anjou and the Breton peninsula... oriented at once to the sea and to the land... city of a wealthy factory-owning bourgeoisie and capital of a rural aristocracy" (André Siegfried, *Tableau politique de la France de l'Ouest*). It was a centre of left-wing activism, where there had been major strikes by workers in 1905 and 1907, and right-wing groups were also strong. So much confrontation and juxtaposition, such different realities, have a natural legacy, Le Pichon and others suggest, in Surrealism.

Nantes also seemed a stranger, a more magical place than most. Julien Gracq, in *Lettrines 2*, reflects that Breton, like him, had known "a town still combed, like a sandbank, by the long, living fingers of the Loire and the Erdre." A more characteristically urban structure inspired André Pieyre de Mandiargues, who was associated for a time with Surrealism. *Le Passage Pommeraye* (in *Le Musée noir*, 1946) involves the famous shopping arcade, linking streets at different levels, which opened in 1843. The blurred outlines, marsh plants, humidity and "opaline and glaucous" colours of the Passage remind Mandiargues' speaker of the "deep-ocean scenery of *Twenty Thousand Leagues under the Sea*, where divers, directed by Captain Nemo, hunt turtles and sharks between the colonnades of a submerged Atlantis." He encounters, instead, a mysteriously familiar woman who pronounces in the deserted gallery the single, echoing word "Echidna" ("the *i* deep, the final syllable suspended in the air, the *ch* guttural like a *k*"). She leads him out of the Passage towards a bizarre and disturbing fate in a narrow house near the port.

André Breton in Nantes: "ces gais terroristes"

André Breton was sent to Nantes in July 1915 to work as a medical auxiliary at a hospital recently set up at 2 Rue du Bocage. The city was promising: "perhaps, with Paris, the only town in France where I had the impression that something worthwhile could happen to me" (*Nadja*, 1928). The most important thing that happened was that he met Jacques Vaché in February or March 1916. Vaché, who had spent much of his childhood and adolescence in Nantes, was a patient at the hospital, recovering from a leg-wound. (At this stage of the First World War wounded French soldiers were often sent to their home town.) He had an immense influence on Breton, although it is difficult to know how many of the details Breton later invents or exaggerates.

At the hospital Breton became aware of the patient's unusual behaviour: "each morning he spent a good hour arranging one or two photographs, bowls, a few violets, on a little table with a lace cover." His opinions were less pacific. He was opposed to all sentimentality, to poetry, and in fact to most things. He either did not know or did not like the poets cherished by the young Breton—Rimbaud, Apollinaire—and was suspicious of Cubism. Vaché believed in a more active kind of performance, dictated partly by the desperate conditions, the need to live in the moment, of 1916. "Writing, thinking were no longer enough: at all costs one had to give oneself the illusion of movement, of noise." So as soon as he came out of hospital he took a job unloading coal on the Loire. And in the evenings he spent freely, wandering from café to café, cinema to cinema to see parts of different films. He and Breton often dined at La Cigale, the restaurant in Place Graslin which opened in 1895. The extravagant Art Deco interior survives in what Julien Gracq calls this "bonbonnière [sweet box] de la belle Époque". Sometimes at the cinema they would slice bread, open wine and talk loudly as if they were at a dinner-party, to the understandable and intended fury of the rest of the audience. In the streets of Nantes Vaché wore different costumes: Lieutenant of Hussars, airman, doctor. Perhaps more worryingly, he kept a young woman sitting for hours, "silent and unmoving", in the corner of his room while he entertained Breton. At 5 o'clock she made some tea and he thanked her by kissing her hand. He claimed that they slept in the same bed but without having sex. The two men were collaborating more actively, as Mark Polizzotti says in his biography of Breton (1995), on "the myth of Jacques Vaché, and through him on one of the central myths of a Surrealist movement yet unborn." Breton in *Les Pas perdus* calls them "ces gais terroristes." Later in Paris, if Breton can be believed, Vaché threatened to take the terrorism one stage further when, dressed this time as a British officer, he prepared to fire his pistol into the audience of Apollinaire's play *Les Mamelles de Tirésias*. His friend somehow stopped him.

Vaché's influence on Breton continued in letters from the Front after his return to the army. He wrote, at once passionate and insouciant, about his dream of joining, dressed in red, a futile "Chinese secret society in Australia". He would star in a film as an adventurer wearing fine riding-breeches, close-shaven, with beautiful hands and a solitary ring; it would all end "in a fire, or in a salon". In fact the most joyous of terrorists died of an opium overdose, in January 1919, at the Hôtel de France in Nantes. It was probably suicide; Breton interpreted his death as a grand proto-Surrealist gesture. In reality Breton could never be as unsentimental and stylish as Vaché. There is evident affection as well as surrealism in his tributes to "a man more beautiful than a reed-pipe", one at whose neck shone "a jewelled waterfall" which may have been the Amazon. "Vaché est surréaliste en moi," he said.

Nantes Cathedral

It took four centuries, from the fifteenth to the nineteenth, to complete the Cathédrale St.-Pierre-et-St.-Paul. (There were earlier churches on the site, one of them celebrated by Venantius Fortunatus in the sixth century for its impressive height and fortress-like appearance. Vikings sacked it nevertheless.) Large-scale restoration after a major fire in 1972 explains its present fairly pristine appearance.

The architecture has had its critics. Henry James noted the "stunted towers"— though no doubt they seemed high enough to the two students who climbed up to attach a tricolour to the lightning conductor in defiance of the occupying Germans on the night of 10-11 November 1940. Elise Rose in *Cathedrals and Cloisters of Northern France* (1914) diagnoses decadent Gothic, exhibiting "at times, a stiffness in guise of simplicity, and poverty of invention with profusion of ornament". The narthex is out of harmony with the nave, the apse exudes uninspiring "quiet orderliness", the general effect is confused. Rose does admire the "very white and lofty nave," with its "numbers of sharply cut, clustered columns".

Like most commentators, however, she is clearly more enthusiastic about the tomb of François II, last independent Duke of Brittany, and his wife Marguerite de Foix. This was erected between 1502 and 1507 for the duke's daughter, Anne of Brittany, by Michel Colombe, who also worked on the tomb of her royal children at Tours. It stood in a Carmelite chapel, was hidden during the Revolution, and was installed in the south transept of the cathedral in 1817. The effigies, in Carrara marble, are graceful enough tributes: "the quiet couple," James calls them. But more attention has generally been paid to the four allegorical female figures at the corners of the monument. They represent Strength, Justice, Temperance and Prudence. Strength, in armour, strangles a small dragon of Evil which has infested the tower of Good. Justice holds her usual sword and balance but indicates mercy by covering the sword-point with the scarf attached to her crown. She is said to be modelled on Anne of Brittany. Temperance holds a horse's bit with which to rein in the passions and a clock to remind us that "To everything there is a season, and a time to every purpose under the heaven" (*Ecclesiastes* 3.1). Prudence holds a compass and a mirror, the latter standing for wise reflection. The back of her head has the face of a bearded man; Prosper Mérimée explains that "this is probably designed to show that wisdom is founded on experience," but did not think it was worth expressing such a fine axiom if it meant sculpting a "monstrosity".

Opposite this tomb, in black and white marble, is the cenotaph (1879) of General de La Moricière (1806-65), servant of France in its colonial wars in North Africa, and then of the Vatican. It prompts Henry James to consider the difficulty of making a modern tomb, in semi-Renaissance mode, carry the same sort of conviction as its predecessors. It is a fine work, carefully studied; perhaps too carefully. It "has every merit but the absence of a certain prime feeling. It is the echo of an earlier time,—an echo with a beautiful cadence." A work which perhaps responds more creatively to earlier art is Alain Thomas' Nativity triptych of 2003-4 in the chapel of the Sacré-Coeur. The bright colours, the snow and the deep blue night sky suggest a Christmas card or Advent calendar. Figures and buildings are naïve, upright. Mary kneels in light blue, Joseph stands in darker colours. The Magi and other travellers come in orange, green, gold (some gold-leaf is used), pink and blue. In celebration of peace people and animals move together towards the stable. There is a circus atmosphere—no solemnity. In the foreground a toucan and a raccoon fraternize joyfully.

Thomas often paints toucans; the largest and best known (1996), perched amid Amazonian vegetation, is frescoed on a wall in Rue Fanny-Peccot, opposite the Town Hall.

NANTES: MUSÉE DES BEAUX-ARTS

Gustave Flaubert in 1847 inveighs, with humorous bravado, against the Nantes museum's irritating fondness for tin-plate vine-leaves. These, like the more familiar fig-leaves, were used to cover nude statues' privy parts. They look like "devices to prevent onanism": this "shameful, maleficent" underwear "shining like saucepans".

By the time the museum moved into the present building at the end of the nineteenth century the curators' attitudes were more enlightened and the collection was rich in works by Flaubert's contemporaries. Orientalists such as Jean-Louis Jérôme are well represented and there are pieces by Corot and Daubigny. Horace Vernet's *La Ballade de Léonore* (1839) is a dramatic digest of Gottfried August Bürger's popular Gothic poem *Lenore*, where the ghost of Lenore's lover, a soldier, carries her off. (The piece was translated by Scott, Nerval and Hugo, and set by Schubert.) In the painting the horse breathes fire and the black-armoured spectre rides on as the girl, with dawning horror, pulls up the visor to reveal the skull. An unearthly light shines from the eye-sockets. The teeth are set. The horse leaps gothically over the tomb-effigy of a medieval king. The spectre's armoured left hand grasps the girl's right hand, weak in its lacy ornamental cuff, silvered by the moonlight.

Costumes and moeurs are very different in James Tissot's modern-dress (early 1880s) versions of the story of the Prodigal Son. Tissot was born in Nantes and was soon to return to France after his successful decade in England. After travelling to exotic foreign places—Tissot's excuse for some fashionable *japonisme*—the prodigal returns, in the third picture, to kneel barefoot with his arms round his father at the docks. But in the fourth and last of the sequence, "The Fatted Calf", we meet him dressed in a sober suit, sharpening the knife for the joint and looking the part of a good, calm bourgeois. He sits in comfort with his parents, sisters and dog beneath a riverside pergola. His brother, to whom one member of the party tries to whisper an explanation, looks suitably resentful and incredulous as he comes up from a boat on the river. He is already a respectable figure, and wears the brimless blue-and-white cap of Tissot's rowing-club at Henley.

But much the most talked-about nineteenth-century piece in the gallery is Ingres' *Mme de Senonnes* (1814). Louis Aragon, in a discursive essay published in *Henri Matisse: a Novel* (1971), describes the painting and its erotic charge. Sitting on a yellow sofa in a plum-to-crimson dress, with her neck, shoulder and cheek reflected in the mirror behind her, she gazes directly "from the perfect oval that is her face, only slightly distorted by the pendant earring on the left side, like a balance tipping slightly on its rod, above that Empire-style décolleté whose opulent bareness is emphasised by the dark velvet of the dress" (Jean Stewart's translation). The "three flimsy ruffles of Italian lace" suggest, instead of concealing, "that swelling of the throat for which Matisse had a lifelong, and Ingres a frequent, predilection". "Physical anomaly" becomes "the very expression of sensuality".

Work from earlier periods includes Georges de La Tour's treatment of St. Peter's denial of Christ (1650). Soldiers dice in the red glow of a brazier. Old Peter is questioned, at left, by a woman holding a candle; its light shines pitilessly on his "No, not me!" face. There are airy eighteenth-century entertainments by Lancret and the like. The twentieth century is also very variously present: Kandinsky, Sérusier and Sonia Delaunay. Jean Metzinger (1883-1956), born in Nantes, later a Cubist, contributes an experimental pointilliste sunset over the Château de Clisson and the Loire. Gaston Chaissac (1910-64) recovers rejected objects, transforming a piece of metal into *Person with Two Blue Eyes* and painting the Last Supper, aptly, on a kitchen table-top. In *Spunkland* (1997) Gilbert and George stand before a landscape of magnified spermatozoa.

GILLES DE RAIS: "THE PSYCHOPATHIC URGENCY OF HIS PRIVATE NEEDS"

The Pays de Retz is an area south of Nantes and the Loire, once part of Brittany. "Retz" is another form of "Rais", the name made notorious by the serial child-killer Gilles de Laval, Baron de Rais (1404-40). Many Bretons would be happy not to claim him for their own, but he had extensive estates in Brittany as well as Anjou and had family connections with the duke. Horror, psychological curiosity and the Breton tradition that he is the original Bluebeard—though Bluebeard usually preys on wives, not children—force us to remember Gilles de Rais. There is no one explanation as to how an immensely wealthy aristocrat and soldier, the companion of Joan of Arc in her early successes against the English, declined in the 1430s into a life of terrible crime. One romantic theory has him traumatized by his beloved Joan's death, but there is no evidence for this. There have been some attempts to argue that his crimes were exaggerated or invented by his enemies, but there is all too much evidence to the contrary.

Gilles' life was always one of excess. As an orphan child he had been used to further the ambitions for territory and power of his grandfather, Jean de Craon. His wealth and lands were seemingly limitless, and his kinsman's main lesson to him was, as Jean Benedetti puts it in *Gilles de Rais: the Authentic Bluebeard* (1971), "that the Rais family was not subject to the laws of God or man." Tradition has the child, in the castle of Champtocé-sur-Loire, between Angers and Ingrandes, already "dressed like a king and behaving like a tyrant". Benedetti sees Joan as appealing to his love of the dramatic and his military exploits as an outlet for his murderous tendencies—"the psychopathic urgency of his private needs had been concealed by the general brutality of military practice." Yet in apparent contradiction to such brutality were his generosity to complete strangers and his religious devotion. Gilles lavished money and attention on the collegiate church of the Holy Innocents at Machecoul, his principal home in the Retz. He paid for splendidly dressed choirboys (inevitably) and chaplains, gold censers and chalices, and a silver reliquary for the head of St. Honoré. It is to be feared that Gilles' devotion to this object was connected with his unpleasant habit of decapitating his victims. Perhaps he thought that honouring a holy head could somehow atone for this, cancel it out.

At the same time that he was worshipping in the church of the Innocents, Gilles was murdering fresh innocents. Between 1432 and 1440 he sexually abused and then killed at least sixty children, possibly two hundred or more, mainly boys, some girls. This happened mostly, it seems, at Machecoul, where the grey ruins of his castle survive. He was also involved, allegedly, in alchemy and black magic; in his detailed confession he talks of making a pact with the Devil, written, Dr. Faustus-fashion, in his own blood, but denies that he handed over his soul.

At last in 1440 Gilles de Rais and several of his companions had been arrested by the Bishop of Nantes for heresy, witchcraft, murder and sodomy. After initial defiance they confessed their crimes. Gilles was publicly hanged and his body burnt on the Île de Biesse, now part of Nantes, on 26 October 1440. He played his final dramatic role as "the perfect penitent" (Benedetti) and left us puzzled still.

St.-Nazaire

Jules Verne, who grew up in Nantes, first sailed down the Loire estuary to St.-Nazaire in 1840, when he was twelve. He remembered it later as a village with a small pier, a church and a few "houses or tumbledown tenements". It grew very rapidly into an industrial port city—its first deepwater harbour opened in 1856, joined by the Penhoët harbour in 1881—although Julien Gracq could still write about its "flock of white and grey houses, scattered across the heath like sheep, but gathered more closely in the centre, as if bound together by fear of the great gusts of wind from the sea" (*Liberté Grande*, 1958, remembering the 1930s). Gracq always imagined it as "badly anchored". This impression increased when he saw the liner *Normandie*, which was built in St.-Nazaire, looming over the low houses like the nave of a floating cathedral. (Gracq plays on the double sense of *nef* as "nave" or "ship".)

The *Lancastria*, a Cunard liner converted as a troopship, has sadder associations. On 17 June 1940, two weeks after Dunkirk, it dropped anchor

ten miles off St.-Nazaire. Smaller ships and boats brought more than 6,000 soldiers, airmen and refugees out from the port to board her. Just before 4.00 p.m. the *Lancastria* was hit four times by a German Ju-88 bomber. It was swiftly obvious that the damage was irreparable. Many people were trapped in the hold. Others, in the sea, choked on oil, drowned or were machine-gunned. Survivors remember those on the upturned hull, about to sink, bravely singing "Roll out the Barrel" and "There'll Always be an England". Up to 4,000 people died. About 2,500 were rescued by British and French boats and taken either on to England or back to the coast. Winston Churchill, wanting to keep up national morale after Dunkirk and before the Battle of Britain, ordered news of the sinking to be suppressed; he felt that "the newspapers have got quite enough disaster for today at least." Some newspaper reports did appear but on the whole the concealment of this, the greatest loss of life in British maritime history, was successful.

St.-Nazaire saw further action during the next few years. Its ship-yards, factories and massive concrete U-Boat base (which now contains the Tourist Office) were a frequent target for Allied bombing. Putting the port out of action became an urgent priority because it was the only Atlantic port with facilities for the repair of the much-feared German battleship *Tirpitz*. Operation Chariot, a daring and successful British raid, followed. Early in the morning of 28 March 1942 HMS *Campbeltown* rammed the dock floodgate. Commandos landed from *Campbeltown* and the accompanying launches to sabotage the dock machinery. The following morning, as planned, the ship exploded, destroying the gate and killing 360 Germans. On the 30th a second explosion prompted panic-stricken attacks on shipworkers and other civilians by German soldiers; mass reprisals were narrowly averted. In the original attack 169 commandos and sailors were killed, 215 were captured and the remaining 227 returned to England— five of them more slowly than the others, having walked and cycled to Gibraltar. Those who died are commemorated by a monument, and a cannon from *Campbeltown*, in Place du Commando.

Unlike the dock, the U-Boat base, which had still been under construction at the time of the raid, continued to threaten Allied shipping. The pocket around St.-Nazaire was one of the last places in Europe where the occupiers surrendered: on 11 May 1945, twelve days after Hitler's suicide. By this time, however, much of the population of what was left of the city had been evacuated. Rebuilding was an immense undertaking. Some people felt that post-war St.-Nazaire was an ugly, soulless place. But a new building programme in the 1990s created an airier, more evidently maritime city. The novelist Jean Rouaud, in his preface to Charles Nicol's book about St.-Nazaire (2004), celebrates the modernity of a logically planned city looking out towards America: more New York than Nantes, he claims. Continuing from an earlier age, the ship-building industry remains active. The 150,000-ton, £550 million *Queen Mary 2* was built at the Chantiers de l'Atlantique and delivered to Cunard in 2003.

LOIRE-ATLANTIQUE: THE ESTUARY

On the Atlantic coast and the Loire estuary it often rains. According to Jean Rouaud's novel *Les Champs d'honneur* (1990), the drizzle is so persistent that natives do not even notice it. Rain becomes a companion. And it makes good business for opticians: people who are for ever having to wipe their glasses with "a shirt-tail, the corner of a restaurant tablecloth, or the clean corner of a scrunched-up handkerchief", are likely to drop and break them. One of the rainy set-pieces of the early part of the novel involves the Citroën 2CV erratically driven by the narrator's chain-smoking grandfather. "When it was raining hard, which cannot be considered exceptional beside the Atlantic, the 2CV, shaken about in the squall, labouring against the wind, letting in water on all sides, was not unlike a dilapidated coaster which had embarked, ignoring the weather-warning, on too rough a sea."

Rouaud's humour leads into a compassionate exploration of several lives. The novel is structured more by memories and associations than by chronology. It often returns to the First World War, but is as concerned with those like "la petite tante" who live and die in the "fields of honour" of civilian life as with those who suffer in war. The characters' and the generations' overlapping and interlacing experience give a surprising density to the small town of Random, based on Campbon, roughly half-way between Nantes and St.-Nazaire. Rouaud's other semi-autobiographical works include *Le Monde à peu près* (1996), which deals with a fatherless boy's unhappy but defining experience of a boarding-school in St.-Nazaire.

Despite the risk of Rouaud's rain, the estuary as it merges with the Atlantic provides some popular seaside resorts. Sunbathing, the great craze of the 1920s and 1930s, flourished unstopped by the complaints of the *curé* of Piriac-sur-Mer, on the rocky Côte Sauvage west of the estuary. In his parish bulletin for 29 July 1934 he considered the strangeness of the human desire to cook oneself: "a pair of shoulders is not worth looking at, at the end of the holidays, unless it has been turned golden, peeled, browned, grilled, pierced even, by the sun! ... Suffering for the sake of being roasted, there is the ultimate *chic*." The sight of roasting flesh was not the only kind of suffering visited on the curé, whose bulletins are quoted in Johan Vincent's book of 2007 on coastal tourism in the area. Earlier in the summer he had asked parishioners not to recommend visitors to apply to him ("poor devil") for information on holiday villas and chalets in Piriac.

The priest's problem should, at least, have been temporary. Increasing numbers of agencies and tourist offices had been opened, even, Vincent points out, in Piriac. The coast was filling up. Just beyond St.-Nazaire is St.-Marc, where Jacques Tati filmed the exteriors for *M. Hulot's Holiday* (1953). The anarchic, gangling Hulot is able to relax, on the beach or the tennis-court, as other holidaymakers, bound by class and convention, cannot. The coast continues towards the busy beaches, streets and casinos of Pornichet and La Baule, fashionable bathing centres especially between the wars. But there is also a hinterland of small villages, some megalithic remains, and the vast salt marshes between Le Croisic and Guérande. As J.W.C. Hughes succinctly explains in *Bradshaw's Illustrated Hand Book to Brittany* (1867), "the country is cut up by dykes and banks, into reservoirs, for the manufacture of salt by the evaporation of sea water." Salt, together with wine, made Guérande a wealthy town at the end of the Middle Ages. After salt decreased in value and the town became less accessible from the sea, it retained its near-mile of ramparts, four gates and air of a miniature city from a book of hours.

Balzac visited Guérande only once, in 1830. But in *Béatrix* (1839) he is very clear about its appearance and imaginative significance as "a magnificent jewel" preserved from the feudal past. It is still "encircled within its mighty walls; its broad moats are full of water, its battlements are complete, no shrubs have grown over the loopholes... There are three gates, where the rings of the portcullises are visible; you can enter only by crossing a wooden drawbridge, clamped with iron, which is no longer raised but still could be." Social distances are maintained between bourgeoisie, nobility and clergy. *Paludiers* (salt-workers in the marshes), farmworkers and sailors are still sharply distinguished by their costumes. The Revolution has had no impact here: Guérande "is still a town apart, fundamentally Breton, fervently Catholic, silent, self-contained, where new ideas do not penetrate far."

The marshes, separated from the town by a band of lush vegetation are, says Balzac's narrator, like a desert. Equally bleak places, nearer the sea, are the setting for Balzac's story "Un Drame au bord de la mer" (1834). The disturbed, mentally and emotionally hyperactive Louis Lambert—subject also of the novel named after him—has come to Le Croisic and the salt marshes in search of peace of mind. But by the sea he encounters a man so much more radically disturbed than himself that all hope of calm is shattered. The old fisherman, whose terrible story we are about to hear, sits as immobile as the granite columns around him, staring into the dazzling ocean. His face is marked by "age, the rough work of the sea, grief, and coarse food, and blackened as if by a thunderbolt".

PORNIC: "SUCH A SOFT SEA AND SUCH A MOURNFUL WIND"

Pornic, on the coast of the Pays de Retz, about twelve miles south of St.-Nazaire and the estuary, is noticed by Baedeker's *Northern France* as "a small sea-port" with "many pleasant villas. In the neighbourhood are several small sheltered coves, with fine sandy beaches." It remains popular for its boats, beaches and seafood.

Robert Browning stayed in the village of Ste.-Marie, near Pornic and now part of the same *commune*, in the summers and early autumns of 1862, 1863 and 1865. On 18 August 1862 he described the area and his life there in a letter to his friend Isa Blagden:

> This is a wild little place in Brittany... close to the sea—a hamlet of a dozen houses, perfectly lonely—one may walk on the edge of the low rocks by the sea for miles—or go into the country at the back. Pornic is full and gay enough at half an hour's distance. Our house is the Mayor's, large enough, clean and bare. I sit in my room all day and walk of an evening... The place is much to my mind; I have brought books, and write; I wanted a change.

Blagden had shared with Browning, the previous summer, the nursing of Elizabeth Barrett Browning during her last illness in Florence. Now, although he said he longed for Italy, he was looking for somewhere without past associations. At Ste.-Marie he was with his father, sister and son but also spent much time alone. His holidays here were therapeutic: both a salve for bereavement and a rest from his busy social schedule in London. There he seemed increasingly to become, as Henry James would later put it, "two Brownings": on the one hand a hearty, talkative dinner-guest, "the accomplished, saturated, sane, sound man of the London world and the world of 'culture'", on the other a solitary, sensitive and challenging poet. Here, living with "such a soft sea and such a mournful wind", the divide was less evident.

The maritime bareness provides a setting for "James Lee's Wife", one of Browning's many studies of imperfect or ill-matched love. A woman reflects, by the window, on the change of season:

> Ah, Love, but a day
>> And the world has changed!
> The Sun's away,
>> And the bird estranged;
> The wind has dropped,
>> And the sky's deranged:
> Summer has stopped.

Her husband's love, unlike hers, proves as changeable as the seasons. Their fire is made of "shipwreck wood" and she imagines sailors cursing the red shaft it casts over the sea, the "warm safe house" and inhabitants. But the coast of France is "bitter" for her, by the fire, as well as for those whose shipwreck made it possible. On shore she wanders among bare, iron-like rocks. She looks out from the doorway in what might stand as a separate sea-poem:

> The swallow has set her six young on the rail,
>> And looks sea-ward:
> The water's in stripes like a snake, olive-pale
>> To the lee-ward,—
> On the weather-side, black, spotted white with the wind.
>> "Good fortune departs, and disaster's behind,"—
> Hark, the wind with its wants and its infinite wail!

Pornic: Browning's "wild little place"

Ten years later Browning set a longer and more morally complex poem in and near Pornic. The starting-point of *Fifine at the Fair* (1872) is Elvire's question to Don Juan, in Molière's *Dom Juan*, about the weakness of his defence of adultery. Browning's modern don knows his Elvira's excellence but is drawn to Fifine, a gypsy girl with "sunshine upon her spangled hips" and "lithe memorable limbs" who is performing at the fair of St. Gilles. His long monologue is an attempt to persuade himself, as much as Elvira, of the virtues of bidding "a frank farewell to what—we think—should be,/And, with as good a grace, welcome what is—we find". (The fractured syntax suggests his real uncertainty about his own arguments.) Eventually he leads her to a local "Druid monument", a "construction gaunt and grey". Learned men and the curé have some ingenious theories about its origins and purpose, but its primal connection with sex and fertility is evident in local tradition: "why, go and ask our grandames how they used/To dance around it" until the curé "disabused their ignorance, and bade the parish in a band/Lay flat the obtrusive thing that cumbered so the land."

In 1865 it was no megalith but the church at Pornic which was laid flat. It was demolished and replaced. At the same time early medieval "pillar-ornaments, column-heads with quaint figures", were being removed, as Browning told Blagden, from the church at Ste.-Marie. The resulting gaps were smoothed and whitewashed, and the old ornaments flung "where they now lie, on a heap of stones by the road-side—where my father [a keen amateur artist] goes to draw them in his sketch-book—groaningly." Few of the inhabitants groaned, if we can credit Browning's verdict on them as "good, stupid and dirty, without a touch of the sense of picturesqueness in their clodpoles".

Le Croisic: "a fine fierce sea, and driving sands"

The fishing-port of Le Croisic, at the tip of the Guérande peninsula, north of the Loire estuary, faces out to the Atlantic. It was especially prosperous in the sixteenth and seventeenth centuries, when it became the main local port, superseding Guérande where the harbour had silted up. Some fine, substantial houses survive from this period. Then cod was the main catch for the fishing fleet; in the nineteenth century it was sardines and later, as still today, mainly prawns, crabs and lobsters; not surprisingly, there are many good fish restaurants. These, the "exuberant, noisy and smelly fish market" (Vivian Rowe) and the beaches continue to attract visitors. At one time they also came, in large numbers, to experience the benefits of hydrotherapy. In 1844, "at the very edge of the Ocean" at St.-Goustain beach, a "Sea-Bathing and Marine Hydrotherapy Establishment" was set up. The buildings continued to serve various medical purposes until as late as 2000, when they became a "complexe hotelier et touristique".

In 1855 Dr. Armand Trousseau's *Notice Médicale sur les bains de mer du Croisic* detailed and recommended the establishment and its methods. Sea-bathing was practised here and had its benefits, but could not be controlled by the medical attendant, and so seawater was diverted into a swimming-pool where it could be better regulated. Elsewhere on the site desalinated water was used as a remedy for scrofula and "syphilitic conditions". Another treatment was a "bath" in warm sand. In case would-be patients were still hesitating, Trousseau went on to list some of the "distractions" which the resort could provide, including billiards, concerts, shooting with cross-bow or pistol, horse-riding, donkey-riding, well-shaded walks and a fine kilometre-long pier. One may suspect that Trousseau was paid a retainer by the establishment; he was, however, a respected Paris clinician. He seems to have been genuinely impressed with everything about Le Croisic. The beach was sandy and without pebbles and had pretty beach-huts. "Expert masters" supervised bathing and gave swimming lessons. Each year "choice society" established itself at Le Croisic for the season—but not so choice, apparently, as to be put off by the "several hundreds" of extra travellers for whom new facilities had recently been provided. And locally the air and the temperature were "so healthy, that there have never been any epidemic or contagious illnesses"; many people who lived in this paradise survived, "without infirmities, into the most extreme old age". Indeed another pamphlet, in 1861, claimed that there was a local proverb to the effect that "At Le Croisic the men have difficulty getting round to dying, but as for the women, they have to knock them over the head."

Hydrotherapy was still flourishing when Robert Browning stayed at Le Croisic during the late summers of 1866 and 1867. He found "the little town and surrounding country... wild and primitive, even a trifle beyond Pornic perhaps". He had stopped going to Pornic, south of the estuary, because he associated it too much with his father, who had died in June 1866. Browning wrote two poems connected with Le Croisic, "that land-strip" washed by waters, "the spit of sandy rock which juts/Spitefully northward." "Hervé Riel" tells the story of an unjustly forgotten "Croisick-ese" naval hero, and "The Two Poets of Le Croisic" concerns two terrible writers who became famous—equally unjustly.

The theme of what time does and does not preserve is taken up also in "The Two Poets" with reference to a local menhir, probably the one in Avenue de la Pierre-Longue, which, like the stone in Pornic, had been used in fertility rites. In a letter of February 1867 Browning reflects further on this aspect of Le Croisic, before turning back to the ocean which has at last absorbed the mighty Loire:

> Croisic is the old head-seat of Druidism in France... : the people were still Pagan a couple of hundred years ago, despite the priests' teaching and preaching, and the women used to dance round a phallic stone still upright there with obscene circumstances enough,—till the general civilization got too strong for this. Close by is the strange, solitary Bourg de Batz... The whole district is wild, strange and romantic, with a fine fierce sea, and driving sands.

Further Reading

Barral i Altet, Xavier *et al. La Cathédrale du Puy-en-Velay*. Paris: Seuil, 2000.

Auffret, François, *Johan Barthold Jongkind, 1819-1891: Biographie illustrée*. Paris: Maisonneuve, 2004.

Caraes, Jean-François *et al. Loire-Atlantique*. Paris: Bonneton, 1998.

Châteaux de la Loire: le guide vert (2006); translated as *Châteaux of la Loire*, Clermont-Ferrand: Michelin, 2006.

Edmondson, John, *Traveller's Literary Companion to France*. London: In Print, 1997.

Ford, Edward, *Alain-Fournier and Le Grand Meaulnes (The Wanderer)*. Lewiston, NY: Edwin Mellen Press, 1999.

Gildea, Robert, *Marianne in Chains: in Search of the German Occupation, 1940-1945*. London: Macmillan, 2002.

Goldring, Douglas, *The Loire: the Record of a Pilgrimage from Gerbier de Joncs to St. Nazaire*. London: Constable, 1913.

James, Henry, *A Little Tour in France* [1885], ed. Leon Edel. Penguin: Harmondsworth, 1985.

Macnab, Roy, *For Honour Alone: the Cadets of Saumur in the Defence of the Cavalry School, France, June 1940*. London: Hale, 1988.

McNeill, John, *Blue Guide: the Loire Valley*. London: A. & C. Black, 1995.

Mérimée, Prosper, *Notes de voyages*, ed. Pierre-Marie Auzas. Paris: Hachette, 1971.

Parker, John, *Interpretations of Rabelais*. Lewiston, NY: Edwin Mellen Press, 2002.

Robb, Graham, *Balzac: a Biography*. London: Picador, 1994.

— *The Discovery of France*. London: Picador, 2007.

Rose, Elise Whitlock, *Cathedrals and Cloisters of Midland France*. London and New York, 1907.

—, *Cathedrals and Cloisters of Northern France*. London and New York, 1914.

Rowe, Vivian, *The Loire* [1969]. London: Eyre Methuen, 1974.

Speaight, Robert, *The Companion Guide to Burgundy* [1975]. Revised edition by Francis Pagan. Woodbridge: Companion Guides, 1996.

Voss, Roger, *Wines of the Loire*. London: Faber, 1995.

Wade, Richard, *The Companion Guide to the Loire*. London: Collins, 1979.

Warner, Marina, *Joan of Arc: the Image of Female Heroism* [1981]. London: Vintage, 1991.

Warrell, Ian, *Turner on the Loire*. London: Tate Gallery, 1997.

Warren, W. L., *Henry II* [1973]. Revised edition. New Haven and London: Yale University Press, 2000.

Wharton, Edith, *A Motor-Flight Through France* [1908]. London: Picador, 1995.

Wheeler, Bonnie and John Carmi Parsons (eds.), *Eleanor of Aquitaine: Lord and Lady*. Basingstoke: Palgrave, 2002.
303: Arts, recherches et créations. La Loire. Nantes: Association 303, 2003.

WEBSITES:
http//www.chaumont-jardins.com
http//estuaire.loire.free.fr
http//www.festivaldeloire.com
http//www.france-for-visitors.com/loire
Histoire et patrimoine des rivières et canaux. http://projetbabel.org/fluvial
http.//www.rivernet.org/loire

Index of Literary & Historical Names

Du Bellay, Joachim, 69-70, 155-6
Du Camp, Maxime, xv
Du Guast, Michel, 86
Duban, Félix, 84
Dubuffe, Claude-Marie, 79
Dumas, Alexandre *père*, 67, 94, 153-4
Dunlop, Ian, 69
Dunois, Jean d'Orléans, Comte de, xix, 61
Dupin, Claude, 108
Dupin, Louise-Marie-Madeleine, 108-9
Dupin de Francueil, Louis-Claude, 109
Duplessis-Mornay, Philippe, 157
Dupuis, Pierre, 64
Duras, Marguerite, 27
Durupt, Charles-Bathélémy, 85-6
Dutton, Ralph, 115

Eleanor of Aquitaine, Queen of England, 141-3, 150-2
Erasmus, Desiderius, 149
Estrées, Gabrielle d', Duchesse de Beaufort, 123
Euvé, Michel, 96
Evelyn, John, xxii, 78, 90, 125, 144-5, 146

Fenwick, Hubert, 130
Flaubert, Gustave, xi, xii, xv, 83, 84, 97, 196
Flower, John, 39
Foltz, Captain, 160
Fontaine, Axel, 92
Foulques III Nerra, Count of Anjou, xix, 132, 165
Foulques V, Count of Anjou, 165
Fouquet, Jean, 65, 111
Fournier, Henri-Alban, *see* Alain-Fournier
Fourré, Maurice, 156
Foyatier, Denis, 62
Fragonard, Jean-Honoré, 172
François I, King of France, 78-9, 84,

100, 103, 104, 130
François II, King of France, 63-4, 91, 98
François II, Duke of Brittany, 185, 195
Francis, R. A., 42, 43

Galbert, Gabriel de, 160
Gambetta, Léon, 114
Gambini, Jules, 28
Gambrinus, 22
Gans, Deborah, 15
Gaulle, General Charles de, 50-1
Gautier, Théophile, 124
Gauzlin, Abbot, 55
Gechter, François, 144
Genet, Jean, 152-3
Genevoix, Maurice, xii-xiii, 58, 75-6
Geoffrey V Plantagenet, Count of Anjou, 140-1, 142, 143
Geoffrey Plantagenet, Duke of Brittany, 142
Gérard-Séguin, Jean-Alfred, 124
Gibbon, Edward, 150
Gilbert and George, 197
Girolamo da Fiesole, 120
Girouard, Mark, xix, xx, 176
Godefroy de Bouillon, 23, 133
Goldman, James, 142-3
Goldring, Douglas, 2, 2-3, 4, 5-6, 20, 78, 113
Gonzague, Louis de, Duke of Nevers, 27-8
Gorky, Maxim, 44
Goscinny, René, 59-60
Goutnova, Sacha, 96
Goyen, Jan van, 123
Gracq, Julien, 24, 68, 74, 185, 186, 192, 193, 199
Graslin, Jean-Louis, 186
Gregory of Tours, 116
Gresset, Jean-Baptiste-Louis, 26-7
Groslot, Jacques, 64
Guardi, Francesco, 172

Index of Places & Landmarks